The
Development
of Modern
Christianity

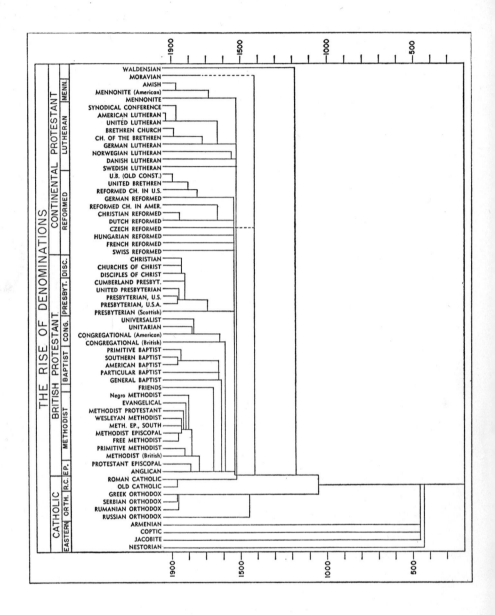

THE RISE OF DENOMINATIONS

The Development of Modern Christianity

SINCE 1500

Frederick A. Norwood

ABINGDON PRESS

New York • Nashville

THE DEVELOPMENT OF MODERN CHRISTIANITY

Copyright © MCMLVI by Pierce & Washabaugh

Library of Congress Catalog Card Number: 56-5371

SET UP, PRINTED, AND BOUND BY THE
PARTHENON PRESS, AT NASHVILLE,
TENNESSEE, UNITED STATES OF AMERICA

Preface

THE PRIMARY PURPOSE OF THIS BOOK IS TO PORTRAY BRIEFLY THE DE-velopment of Christianity in the context of modern history. The secondary purpose is to show how, in this development, many different churches and sects came into being, and how, especially in our day, these are manifesting an inner and continuing unity through the Ecumenical Movement.

A diligent attempt has been made to limit the book in length and in elaboration of detail. In spite of the risks of superficiality and vagueness, the primary consideration of concise introducton has been maintained. Such a book as this, if used as a text, invites extended reading in sources and secondary works. To that end the text has been restricted, and selected reading lists have been appended to each chapter. A textbook should be an invitation, not a barrier, to broad reading.

Recently students of church history have become aware that the modern period has not been given the attention, especially in survey courses, that it deserves. This really means neglecting the Protestant heritage. Within a modest scope this book seeks to redress the balance. The consequent neglect of the earlier periods is owing not to a judgment of their unimportance but rather to the fact that they have already been well and repeatedly treated.

Likewise, many earlier books have failed to integrate European church history with the broader panorama of the world stage, including American church history and the history of missions. Although it is impossible here to present all the global stage with comprehensiveness as well as clarity, it must be made plain that a major aspect of modern church history is the expansion of the faith.

A further consideration is the relation of the history of Christianity to the political, social, and cultural environment in which it lives. Religious traditions are not nurtured in a vacuum. Nor can the secular aspects be understood apart from the religious influences that participated in their origin. Hence the Reformation must be related to the political-power factors of Holy Roman Empire and territorial princes, the Wesleyan Revival to the Industrial Revolution, and the papacy of the early nineteenth century to the rise of romanticism. This book attempts to destroy the popular illusion that religion occupies but one compartment of history.

Many efforts have been made to set forth the rise of denominationalism. In some cases the theme is lost in a welter of facts. In others the handbook approach ignores the unbroken historical stream in which denominations exist. This book seeks to describe the main ecclesiastical traditions in the proper context of historical development. Hence, the name of each organization, as it first appears, is italicized in the text. Since one is easily lost in the differentiation of multiform species, attention is centered on denominational genera.

And then finally, emphasis is placed on the reunions and associations that comprise the Ecumenical Movement and give visible expression, however imperfectly, to the unity of the City of God, the communion of the saints. "And they shall all be one."

Many have helped in the making of this book. The library staff of Garrett Biblical Institute have assisted with unremitting resourcefulness and patience. Appreciation must be expressed to Roland H. Bainton, Don W. Holter, David C. Shipley, Matthew Spinka, and William Toth, who have read various chapters, and to Edmund D. Soper, who read the entire manuscript. Their kind but pointed suggestions have made possible a better book. A less tangible but equally significant debt of gratitude the author wishes to express to his professors in graduate studies at Yale University, especially Roland H. Bainton, Hajo Holborn, and Kenneth S. Latourette, and to Hastings Eells, H. C. Hubbart, and C. E. Van Sickle, who first made history a living thing at Ohio Wesleyan University.

FREDERICK A. NORWOOD

Contents

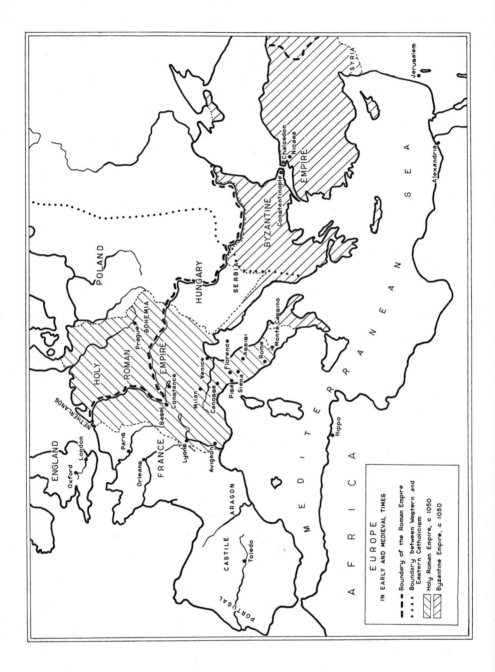

EUROPE
IN EARLY AND MEDIEVAL TIMES

- - - Boundary of the Roman Empire
· · · · Boundary between Western and
         Eastern Catholicism
///// Holy Roman Empire, c 1050
\\\\\ Byzantine Empire, c 1050

CHAPTER I

From Revelation to Reformation
[100-1500]

A. The Early Church

SCARCELY A RIPPLE OF CONCERN WAS PERCEPTIBLE IN ROME AS REPORTS came in of dissension in Judea over the agitation of certain Galileans. After such news as the Roman procurator, Pontius Pilate, thought worthy of report had been sent through channels, little of an untoward nature was apparent. Moreover, the Governor of Syria could be counted on to take care of any exigency that threatened to get out of hand. The Emperor Tiberius had many other responsibilities—important ones. The Romans never could understand the Jews anyway.

A generation went by before the center of the Empire became acutely aware that out of Judea, the least of the provinces of the world dominion of Rome, had arisen a movement that was escaping from the confines of Jewish culture and was spreading through Greek cities and even to Rome itself. All that went on between the death of Jesus and the death of Paul we do not know, simply because most of such few records as were made are lost. What happened to the Apostles? With the exception of some slight information in the book of Acts and scattered references elsewhere, we do not know. Their history has been lost, and as a result their legend has been found. It has provided a neat and geographically delineated province for each. Some of it may be true. We do not know.

But we do know this: From the depths of the Crucifixion and the heights of the Resurrection rose by the time of Pentecost a congregation of the followers of Jesus, whom they now called the Christ. They followed in his Way, under the guidance of the Holy Spirit. First in Jerusalem, then in Palestine, then throughout the provinces of the East, finally around the Mediterranean world, this little congregation spread and multiplied until one day—in law at least—none but Christians were to be found in the civilized world of Rome. In the earliest years the followers of the Way—as they liked to call themselves—were scarcely aware that they were Christians. They remained within the general framework of Judaism, adhered to the regulations and customs of the Old Testament, and sought at the same time to express their faith in Christ as the Anointed One, the Messiah. The implications of this new faith were slow in development.

1. Christianity Tried. Down to the fourth century Christianity was illegal. To be a Christian was against the law. If a man went to church, he did so covertly, avoiding attention. The Romans looked unfavorably on Christians for a variety of reasons, some of which were valid. Many unfounded charges were laid against them, including antisocial behavior, cannibalism, and even atheism. Behind it all lay the knowledge that Christians were exclusive, unwilling to share in the large family of pagan deities widely accepted by intelligent men. The Christians would worship one God and one only. They did not admire the broad-minded benevolence which prompted the Emperor Alexander Severus to place a bust of Christ on his private altar, along with images of other prominent deities. And then, Christians were peculiar. They were— well, different. They rejected widely accepted customs and insisted on doing things their way. They even objected to the rite of venerating the image of the emperor with a pinch of incense. Being peculiar, they were suspect. Being suspect, they were dangerous. Although they had preserved the saying of their leader, "Render unto Caesar the things that are Caesar's," they also maintained, "We must obey God rather than men." Such people could expect no consideration in the Roman Empire, which had to look after all her subjects. Law, proper order, and discipline required that the Christians be put down.

Persecutions were sporadic for several generations. At first they were entirely local and unplanned. By 250, however, the Emperor Decius decided that an all-out effort must be made to eradicate the pestilent sect. By now Christians were numbered even among governmental officials. Many influential and well-placed individuals were favorably disposed to the new doctrine. If the ancient integrity of Rome was to survive, the insidious infiltration of this alien and cowardly religion must be stopped. Two years previously Rome had celebrated the one thousandth anniversary of its foundation. Should the truly admirable achievement of a millennium be lost? Should the strength of the Empire be weakened from within at a time when bastions on the frontiers were already feeling the pressure of imponderable forces of barbarism? Decius therefore decreed the first general persecution, a fearful period in which Christians were sought out, exposed, denounced, and forced either to abjure the faith or to suffer terribly, even to death. Many did heroically "confess" with their lives. Others, willing but weak, "lapsed" in one way or another, sometimes with the friendly connivance of local officials.

Other periods of persecution followed. Not until 313, when the Edict of Milan, issued by the Emperor Constantine, decreed toleration throughout the Empire, could Christians relax and sleep peaceably.

During these early years the Roman state was not the only problem besetting the leaders of the new faith. There were ambitious rivals without and insistent critics, soon to be labeled heretics, within. First, but probably least dangerous as a rival, was the official Roman religion supported by the state, featuring a gallery of gods and goddesses largely borrowed from Greek mythology. More important were the mystery and fertility cults imported from the East. These were religions that promised many benefits akin to Christianity, including present prosperity, future felicity, and life everlasting, sometimes even with a dying and rising god through whom all men might win salvation. On the other hand a real challenge came from the Roman and Greek philosophers, in the tradition of Plato and Aristotle. The men of Athens had been slightly amused at the ridiculous figure of an Asian Jew delivering an oration on some incomprehensible topic. It is amazing that Paul found *any* followers in the ancient capital of rational thought. "What has Athens to do with Jerusalem?" asked Tertullian, one of the most outspoken defenders of the way of Christ.

The ramparts might be well manned against rival religions, but what about the traitors who bored from within—those who would distort or adulterate the Christian faith beyond recognition? Already heresy was a growing problem. Judaizers (Jews in Christian garb), Gnostics (pagans in Christian garb), Syncretists (wearing the coat of many colors), had entered the Christian fold from early times. Persian

dualism and other oriental principles got in through Manichaean teachings. If the apologists—as the champions of Christian truth were called
—effectively defended Christianity from pagan rivals and critics, writers
like Tertullian and Cyprian set out to protect the nascent church from
heretics. The former, while he denounced the use of force, was not above
quoting scripture against the incorrigible obstinacy of the Gnostics. And
although Cyprian said we should seek to become wheat and leave the
tares to God, he cut off all who differed with him and said, "Outside the
Church is no salvation." Theologians like Irenaeus, Clement of Alexandria, and Origen set about the definition of the faith as held by the
"orthodox" or true believers. The stage was set for the great trinitarian
and christological controversies of the fourth and fifth centuries. The
first of these controversies dealt with the central problem of God as one
God, yet also Father, Son, and Holy Spirit. How could God be three
"persons," yet one? The other controversy raised the issue of the nature
of the person of Christ. Is he human, or divine, or a combination of
both?

In these very first centuries, therefore, a tendency toward diversity,
if not yet division, appeared within the Christian fold. This tendency
will constitute one of the chief themes in the long story that follows
and finds modern expression in some 250 denominations. But along
with this increasing diversity grew a sense of spiritual unity through
faith in Christ, binding Christians together in a fellowship of belief,
worship, and service. Against this one Church, transcending the
divisiveness of all churches, all the powers of earthly rulers could not
prevail.

Before we take leave of these early Christians of the persecuted
Church, let us pause over the appealing picture painted in that matchless document, the Letter to Diognetus, probably written early in the
second century:

Christians cannot be distinguished from the rest of the human race by
country or language or customs. They do not live in cities of their own;
they do not use a peculiar form of speech; they do not follow an eccentric
manner of life. This doctrine of theirs has not been discovered by the in-

genuity or deep thought of inquisitive men, nor do they put forward a merely human teaching, as some people do. Yet, although they live in Greek and barbarian cities alike, as each man's lot has been cast, and follow the customs of the country in clothing and food and other matters of daily living, at the same time they give proof of the remarkable and admittedly extraordinary constitution of their own commonwealth. They live in their own countries, but only as aliens. They have a share in everything as citizens, and endure everything as foreigners. Every foreign land is their fatherland, and yet for them every fatherland is a foreign land. They marry, like everyone else, and they beget children, but they do not cast out their off-spring. They share their board with each other, but not their marriage bed. It is true that they are "in the flesh," but they do not live "according to the flesh." They busy themselves on earth, but their citizenship is in heaven. They obey the established laws, but in their own lives they go far beyond what the laws require. They love all men, and by all men are persecuted. They are unknown, and still they are condemned; they are put to death, and yet they are brought to life. They are poor, and yet they make many rich; they are completely destitute, and yet they enjoy complete abundance. They are dishonored, and in their very dishonor are glorified; they are defamed, and are vindicated. They are reviled, and yet they bless; when they are affronted, they still pay due respect. When they do good, they are punished as evildoers; undergoing punishment, they rejoice because they are brought to life. They are treated by the Jews as foreigners and enemies, and are hunted down by the Greeks; and all the time those who hate them find it impossible to justify their enmity.

To put it simply: What the soul is in the body, that Christians are in the world.[1]

2. Christianity Triumphant. As the Emperor Constantine stood among the dead after the battle of October 27, 312, what did he think of Christ? Or did he think of him at all? The ancient church historian Eusebius tells an engaging story of how, one afternoon, in the presence of the whole army, the Emperor had a vision of a shiny cross in the sky, accompanied by the words, "In this sign conquer." The next night in a dream he was instructed to affix this sign on his standard. Having done so, he entered into battle against his rival for imperial power and defeated him. Was Constantine converted to Christianity upon this occasion? Or was he merely the astute politician who recognized

[1] From *Early Christian Fathers,* edited by Cyril Richardson. The Westminster Press, 1953. Used by permission.

the value of the new religion for his own purposes? This moot question has not yet received its final answer. But the results of the Emperor's favorable experience are manifest.

Christianity ceased to be persecuted. It became one of the freely tolerated religions of the Empire. From this time the church occupied an ever more influential position until that other day arrived, November 8, 392, when another emperor, Theodosius, put his hand to a decree forbidding anyone, even in private, to offer sacrifice, to honor the *lares* by fire, *genii* by libations, *penates* by incense, or to adore idols, construct altars of grass, or in any other way to worship any deity other than God the Father through his Son Jesus Christ. The only non-Christian faith excepted was Judaism.

In 394 the last Olympic games, symbol of Greek humanism, were held, and then passed out of existence, to be forgotten until our times. By 529 the last light of pagan philosophy, the once famed school of Athens, was snuffed out, foreshadowing the gathering darkness attendant upon the dissolution of the Roman Empire itself. Thus, as that ancient institution embraced in marriage of church and state the new and vibrant Christian faith, it at that moment felt the coldness of limb and stiffness of countenance that mark approaching death. As the emperors abandoned the West and moved the capital of the Empire into a world of Byzantine splendor in the East—Constantinople —the bishops of Rome stepped forth as at once the champions of Christianity and the defenders of what was left of ancient civilization, ready and able to adjust to the barbarian forces slowly stifling the antique world.

In the course of its triumph the Christian faith was congealed into an institution. Fathers like Ambrose, bishop of Milan and defender of the church against encroachment by the state; Jerome, monk and translator of the Bible into Latin (the Vulgate) ; and Augustine, theologian extraordinary, adversary of the Donatists, Manichaeans, and Pelagians, and author of *The City of God* and of the *Confessions,* one of the first great spiritual autobiographies—these men helped forge an ecclesiastical structure, a doctrinal standard, and a moral discipline characteristic of Christianity in its many branches to this day.

The new prestige of the church is illustrated by the story of Ambrose and the Emperor. Theodosius in a rage had massacred seven thousand people of Thessalonica. Returning to Milan, he sought to enter the church for mass. But he was met at the door by Ambrose, who told him, "You cannot enter here with hands soiled by human blood." And even the Emperor had to do penance before he was admitted to communion.

Gradually, then, the faith congealed. The process involved both good and evil for the church—good because formation of structure was necessary for survival in the midst of so many conflicting forces, evil because solidification meant exclusion of forms of the faith that did not accord with the rigid standards of "orthodoxy." The result was widespread division and schism.

The main channel for the development of churchly standards was the ecumenical or universal council. Seven of these are accepted by the three main branches, Roman Catholic, Eastern Orthodox, and Protestant, in their formulation of fundamental doctrine. These are: Nicaea (325), Constantinople (381), Ephesus (431), Chalcedon (451), Constantinople (553), Constantinople (680-81), Nicaea (787). Of these, two are probably the most significant, Nicaea (325) and Chalcedon. The issues fought out in these councils had their roots in differences already noticeable in New Testament times and already formulated by theologians of the second and third centuries. Early creeds defined God in terms of Father, Son, and Holy Spirit, and the Son was widely regarded as both divine and human. The problem in each case was to arrive at a proper understanding of the relationships of three in one (the Trinity) and two in one (Christ). The problem considered at Nicaea was presented when one Arius, an aged priest of Alexandria began to teach that Christ, although divine, was less than God. His opponent, Athanasius, defended the view that Christ was fully God, equal with the Father in the Trinity. The Emperor Constantine, who had embraced Christianity as a cement that would help hold the Empire together, was shocked to discover that this cement was itself cracking. He called a council at Nicaea in 325 to decide the issue. Arianism was condemned and Christ was described as "God of God, Light of Light, very God of very God, begotten not made, being of one substance with the Father." Thus arose the *Arian* heresy that continued to trouble the church into the Middle Ages and has influenced Christian thought to this day.

A further difficulty then arose over the nature of the second Person of the Trinity. When the bishop of Alexandria began to use the term "Mother of God" with reference to the Virgin Mary, Nestorius, bishop of Constantinople, rejected the term. He was therefore charged with denying the full divinity of Christ. Nestorius ended his tragic days in exile, but *Nestorianism* continued a vigorous and divisive force, and found expression in a church organization centered in the Persian Empire. Its supporters had difficulty in accepting the doctrine of two complete natures, divine and human, in one person. This question was not resolved until 451, when the Council of Chalcedon decided, after considering the difficult problems revolving around the terms substance, hypostasis, person, nature, that Christ was

the same perfect in Godhead and also perfect in manhood; truly God and truly man, of a reasonable soul and body; consubstantial with the Father according to the Godhead, and consubstantial with us according to the Manhood; . . . to be acknowledged in two natures, *inconfusedly, unchangeably, indivisibly, inseparably;* the distinction of natures being by no means taken away by the union, but rather the property of each nature being preserved, and concurring in one Person and one Subsistence, not parted or divided into two persons, but one and the same Son, and only begotten, God the Word, the Lord Jesus Christ.[2]

This meant that those who had stressed the divine nature of Christ as over against his human nature were excluded. They formed several branches of *"Monophysite"* Christianity, including most of Egypt, Ethiopia, and Syria, and part of Armenia. Since the Chalcedonian formula stood firmly on Christ's divinity *and* humanity, neither Nestorians on the one hand nor Monophysites on the other could accept the settlement. Both of these dissident groups were strongly influenced by political factors as well as theological. The history of the *Armenian Church,* for example, is inextricably tied up with the national history of the Armenians. In Egypt rose the *Coptic Church,* in Syria the *Jacobite Church,* in Ethiopia the *Abyssinian Church,* all of which survive to this day.

[2] Philip Schaff, *The Creeds of Christendom* (New York: Harper & Bros., 1877), II, 62.

In addition to the divisions that came from theological-political conflicts others arose from questions of organization and discipline, also with political overtones. Even in the early period the *Montanists* had, through extreme asceticism (severe, self-denying discipline), broken with the main tradition. In the time of Augustine the *Donatists* also split over the question of discipline, especially the validity of sacraments administered by a priest of impure life. The Donatists said that baptism and ordination by an immoral priest were worthless. Their immediate concern was over those who had betrayed the faith during the Diocletian persecutions by destroying Scriptures or denying they were Christians. Such conduct disqualified priests in their rigorous discipline. In answer Augustine and others recognized that such a contingency would undercut the whole doctrine of sacraments as channels of grace, and maintained rather that they are valid if administered correctly by persons of proper ordination. All these schismatic groups died out during the early Middle Ages.

Partly as a result of the various problems of doctrine and discipline, the church developed standards of authority. From the original organization of presbyter and deacon evolved a complicated and impressive edifice of bishops, archbishops, metropolitans, patriarchs, and finally the pope. Five patriarchs continued to claim special apostolic authority, four of them in the East—Jerusalem, Antioch, Alexandria, Constantinople. The last of these achieved greater prestige because he was associated with the political power of the Eastern emperors. His major rival was the patriarch of the West, the bishop of Rome, who claimed, and was granted in a measure, supreme authority over the whole church, by virtue of his office at the traditional heart of the Empire and his succession from the chief of the Apostles, Peter. The interpretation of Matthew 16:18 by the bishops of Rome continued for them the power granted to Peter by Christ. This interpretation was not acceptable to the four patriarchs of the East, who would give to their Western brother no more than a sort of honorary pre-eminence, if that. The story of how this difference, together with theological and political factors, led to the historic schism between East and West is part of the story of the Middle Ages. But the seeds of the division were laid in the early church. Throughout the time of Popes Leo I (mid fifth century) and Gregory I (end of sixth), both termed "the Great," the bishops of Rome developed the theory of papal supremacy within the church. The outworking of this theory is also part of the medieval story.

B. The Medieval Church

1. Rise of the Roman Catholic Church. There is a big difference between 250 and 1076. In the former year the bishop of Rome was imprisoned by the emperor and died there; in the latter the bishop of Rome, now pope, kept the emperor waiting penitent outside a castle for three days while he deliberated on proper judgment. The difference is explained by the rise of a powerful institution, the *Roman Catholic Church,* in many ways the epitome of the Middle Ages.

The story of the bishops of Rome does not begin with Gregory I, the Great (590-604); but he has been called with some justification the "first of the popes." Foundations for papal authority had been laid during the great doctrinal controversies of the three preceding centuries; but not until the Roman Empire had dissolved in the midst of the barbarian invasions did the bishops of Rome come into their own as almost the sole surviving authority of any kind in the West. Whereas the Eastern patriarchs were repeatedly hampered by rivalries among themselves and by the continuing Roman imperial authority in Constantinople, the "patriarch of the West" was relatively free to operate in not only spiritual but also temporal affairs.

The position of Gregory I is illustrative. During his pontificate he had to look after the feeding of the people of Rome during famine, fend off the growing threat of Lombards in northern Italy, administer the large and scattered papal lands—all this in addition to his responsibilities as bishop of Rome, patriarch of the West (Italy, Gaul, Spain, Britain), and universal pope over the whole church.

This last was a touchy point, for the patriarch of Constantinople had called himself "ecumenical patriarch." Gregory with elaborate humility took to himself the title "servant of the servants of God." His interests ranged from promotion of the Christian mission to England to negotiations with the church in the East. His influence was felt in all aspects of church life—in preaching, liturgy, church music; in the discipline of clergy and monks; in administrative organization; in doctrine, especially popular belief and biblical interpretation; and in missionary expansion.

The mission to England under Augustine (not to be confused with the early-fifth-century bishop of Hippo) is one of the high lights. This Augustine planted Roman Christianity in Britain, where already a non-Roman form had been brought from Ireland. The casting of this bread upon the waters brought back returns within a century, when numerous missionaries from England moved to the Continent for missions among the still pagan people of central Europe.

Gregory also helped set the tone of popular Roman Christianity for the Middle Ages and, to some extent, for that church in our own day, with his development of such aspects as saints, miracles, allegorization of the Bible, purgatory, angels and demons, and semi-Augustinian theology.

During the Middle Ages monasticism was taking root in western Europe. Originating in the ascetic, antisocial, and otherworldly atmosphere of the East, exemplified by the flight of Anthony to the desert in Egypt, in the West it was transformed into a vigorous, active, and socially significant form of Christian devotion. Preserving the ideals of contemplation and escape from worldly sin, Western monasticism added the emphases on communal living, scholarly study, work, and finally, with the appearance of the friars, religious and social service among men living in the sinful world.

In this Western development Benedict, who founded the mother monastery of the Benedictine Order, Monte Cassino, about 529, is most important. His Rule, with its balanced regimen of work, worship, study, and rest, became the model for monastic establishments in Europe. From this beginning sprang in the next centuries the Cluniac monastic reform, the austere Carthusians, the Cistercians famous for St. Bernard and for sheep raising, and many other lesser orders.

With some radical changes of fortune, ebb and flow, the church of Rome developed down to the time of Gregory VII (1073-85), already famous as Hildebrand, ecclesiastical statesman. Under this vigorous pope the church was confirmed in its power and influence in society, and the papacy was confirmed in its authority both within the church and in secular affairs. Symbols of these achievements are (1) the institution of clerical celibacy, and (2) the humiliation of the Holy Roman Emperor Henry IV at Canossa. Gregory did not invent celibacy, which had been advocated in some circles from early times. But he did effectively enforce this rule, thus demonstrating his growing disciplinary authority. The affair involving Henry IV concerned investiture—that is, the installation of ecclesiastical officials and investment with the symbols of their authority. The trouble lay in the question as to who should do the investing, the pope or the emperor.

This problem involved feudalism, a fundamental medieval institution that can best be understood along three lines. It was at once a system of land tenure, a form of political organization, and a bond of personal loyalty. In its economic aspect it meant the separation of the functions of ownership and use of land. The owner, or overlord, did not actually work or control all his land; the user, or vassal, did not own the land he controlled and used. Each, overlord and vassal, bound in mutual contract, owed certain services to the other. Out of this situation grew the typical fief, which was held and used by a vassal as a grant from his overlord in return for military and other services, and in the possession of which the vassal was protected by the overlord. In this way feudalism took on a political aspect, involving mutual relations from the lowliest vassal-knight to the mightiest king. Many leaders figured as both overlord and vassal, subdividing fiefs they held from an overlord among vassals of their own. In the third place the two were bound together in the personal bond of loyalty, in which the vassal became the overlord's "man" (not in the sense of servant or underling).

In this system the church was deeply involved. Bishops and abbots were overlords and vassals, not so much of each other as of secular princes. Now the obvious question is: When a bishop is appointed to a see in, say, Germany, who nominates, elects, and invests him? Aside from the cathedral chapter, what are the rights of the pope, his spiritual overlord, and the emperor, his temporal overlord? This issue lay beneath the conflict that led Henry IV to Canossa in the year 1077.

In this episode, after a series of denunciations from both sides, the Pope, Gregory VII, excommunicated the Emperor and released his subjects from their bonds of allegiance. Unable at the time to stand against this power, Henry crossed the Alps and sought a personal consultation with Gregory, who kept him waiting outside, barefoot and in penitential garments, for three wintry days, while he decided what should be done. Canossa was the location of the event and has become the symbol of the victory—temporary, it turned out—of papal authority over imperial. The stage was set for the great age of faith, the thirteenth century, in which papal authority in the person of Innocent III, dogmatic authority in the person of Thomas Aquinas, and monastic discipline in the forms of Franciscans and Dominicans, combined to provide a glimpse of a majestic ideal, *respublica Christiana,* the universal Christian empire, in which all men, even emperors, should give prime allegiance to the vicar of Christ, the lord pope, who wielded the awful power of God himself.

2. Rise of the Eastern Orthodox Church. Before this, however, an episode had occurred that damaged considerably the ideal of the Christian unity of civilization. This was a division between the Eastern and Western churches. The trouble had been long brewing, ever since the seat of empire had been transferred from Rome to Constantinople in the fourth century. There were doctrinal, political, economic, and purely personal aspects. The church in the East continued to be dominated by the authority of the Byzantine emperors, although the theory of co-ordinate spheres, temporal and spiritual, survived. In the West imperial authority disappeared, and, when revived from the ninth century on, never succeeded in completely dominating the church, over which the pope increasingly ruled supreme. The mere fact that after 800 there were *two* empires—impossible in theory—suggested two churches. Economic disparity between the flourishing East and the barbarous West increased the differences. Doctrinal difficulties between the activistic, Latin-speaking West, with its concerns for the doctrine of man and sin, and the passivistic, Greek-speaking East, with its concerns for contemplation and the doctrine of the Incarnation, took forms rather obscure to modern minds, but fundamental to the diverging theological paths of the time. And then the personal struggles for prestige and power, four-sided between Eastern and Western emperors and Eastern and Western prelates, led to hard feeling and then to growing suspicion and hatred. It all came to a head in 1054, when legates of the pope dramatically laid on the altar of the great church of Hagia Sophia in Constantinople a bull of excommunication against the patriarch, who in his turn a few days later in solemn assembly excommunicated the legates. Although this did not mark the final breach, which was postponed until the middle of the fourteenth century, in practice there were now two major churches, and also the ancient heretical churches already described. The seamless robe of Christ had been rent! Here was no slight imperfection on the universal robe, such as ancient and medieval heresies marked. Here was a clear and complete division and separation. Amazingly, the theory of the one true Church persevered, even as applied to earthly institutions, down to our own day. But from this time has existed in Christendom not one Catholic Church, but two, both claiming to be catholic—that is, universal. The dream of temporal catholicity might persist; the fact of division was irretrievable.

By the end of the eleventh century the church already exhibited four forms of diversity: (1) schism between East and West, (2) ancient though small schismatic churches springing from doctrinal and disciplinary controversies, (3) non-institutionalized "heretical" movements, and (4) monasticism, with its principle of a double ethic, the higher for monks who would follow the counsels of perfection, the lower for ordinary mortals who hoped for salvation in spite of their own sinfulness through the sacraments and ministry of the church. More divisions were to follow from "heretical" movements of the high and late Middle Ages and from the final outworking of the monastic movement in the orders of friars—all these before the many and deepreaching divisions of the Reformation.

3. The Medieval Ideal of Christian Roman Empire. In spite of actual division the Western church continued to act as if the seamless robe were still whole. The claim to universal world dominion in the name of Christ came closer to realization during the pontificate of Innocent III (1198-1216) than at any other time in history, before or since. Not only was the Pope regarded as supreme in the church, which was one and indivisible, but also he was widely recognized as superior even in temporal authority over any kings or princes whatsoever. With few exceptions the mere threat of excommunication was sufficient to bring even the most recalcitrant ruler to submission. The king of France, stubborn Philip Augustus, was forced to take back his divorced wife and restore confiscated church lands. The Pope arbitrated between two claimants to the imperial crown. He re-established and extended direct papal political control over much of Italy. He subdued with excommunication and interdict King John of England, who sur-rendered his entire kingdom to Innocent and received it back as a vassal ruling under the direction of papal legates. He was feudal suzerain over such exalted vassals as the kings of Aragon, Portugal, Po-land, Hungary, and Serbia. His control of the hierarchy and the church at large was equally thorough. Papal monarchy was a reality under this able, vigorous, persistent, and ambitious prelate.

The Fourth Lateran Council of 1215 set the doctrinal structure of the Middle Ages. The culmination of the monastic movement came in this period, with the formation of the two orders of friars, the Francis-cans and the Dominicans. Both Francis and Dominic were children of their age, both fully medieval. But the former has achieved universal appeal beyond the Roman Catholic Church and beyond the Middle Ages, whereas the latter has remained bound within the confines of both. The Franciscans became the humble followers of Jesus, trying by means of biblical primitivism to revive the Apostolic Way. In so striving they released creative forces that led within a century to "heretical" movements, such as the *Fraticelli,* which broke with the church. The Dominicans, on the other hand, became the *domini canes,* the hounds of God, devoted to the principles of Roman Catholic truth and papal authority against heresy and schism. They were tailor-made agents for the contemporary institution for maintenance of orthodox belief, the Holy Office of Inquisition, which awesome instrument for the suppression of heresy was soon to come.

The principle almost universally accepted in the Middle Ages was that there is but one true faith, that this faith is known and defined by the authority of the church through the power granted to the popes through Peter, and that therefore all other faiths are false and heretical.

If a murderer is detested and punished for killing the body, how much more heinous is he who kills the soul—the heretic! The instrument devised to preserve this uniformity of belief was the Inquisition, and the men most qualified to use this instrument were the Dominicans, with their great learning, preaching ability, and hatred of heretics. Free from any ecclesiastical restrictions, unlimited in the exercise of their authority except by the direct action of the pope, the inquisitors struck terror into the hearts of laity and clergy, poor and rich, humble and mighty.

Although technically the papal inquisition was not founded by Innocent, it followed within a generation and truly belonged in the world of faith and authority he embodied. And although it was not established all over Europe, it imposed a seal of silence on most forms of independent thought and action in all matters relating to the church and its dogma. With its secret agents, anonymous accusations, guilt by association, impressive judicial machinery weighted against the defendant, imprisonment without charge, torture, confiscation of goods, and sentence of heavy penance, or even death through the secular arm, it sought to eliminate any variation from orthodox doctrine. It stands as one of the most vigorous attempts ever made to enforce uniformity of thought and belief. It failed.

C. Christianity on the Eve

For over one thousand years Europe had been bemused by the dream of a universal Christian empire—*respublica Christiana*. In the late Middle Ages this dream was rudely broken. The idea, never fully realized at any time, that all Christendom was one, united under the dual sovereignty of the pope, the spiritual ruler, and the emperor, the temporal ruler, dominated the political concepts of men from the days of Augustine of Hippo to those of Marsiglio of Padua. But after heretical movements, the Babylonian Captivity, and the Great Schism had rent the church internally, after the new national monarchs had successfully defied the most vigorous popes, and after insistent demands for reform had led to repeated and largely unsuccessful attempts at purification, never again could even the most starry-eyed visionary maintain the fiction of the seamless robe of undivided Christendom, one in spirit and one in authority. At one and the same time national subdivision and Protestant decentralization took the place of imperial unity and papal catholicity. The result of these tendencies, gathering force in the fourteenth and fifteenth centuries, was the Protestant Reformation.

1. Medieval Heretical Sects. Long before the full force of decline was apparent, ruptures appeared in the façade of Western Christianity. These took the form of "heretical" schisms. They were heretical with reference to the orthodox position of the Roman church, but apostolic in their own interpretation. Insofar as they turned from the authority of the church to the authority of the Bible and from the example of ecclesiastical tradition to that of Christ and his disciples, they may be described as forerunners of the Reformation. Yet they remained essentially medieval. Of them two were outstanding. One has survived to this day.

Most appealing to modern Protestants are the followers of Peter Waldo, who was very much like Francis of Assisi and anticipated him in devotion to the ideal of poverty with his "Poor Men of Lyons." He was familiar with those passages of the Bible advocating a simple life of faith in accordance with the teachings of Jesus. His offense was not so much that he taught poverty—so did Francis—as that he presumed to read and expound the Bible without guidance from the priests. If scholars complained that the Waldenses stumbled over the text, the scholars themselves stumbled as much. G. G. Coulton tells the story of a young cowherd who had lived only one year with a Waldensian family, but already knew by heart forty Sunday Gospel lessons. As it was said of them, "Whatsoever is preached and not proved by the Bible text, they hold for fables." The *Waldenses* are among the few medieval sects that have continued unbroken to the present day. The modern Vaudois of the French-Italian Alpine region have maintained their fellowship as a Protestant group that looks behind Luther and Calvin to their medieval founder, 350 years before.

The *Cathari,*[3] or *Albigenses,* were different from other heretics in

[3] From Greek *katharos,* "pure." They claimed to be cleansed of all sin and worldly interests and so were "perfected."

[25]

that theirs was a religion essentially foreign to the tradition and spirit of Christianity, although it contained strong elements of it. No such thoroughgoing dualism as theirs could be at home in the Christian faith, with its Jewish background of God the creator of heaven and earth and its cherished doctrine of the Incarnation. The Cathari rejected all or part of the Old Testament as reflecting the work of the evil god, Satan, with whom was associated all that is of matter and flesh. The spirit is good; the flesh is bad. Christ could not truly have become man, could not truly have died on the cross. In their effort to withdraw as far as possible from the flesh, some Cathari even resorted to suicide. It is little wonder that other heretics denounced Catharism as vigorously as Catholicism. This heresy, of Manichaean origin, reflecting Persian dualism, was a stranger.

2. *Decline of the Church*. Pope Boniface VIII (1294-1303) embarked on a vigorous program of supervision of the rulers of Europe patterned after the noble precedent established by Innocent III some one hundred years before. But he soon found himself in the position of one who, having corralled the sheep, is driven over the fence by the goats. In two famous bulls (papal letters sealed with a bulla) , *Clericis laicos* and *Unam sanctam*, Boniface had attempted to forbid the taxation of the clergy by secular princes and to establish the universal authority of the papacy. Said the Pope:

Both swords, therefore, the spiritual and the temporal, are in the power of the Church. The former is to be used by the Church, the latter for the Church; the one by the hand of the priest, the other by the hand of kings and knights, but at the command and permission of the priest. Moreover, it is necessary for one sword to be under the other, and the temporal authority to be subjected to the spiritual. . . . And we must necessarily admit that the spiritual power surpasses any earthly power in dignity and honor, because spiritual things surpass temporal things.[4]

When King Philip IV of France, called "the Fair," heard of this, he exploded. Calling to his trusted aide, Nogaret, he set about putting

---

[4] Oliver J. Thatcher and E. McNeal, eds., *A Source Book for Medieval History* (New York: Charles Scribner's Sons, 1905) , 315-16.

Boniface in his proper place. The plot amounted to nothing less than the abduction of the Pope, who was to be captured by Nogaret at Anagni, a small village near Rome. Taken prisoner to France, he was to be tried and deposed and replaced by a pope of Philip's choosing. The plan worked well until Boniface was rescued by his fellow townsmen and conducted to Rome, where, infirm with age and upset by his ordeal, he died about a month later. *Sic transit gloria mundi.* If the symbol of papal supremacy over temporal rulers is seen in the dramatic episode of Canossa, the symbol of the new independence of the national monarchs is observed in the equally dramatic episode of Anagni.

The effects of the disastrous collapse of papal authority under the rising powers in France and England were immediate and apparent. The death of Boniface opened the way for a general attack on the medieval church. When his immediate successor died soon after his election, the cardinals, at Perugia, finally settled on a Frenchman educated in France and at the time archbishop of Bordeaux, who assumed the title Clement V. Under the influence of Philip IV the new pope, to the consternation of the Italians and to the outrage of much of the rest of Europe, refused to go to Rome for his coronation, but chose instead Lyons, where he was crowned in the presence of the French king and delegates from the king of England. This was in 1305, and in that year began the "Babylonian Captivity," as it was called by the Italians, for Clement never went to Rome, nor did his successors—with one brief exception—until 1377. It is called the "Avignonese period," because in 1309 the popes took up residence in Avignon, a city along the Rhone River adjoining France, owned by the king of Naples, who later sold it to the popes. Christendom was treated to the sorry sight of a line of popes subservient to the line of kings who had humiliated the great Boniface and defied the authority of the church.

And that was not all. At Avignon the papacy took on some of its less spiritual aspects, especially the efficient expansion of papal finance under the able John XXII (1316-34). His annual income compared very favorably with that enjoyed by the king of England. During these years new voices of opposition to the old claims of universal papal authority were raised, and new national monarchies like England declared their independence in such statutes as those of Provisors, which forbade the pope to make appointments to ecclesiastical offices in England, and Praemunire, which forbade appeals from English ecclesiastical courts to the papacy. This ran directly counter to the Roman doctrine that the clergy were subject to no national law or king but were primarily under the authority of the supranational papacy.

One of the most direct consequences of the Babylonian Captivity was the Great Schism. Gregory XI, urged to return to Rome by Catherine of Siena and others, decided to end the exile in 1377 by moving back to the eternal city. But having done so, he promptly died, to the confusion of everyone. The cardinals first elected Urban VI, who through utter tactlessness alienated the whole body of cardinals. Repenting of their choice, they declared his election void and chose instead Clement VII, who now took up residence once again in Avignon. (Both of these popes were later declared antipopes and were not counted in the numerical succession.) As Urban refused to accept the reversal, there were now two popes, one in Rome, the other in Avignon, both regularly elected by the same body of cardinals, both claiming universal authority over the whole church. Part of Europe acknowledged the Roman pope, the rest the Avignonese. This, then, was the final catastrophe, for how could anyone pretend to see spiritual unity in the midst of so great temporal confusion? By the time the Council of Constance got around to ending this scandalous duet, it had become a trio, with three popes singing discordantly the same tune. When the council deposed all three in 1417 and elected Martin V, it ended the Schism. But the damage had been done, and powers of dissolution were turned loose throughout the length and breadth of Christendom.

The fifteenth century saw further indications of decline. In the middle decade there sat on the papal throne one Nicholas V, the first of a series of humanist popes. Deeply influenced by the humanistic and secular interests of the Renaissance, he not so much denied or forgot his spiritual calling as added to it a host of extracurricular activities, ranging all the way from the accumulation of the first nucleus of the great Vatican library to the support of worldly secretaries who were busily engaged in undermining the prestige of the papacy and ultimately the validity of Christianity itself. The papacy was itself partially secularized, and in this process joined in uneasy alliance the very forces in the Renaissance that were opposed to a spiritual interpretation of life.

The net result was a decline in spiritual fervor, intellectual vigor, and moral integrity. The latter half of the fifteenth century displayed one of the most discouraging spectacles of religious decline in history, and the papacy led the way. The bottom was reached with Alexander VI, Rodrigo Borgia. Secular, immoral, venal, with single-minded devotion he sought to transform the Papal States into an enlarged inheritance for his son, Cesare. All these fine plans, however, were brought to nought by his death in 1503 and the election of his bitter enemy, Julius II, one of the most successful generals ever to sit on the throne of St. Peter.

Following the lead of the papacy, yet always eager to show the way, high prelates and low servitors participated in the general decline of the church. Wealth; nepotism—favoritism shown to relatives, especially in patronage; simony (from Simon Magus) —the buying or selling of church office or privilege; avarice; immorality; all became, not universal, but certainly widespread.

3. Denunciation of Evils and Demand for Reform. Desperate indeed were the voices raised in protest against the insidious decay. One crying in the wilderness was Catherine of Siena (d. 1380). She yearned for the return of the popes to their ancient seat in Rome, stood as the conscience of the church against the abuses and evils she saw everywhere about her. While urging Gregory XI to come home, she warned him to "drive out of the sheepfold those wolves, those demons incarnate, who think only of good cheer, splendid feasts, and superb liveries." Men of integrity like the great ecclesiastical statesmen Pierre d'Ailly and Jean Gerson struck hard blows at all the accumulated evils of their day, nepotism, annates, indulgences, jubilees, reservations (of revenues from vacant sees), simony, abuse of visitations, fees for everything, and, of course, the injury wrought on France.

Less restrained and more bluntly to the point were the words of many critics in the fifteenth century. Quite early the author of *De Ruina Ecclesia* portrayed Christ judging his latter-day disciples:

The supreme pontiffs, as I know, are elected through avarice and simony; and likewise the bishops are ordained for gold. The old proverb, "Freely give, for freely ye have received," is now most vilely perverted and runs, "Freely have I not received and freely will I not give, for I have bought my bishopric with a great price and must indemnify myself impiously for my outlay." If Simon Magus were now alive, he might buy with money not only the Holy Ghost, but God the Father and Me, God the Son.[5]

Laymen were no less vociferous in denunciation. Geoffrey Chaucer (d. 1400) more than once pointed the finger of scorn at the clergy. Before describing a friar in bitter tones, he drew a satirical picture of a monk:

> He was a lord ful fat and in good poynt;
> His eyen bright, and rollyng in his heed,
> That stemed al as doth a furnace red;
> His bootes souple, his hors in gret estate.
> Now certeinly he was a fair prelate.
> He was not pale as a for-pyned ghost.
> A fat swan loved he best of eny roast.
> His palfray was as broun as is a berye.[6]

These altogether typical individuals stood in stark contrast to the ideal priest:

> A good man was ther of religioun,
> And was a poore Parson of a town;
> But riche he was of holy thought and werk.
> He was also a lerned man, a clerk
> That Christes gospel gladly wolde preach;
> His parishioners devoutly wolde he teach.
>
> . . . .
>
> This noble ensample unto his sheep he gaf,
> That ferst he wroughte, and after that he taughte.
>
> . . . .
>
> He wayted after no pompe nor reverence,
> Nor made himself spiced in conscience,
> But Christes love, and his apostles twelve,
> He taught, and ferst he folwed it himselve.[7]

---

[5] Quoted in Alexander Flick, *The Decline of the Medieval Church* (London: Kegan Paul, 1930), I, 336.

[6] *The Canterbury Tales* (New York: E. P. Dutton & Co., 1930), Everyman's Library, pp. 5-6.

[7] *Ibid.,* pp. 12-13.

Extremely bitter were the gravamina, or lists of grievances, submitted at meetings of the imperial diet in Germany from the middle of the fifteenth century. This spirit was still violent in 1518, when Cardinal Cajetan proposed to the Diet of Augsburg a tax on the clergy and laity to be used against the Turk. The sharp answer he received pointed out that the real enemy of Christianity was not the Turk, but the "hound of hell" in Rome. This same attitude is clear in the famous *Letters of Obscure Men,* published 1515-17 in Germany, a successful satire on sinful and obscurantist tendencies in the church.

All the reformers before the Reformation, from Wyclif and Huss through Savonarola to Ximenes and Erasmus, were at one in their denunciation of the evils rampant in the church they all loved so much. These accumulated criticisms and demands for reform could not remain without effect. From time to time various attempts were made to correct abuses, purify the church of evil influences, raise the standards of the clergy, and generally improve the spiritual quality of life. With few exceptions these efforts were without avail or of only local and temporary effect.

Two men at least, one an Englishman of the fourteenth century, the other a Bohemian of the fifteenth, set about starting something. John Wyclif (d. 1384) and John Huss (d. 1415) are symbols of the crying need for real root-and-branch reform—not a spring house cleaning but a reconstruction.

An Oxford scholar, teacher, priest, and theologian, Wyclif started by attacking some of the cherished privileges and practices of the medieval church. He began to criticize the clergy for their concern with secular affairs, especially their attempts to control magistrates and rulers. Rather, he said, it is for the clergy to attend to spiritual things; and if they fail in their high calling, the magistrates should discipline the priests. Later he attacked certain aspects of papal authority and denied any biblical foundation for the mendicant orders. In 1382-84 he made English translations from the Latin Vulgate, against the express opposition of the hierarchy to putting the Bible into the hands of the common folk, whom, it was thought, it might corrupt.

The storms against him occasioned by these teachings, however, were as nothing to the gale loosed when he tampered with the doctrine of transubstantiation, which made of every mass a miracle. The power to change the consecrated bread and wine of the Lord's Supper into the very body and blood of Christ was the central point of the medieval exaltation of the office of priest. Only the priest, through magical powers conferred by ordination, could perform the miracle of the mass. Ordinary mortals could never hope to participate in this great wonder except through the service of the priest at the altar. Fortunate indeed was Wyclif now that he could count on the protection of mighty political figures in the England of Edward III, especially John of Gaunt. Wyclif bravely spoke of the "idolatry of the priests of Baal, who worship gods they have made," and of the presumptuous doctrine that granted to "synners the power to make God." The hatred engendered among the conservative hierarchy was cherished down to the Council of Constance, which ordered his bones be dug up and cast away. This was actually done in 1429, with an unexpected result described by one writer in these words: "They burned them to ashes and cast them into Swift, a neighboring brook running hard by. Thus this brook hath conveyed his ashes into Avon, Avon into Severn, Severn into the narrow seas, they into the main ocean. And thus the ashes of Wickliffe are the emblem of his doctrine, which now is dispersed all the world over." [8] Although he left no organized followers and no institutional monument, his influence is seen in two directions: among the *Lollards* of England, who rose in his time and continued down to the Reformation, and the Hussites of Bohemia, who made use of his teachings and writings.

In one way Huss took up where Wyclif left off, for Huss's first break with the authorities of Bohemia came over the question of Wyclif and his teaching. Educated at the University of Prague and preacher in the great Bethlehem Chapel in that city, Huss is one of the most heroic and colorful figures in Bohemian history. When he became rector of the University in 1409, he was soon in deep water over the issue of Wyclif, whose ideas and writings had been brought in by students. Although the archbishop of the city complied with a papal bull ordering the burning of the Englishman's books, Huss refused and preached a sermon on the following theme:

[8] Thomas Fuller, *The Church History of Britain* (London, 1837), I, 493.

Now is fulfilled the prophecy of Jacob of Taramo that in the year 1409 one should arise to persecute the Gospel and the faith of Christ, for the late Pope, I know not whether he be in heaven or in hell, has written on his wretched parchments to the archbishop to burn the books of Master John Wyclif, wherein are many good things.[9]

An interdict laid on Prague led to further conflict, culminating in the arrest and trial of Huss before the Council of Constance, which met in 1414. Appearing at Constance voluntarily and under safe-conduct from the holy Roman emperor, Huss was imprisoned over the objections of his Bohemian supporters on the argument that safe-conducts do not apply to heretics. At his execution he suffered degradation and humiliation as well as extreme torture in the fire. His ashes, like those of Wyclif, were thrown into the river. Alexander Flick calls it the most momentous event of the century.[10] In commemoration long afterward, three medallions were struck in Prague, showing Wyclif striking a spark from a stone, Huss kindling a fire from the spark, and Luther lighting a torch from the fire. The *Hussites* continued in existence and contributed much to the reformation.

The reference to the Council of Constance draws our attention to another reform movement, genuine even though opposed to the heretical programs like those of Wyclif and Huss. The conciliar movement represents both an attempt to establish—or re-establish—an authority in the church higher than the papacy and an effort to effect purification from above. Both failed. The original occasion for the calling of a general council was the Great Schism. Early in the fourteenth century Marsiglio of Padua in his *Defensor Pacis* had set forth the supremacy of a general council, and now this principle was welcomed as an ideal method of healing the split in the papacy. But the first council, that of Pisa in 1409, was a disappointment, for, although it deposed the two rival popes and elected another, the net result was three popes. The wiser leadership in the Council of Constance successfully ended the Schism and sought to promote reforms badly needed. Successful in dealing with the popes, it was less so in tilting with the devil.

---

[9] Eustace J. Kitts, *Pope John the Twenty-Third and Master John Hus of Bohemia* (London: Constable, 1910), p. 46. Quoted from F. Palacky, *Documenta* (1869).

[10] *Op. cit.,* II, 91.

Jealousies and vested interests prevented any serious house cleaning. The later councils of the fifteenth century accomplished little beyond this. In the midst of general disillusionment the popes succeeded in restoring their supremacy and in repealing all conciliar legislation to the contrary.

A less obvious and more introspective, but nonetheless significant, effort to purify the church came from the late medieval mystics, who were anything but unrealistic dreamers. One of them was Meister Eckhart (d. 1327), a pantheist who taught that direct union with God through mystical experience was more important than ecclesiastical observances. His most distinguished disciple was John Tauler, a more practical teacher whose writings deeply affected Luther. From these beginnings sprang the loosely organized group known as the Friends of God, active in southern Germany and Switzerland, including both clergy and laity. And out of this group came the anonymous *German Theology,* setting forth a doctrine of complete surrender to the will of God. As this doctrine spread into the Netherlands, another group developed under the name "Brethren of the Common Life," who added a semi-monastic discipline to the mystical doctrines of contemplation. Thomas à Kempis (d. 1471), reputedly author of the famous *Imitation of Christ,* learned his simple, mystical, warm faith in this association. One should not lose sight of women mystics, most famous of whom was Catherine of Siena, referred to above. Indirectly, through their emphasis on personal religious experience as against ecclesiastical and liturgical observance, these people provided motivation for reform through the whole church. Unfortunately too few were moved in the direction of real improvement, and the mystics remained individual voices isolated in the midst of a church deaf and blind.

By the end of the fifteenth century, therefore, a long process of trial and error had demonstrated not only the need for reform and the widespread demand for it, but also the failure of numerous attempts to accomplish it. Little wonder that some devout souls despaired of saving the church, so sunk in iniquity and blinded by its own evil. Girolamo Savonarola (d. 1498), the evangelistic monk of Florence in Italy, cried in anguish, "When I reflect upon the priests, I am constrained to weep. . . . A terrible chastisement awaits them. . . . O prostitute church, thou hast displayed thy foulness to the whole world and stinkest unto heaven!" This fiery Christian, who began preaching in the city of the Medici in 1482, led the people in a movement that, before it had spent itself, had overthrown the Medici family, opened the gates to the ambitious Charles VIII of France, denounced the sins of the church from those of the notorious Alexander VI down to the evils rampant in Florence itself, and called down a scourge from God on all sinners. But, as the approach of the invading French army had signalized the rise of Savonarola to power, so its departure marked his fall. He was convicted of heresy and burned at the stake.

A more realistic, but also more negative, program of reform was promulgated in Spain by the redoubtable Franciscan monk and eminent Castilian statesman, Francisco Ximenes de Cisneros (d. 1517). Coming to prominence in the days when King Ferdinand of Aragon and Queen Isabella of Castile, both strong Roman Catholics with a double devotion to the papacy and to their own royal interests, were forging a new national monarchy out of the separate kingdoms left over from the Middle Ages, Ximenes rose to power in both church and state. In 1492, a year of many important events in Spain, he was appointed confessor to her majesty; and three years later he became archbishop of Toledo, a position that carried with it not only the spiritual primacy of Spain but also the grand chancellorship of Castile. From this eminence Ximenes proceeded to reform first his own order, with the result that some one thousand monks, unwilling to submit to the new rigor, are said to have left the country. His reforming zeal penetrated into all sides of the Spanish church, culminating in the re-establishment of the Inquisition in its uniquely Spanish form and efficiency. Influenced by the forces of humanism, which in Italy had been directed as often as not against the church and even Christianity, he supported the scholarly study of the Bible according to the new principles, and thus turned this force to the service of the church rather than against it. The result of this effort was the notable Complutensian Polyglot (that is, a multilingual publication of the Bible from Alcalá), finished in 1517 and published in 1520.

This early Spanish reformation, then, was characterized by the zeal of the Castilian and Aragonese monarchs in serving both royal and ecclesiastical interests, by the vigorous purification of both regular and secular clergy under Cardinal Ximenes, and by the very narrow and conservative outlook that Spanish Catholicism has demonstrated to this day. One notes the publication of a new Bible under scholarly and papal auspices in a country where the reading of the Bible by the laity was frowned upon. And one notes the culmination of this triumphant "reformation" in the often fanatical extremes of the Inquisition.

A more benevolent and irenic, although sometimes also ironic, effort arose from the land far to the north of the Pyrenees, in the Netherlands, where was born Desiderius Erasmus (d. 1536). The greatest of all the Christian humanists, he became the most cosmopolitan citizen of Europe and the most respected advocate of peaceful reform within the church. Broadly educated and well traveled, he drank in all the strong intellectual draughts of that volatile age, and then poured out a heady and spicy literary punch of his own. He was not all things to all men, but his fame brought out all the varied facets of his character. Writes his devoted yet critical biographer and editor, P. S. Allen:

And for those who are interested in human nature—and who is not—there is a gallery of characters, almost as rich as in Theophrastus or in Earle: the bright schoolboy, the reluctant canon, the poor student, the brilliant friend, the horseman, the gay courtier, the anxious traveller, the matchless scholar, courted and besought of kings, yet holding them all at arm's length; finally the master lapped in the devotion of his followers, toiling daily with them in his "mill," now exacting and imperious, laying on them burdens heavy as his own, now charming them with natural, unforced merriment.[11]

In Italy, Basel, England, Freiburg im Breisgau, wherever he went, he brought a friendly and amicable spirit into the often bitter struggles raging over the question of reform. Writing in a smooth Latin style worthy of the ancients, he presented, now seriously, now in gentle satire, the needs and methods of reform peacefully within the framework of the church. Nothing was farther from his mind than a tragic schism, a rent in what he thought should be the seamless robe of Christ.

[11] *Erasmus; Lectures and Wayfaring Sketches* (New York: Oxford University Press, 1934), pp. 26-27.

When Martin Luther approached the point of separation and ex-communication, Erasmus shrank back, unwilling to come forth in the front line of what was now becoming a spiritual war. Twitted over his lack of manly courage, he replied, "Were I a Swiss soldier, that might be a warranted reproof; but since I am a man of learning, and need tranquillity for my labors, it harmeth me not." Living safely rather than dangerously, he continued to exert a powerful influence on the forces for reform. Luther himself had to admit that Erasmus could drive home some shrewd blows, as in *Julius Excluded from Heaven.* He certainly personified a most successful marriage of Christianity with the new humanism, indicating one way in which the profound differences between the Renaissance and the Reformation could, in part at least, be resolved. A most happy and successful illustration of this interaction is found in the scholarly edition of the Greek New Testament, which Erasmus published in 1516, a landmark in biblical study.

His benevolence, his wit, his peacefulness, his universalism, have left their mark on the thoughts of men to this day. "I wish," he said at one time, "to be called a citizen of the world, the common friend of all states, or, rather, a sojourner in all." And yet, on his deathbed, the memory of his native land was too strong, and brought to his lips words of a tongue he had well-nigh forgotten: *"Liever Got."*

For Further Reading

This list, and those following, provide a selected bibliography dealing with topics introduced in the text. Adequate understanding of the development of modern Christianity can be achieved only by broad reading in various materials. With few exceptions only recent publications in English are included.

GENERAL

Case, S. J., *et al.*, eds. *A Bibliographical Guide to the History of Christianity.* Chicago: University of Chicago Press, 1931, 265 p.

Church History. Bibliographical articles on the following subjects help bring Case up to date. *Journals:* XXI (1952), 73-75. *Ancient church history:* XX (1951), 68-71; XXI (1952), 365-67; XXII (1953), 327-29 ff. *Medieval church history:* XXI (1952), 146-49; XXII (1953), 239-42. *Reformation:* IX (1940), 305-40; XIX 1950), 116-128; XVII (1948), 207-40; XVII (1949), 241. *Modern Europe:* XXI (1952), 71-73; XXI (1952), 267-271. *Eastern Orthodox history:* XX (1951), 82-84; XXII (1953), 166-68. *American church history:* XX (1951), 72-74; XXI

1952), 150-52. *Expansion of Christianity:* XX (1951), 85-90; XXI (1952), 345-64; XXII (1953), 50-53; XXII (1953), 329-336.

Bettenson, Henry, ed. *Documents of the Christian Church.* New York and London: Oxford University Press, 1947, 457 p. Predominance of Anglican materials.

Ehler, Sidney Z., and J. B. Morrall, eds. *Church and State Through the Centuries.* Westminster, Md.: Newman Press, 1954, 625 p. Excellent collection of Roman Catholic documents.

Gee, H., and W. J. Hardy, eds. *Documents Illustrative of English Church History Compiled from Original Sources.* New York: The Macmillan Co., 1902, 670 p.

Fosdick, Harry E., ed. *Great Voices of the Reformation.* New York: Random House, Inc., 1952, xxx, 546 p. Popular collection, from Wyclif to Wesley.

Kepler, Thomas, ed. *The Fellowship of the Saints.* New York and Nashville: Abingdon Press, 1948, 800 p. Devotional selections from historical sources.

Mirbt, Carl, ed. *Quellen zur Geschichte des Papsttums und des Roemischen Katholizismus.* Tuebingen: J. C. B. Mohr, 1934, 650 p. Standard, in the original languages.

Schaff, Philip. *The Creeds of Christendom.* New York: Harper & Bros., 1877, 3 vols.

Latourette, Kenneth S. *A History of Christianity.* New York: Harper & Bros., 1953, 1516 p.

Walker, Williston. *A History of the Christian Church.* New York: Charles Scribner's Sons, 1918, 624 p.

Hughes, Philip. *A History of the Church.* New York: Sheed & Ward, 1935, 3 vols. By a Roman Catholic, based on scholarship.

Brinton, Crane. *Ideas and Men.* New York: Prentice-Hall, Inc., 1950, 597 p. Penetrating survey of intellectual history by a general historian.

Fliche, A., and V. Martin. *Histoire de l' Eglise.* Paris: Bloud & Gay, 1948, 26 vols. Magnificent enterprise by modern French Catholic historians; only about one half of the volumes have appeared.

Hauck, Albert. *Kirchengeschichte Deutschlands.* Leipzig: J. C. Hinrichs'sche Buchhandlung, 1887-1903, 5 vols. Standard.

Latourette, Kenneth S. *A History of the Expansion of Christianity.* New York: Harper & Bros., 1939-45, 7 vols.

Schaff, Philip. *History of the Christian Church.* New York: Charles Scribner's Sons, 1882-1910, 7 vols. Old, but generally still reliable.

Neve, J. L., and O. W. Heick. *History of Christian Thought.* Philadelphia: Muhlenberg Press, 1946, 2 vols.

Seeberg, R. *Textbook of the History of Doctrines.* Grand Rapids: Baker Book House, 1952, 2 vols. in 1.

Pastor, Ludwig. *History of the Popes from the Close of the Middle Ages.* St. Louis: B. Herder Book Co., 1899-1953, 40 vols. Standard and exhaustive.

CHRISTIANITY ON THE EVE

Cheyney, Edward P. *Dawn of a New Era.* New York: Harper & Bros., 1936, 389 p. Rise of Modern Europe series, 1250-1453.

Gilmore, Myron P. *The World of Humanism, 1453-1517.* New York: Harper & Bros., 1952, 326 p. Rise of Modern Europe series.

Mackinnon, James. *The Origins of the Reformation.* New York and London: Longmans, Green & Co., 1939, 448 p.

Flick, Alexander C. *The Decline of the Medieval Church.* New York: Alfred A. Knopf, Inc., 1930, 2 vols.

Ferrara, Orestes. *The Borgia Pope: Alexander VI*. New York: Sheed & Ward, 1940, 455 p.

Misciattelli, Piero. *Savonarola*. New York: D. Appleton-Century Co., 1930, 273 p.

McFarlane, Kenneth B. *John Wycliffe and the Beginnings of English Noncon-formity*. New York: The Macmillan Co., 1952, 197 p. Teach Yourself History series.

Workman, H. B. *John Wyclif*. Oxford: Clarendon Press, 1926. 2 vols.

Spinka Matthew. *John Hus and the Czech Reform*. Chicago: University of Chicago Press, 1941, 82 p.

Allen, P. S. *The Age of Erasmus*. New York: Oxford University Press, 1914, 303 p.

Smith, Preserved. *Erasmus*. New York: Harper & Bros., 1923, 479 p.

Phillips, Margaret Mann. *Erasmus and the Northern Renaissance*. New York: The Macmillan Co., 1950, 236 p. Teach Yourself History series.

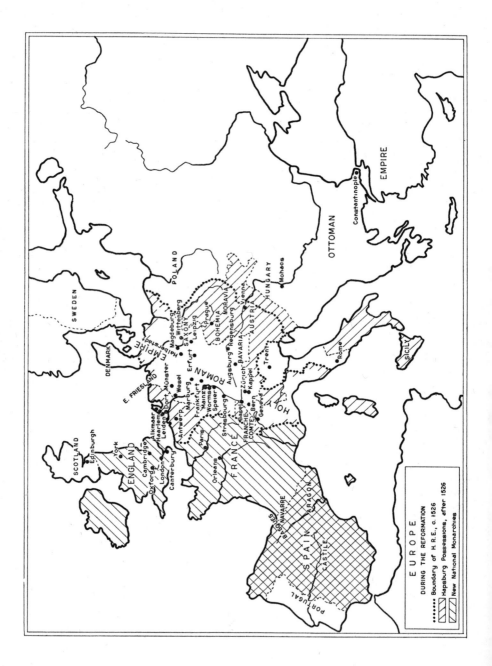

EUROPE
DURING THE REFORMATION

•••••• Boundary of H.R.E., c. 1526
///// Hapsburg Possessions, after 1526
XXXX New National Monarchies

SCOTLAND
Edinburgh•
York•
ENGLAND
Cambridge•
Oxford• London•
Canterbury•

E. FRIESLAND
Alkmaar•
Leiden• Haarlem
Antwerp• Dort• Münster• Wesel•

DENMARK
SWEDEN

EMPIRE
Hildesheim•
Magdeburg•
Wittenberg•
SAXONY Leipzig•
Erfurt• Prague•
ROMAN BOHEMIA MORAVIA
Marburg• Regensburg•
Frankfurt• Augsburg• BAVARIA Vienna•
Mainz• Zürich• AUSTRIA
Worms• Basel• Bern• Kappel• HUNGARY
Speier• FRANCHE- Geneva• Trent• Mohacs•
Strasbourg COMTÉ HOLY

POLAND

OTTOMAN

Constantinople•

EMPIRE

Paris•
Orleans•
FRANCE
BÉARN
BASQUES
NAVARRE ARAGON
SPAIN
CASTILE
PORTUGAL

Rome•

SICILY

CHAPTER II

The Age of Reform

[1500-1648]

A. Luther and Lutheranism

1. MARTIN LUTHER. THE MAN WHO MORE THAN ANY OTHER LET loose the pent-up pressures of reform in the sixteenth century was Martin Luther. He was born about 1483 in Saxony in what is now Germany. He grew up amid rather strict surroundings of home and school. With a B.A. and an M.A. in law from the University of Erfurt, one of the most eminent medieval institutions of the Empire, he was apparently on the threshold of the career his father had hoped for him. And then came—as lives of Luther always tell—the thunderstorm in July, 1505. The crashing of thunder in a world still sunk in fear and superstition was an awful thing. And, as Luther felt the power of an angry deity lashing out *at him,* he cried in terror to St. Anne, vowing he would become a monk if she would save him.

Later holding this vow as binding, he forthwith became a novice in the Augustinian Order. There he devoted himself rigorously to the monastic rule, which was strict but not extreme. This provided for silence in the place of his former volubility, for solitude instead of the boisterous circle of friends, a cell instead of the tavern, discipline instead of amiable indulgence. "If ever a monk gained heaven by his monkery," he wrote later, "I must have done so." He added that he should have martyred himself if he had pursued his regime longer, with watching, praying, studying, and so forth.

He had tried the monastic way of self-help to heaven. This way of attempted righteousness through the sacraments and meritorious works had taught him one thing: He was and remained a miserable sinner in the eyes of God. The Lord required much more of him than he could ever perform. The Judge had him down for what he was. There is no telling what the results might have been for Luther had he not been pulled out of his cell and out of himself.

After a trip to Rome on business of the Order he was assigned to Wittenberg as professor in the new university. The journey of five months to Rome was a sort of seven days' wonder for this provincial Saxon from the "barbaric" regions beyond the Alps. And his responsibilities at Wittenberg kept his mind so full he had little time left for his own condition. Professor of theology, lecturer on Psalms and Romans, pastor of the church, presently district vicar of the Augustinian Order, he was very busy, wholesomely busy.

And in the course of it he found himself—some would say, was found of God. He came to realize through his study of the Psalms that the awful righteous Judge had, for love of the sinner, become the sufferer on the cross. And then, wonderfully, from Romans he finally understood the nature of justification before God. One does not justify himself by good works. One is justified through the grace of God by faith. "As it is written, 'He who through faith is righteous shall live'" (Romans 1:17, Revised Standard Version).

> Did we in our own strength confide,
> Our striving would be losing;
> Were not the right Man on our side,
> The Man of God's own choosing.

Thus Luther put it in his stirring hymn "A Mighty Fortress Is Our God." And thus was established one of the central pillars of the Reformation: justification by faith *alone*. Luther added the last word just to be quite clear about it. Faith in God's saving grace, through our Lord Jesus Christ who died for our sins, faith which is itself a gift of God, faith alone is the base for our justification and redemption. Good works are the fruits of faith, the product of a redeemed life, not the cause of it.

The new pastor at Wittenberg had already been troubled by the problem of indulgences. For Elector Frederick the Wise of Saxony had abundantly endowed his chapel with sacred relics ranging all the way from bones of St. Jerome to a piece of Moses' burning bush. These relics were prized in association with the indulgence authorized by the pope and made available on All Saints' Day each year, when a great indulgence festival was held. But now some of Martin Luther's parishioners came bearing certificates of indulgence entitling them, as they had been told, not only to remission of the temporal penalties for sins repented, confessed, and absolved, but complete remission of all sins. Moreover, they had obtained certificates releasing their late parents from purgatory. Where had they bought these indulgences? They had come, it developed, from outside Saxony, in territory in which the indulgence for St. Peter's in Rome was being offered. The new pastor, concerned about the effect of the practice on the spiritual life of his flock, determined to study anew the doctrine of indulgences and measure its validity. The result was manifest on October 31, 1517, when he posted on the door of the church in Wittenberg his famous Ninety-five Theses.

The doctrine of indulgences arose from the sacrament of penance, which itself developed from the question of postbaptismal sins. One could be baptized only once. If all sinners were lost souls, the churches would be empty and the choir of heaven would never be filled. The sacrament of penance was developed as a solution. Let the repentant individual confess his sins, gain absolution from the priest, and do "penance." In this way the spiritual ledger might be balanced, a credit of meritorious satisfaction against the debit of sin.

In the course of the Middle Ages elaborate penitential schedules were worked out, certain penances for specific sins of defined degrees. Gradually, however, the practice became common of substituting one penance for another. In the time of the Crusades this meant the substitution of the holy work of going on a crusade for the ordinary penance required. One who took the sword in defense of the Cross would gain, according to papal authority, remission of the temporal penalties for his sins. Indulgence, that is, would be granted to crusaders. It was only a small step to include those who, staying home themselves, hired another to crusade in their place. This meant that a payment of money had obtained the benefit of indulgence. After the Crusades the custom of payment persevered and was applied to indulgences proclaimed in jubilee years, for special occasions and purposes, and finally for almost any reason. When the question was asked, by what authority the pope proclaimed indulgences, the answer given was: Through the perfect sacrifice of the sinless One, Jesus Christ who suffered for the sins of all, together with the exceeding merits of the saints through the ages, a treasury of merit was available for aid to frail men and women. This merit could be transferred, through the indulgence system, to ordinary mortals who lacked merit of their own.

Before the time of Luther various extensions and abuses of the system had become widely accepted, including elimination of the factor of repentance, indulgences for the dead, for the chief purpose of raising money, and confusion of remission of the temporal penalty with forgiveness of sins. Abuse in extreme form was contained in the program of the Dominican Tetzel, who came selling the certificates purchased in 1517 by the people whose pastor was Martin Luther.

Although the facts were not then widely known, this particular campaign was loathsome for other reasons also. Albrecht of Brandenburg was an ambitious young man who had already advanced further in the church than he should have, holding at an uncanonical age the two dioceses of Magdeburg and Halberstadt. He now wanted to gain the archdiocese of Mainz, the clerical crown of all Germany. But the dispensation from the pope would cost money, much more money than the previous dispensations, on account of youth and double tenure. Where there is a will, however, sometimes there is a way. In order to pay the enormous fee for this extra special dispensation, he borrowed the money from the powerful banking house of Fugger. To provide for repayment of the loan, the pope, Leo X, granted to Albrecht the privilege of selling indulgences in his territories. This indulgence was to provide funds for the pious work of building St. Peter's in Rome as a mecca for Christendom. In the case of Albrecht, however, the understanding was that half should go to Rome and the other half to Augsburg to repay the Fuggers.

In the Ninety-five Theses submitted for debate Luther took a position on three matters: (1) papal exploitation through the sale of indulgences, (2) the jurisdiction of the pope over purgatory, and (3) the effect of indulgences on the spiritual attitude of the sinner. Quickly Christians divided over the issue and over the man. Augustinians were for him, Dominicans against, Germans for, Italians against, humanists for, scholastics against, plain people and common clerics for, high prelates and potentates against. But these groups were more or less divided within themselves. Efforts from Rome to stifle either the issue or the man were unavailing. At Leipzig in 1519 Luther was forced, through the adroit argumentation of Dr. John Eck, to acknowledge some of the more radical implications of his position. He was forced from reliance on the authority of the pope to the pope better informed. If an informed pope could err, a general council of the church stood as the authority. But even a council could err—as in the case of John Huss, who had ideas "most Christian and evangelical, and these the universal church cannot condemn." There, said Eck triumphantly, you see Luther, self-acknowledged Hussite and heretic.

From an ecumenical council Luther fell back on the authority of the Bible. In matters of faith the Scriptures are our final authority. Search the Scriptures to find the truth. Thus was established another pillar of the Reformation—the sole authority of the Bible.

Luther was undoubtedly taken aback. During the year 1520 he worked out the meaning of his position, expressed in three works of prime importance. These were *To the Christian Nobility of the German Nation, On the Babylonian Captivity of the Church,* and *On Christian Freedom.* "The time for silence has gone, and the time for speaking has come." So he announced his intention as he addressed the German nobles on matters some of which were already close to their attention. Especially there was the matter of the Italian pope's interfering in German affairs. The pope had surrounded himself, said Luther, with three walls, from which he expected to dominate Germany unscathed. One was the exclusion of lay Christians from ecclesiastical affairs. Another was the pope's claim to the sole right to interpret scripture. The third was his claim to the sole right to call church councils. The first of these called forth another central pillar of the Reformation—the priesthood of all believers. Every baptized man, justified by God through faith, is a priest. Through his own witness he ministers to other Christians. He needs neither priest nor sacrament beyond his own direct relation to God. Luther backed away from the radical implications of this doctrine. But it remained in the Protestant tradition, to bring forth much fruit and many denominations.

Now may God help us, and give us all of those trumpets that overthrew the walls of Jericho, so that we may blow down these walls of straw and paper, and that we may set free our Christian rods, for the chastisement of sin, and expose the craft and deceit of the devil, so that we may amend ourselves by punishment and again obtain God's favor.[1]

Particularly was Luther incensed over the practice of kissing the pope's feet. "It is an unChristian, or rather an anti-Christian example, that a poor sinful man should suffer his feet to be kissed by one who is a hundred times better than he." [2] He asked the pope: Who gave him power to exalt himself above God? He then submitted a program of reform in accordance with the political and economic predilections of his fellow Germans: abolition of annates, pomp, temporal power, celibacy, masses for the dead, processions, saints' days and festivals (except Sunday), interdicts, etc. Especially to be reformed were the universities. "Nothing is more devilishly mischievous than an unreformed university." Germans should give attention to their own peculiar vices of dress, usury, and intemperance. He did not fear the consequences of his attack on the papacy. His only concern was that it might be overlooked and forgotten. The violence of the reaction would measure the truth of his position. He concluded with the suggestion that he was not done. "I have another song to sing concerning Rome. If they wish to hear it, I will sing it to them, and sing with all my might. Do you understand, dear Rome, what I mean?" [3]

The "song" took the form of another tract, *On the Babylonian Captivity of the Church,* done in Latin instead of German and directed to churchmen instead of patriots. Here he defined his position on the sacraments, a matter of extreme importance to the whole concept of the ministry, ecclesiastical authority, and the doctrine of the church. In the course of the Middle Ages seven sacraments had been specified. These were officially established at the Fourth Lateran Council, 1215, in which Innocent III also fixed the dogma of transubstantiation. The seven were: baptism, confirmation, the Lord's Supper, penance, ex-

[1] *Works of Martin Luther* (Philadelphia: A. J. Holman Co., 1915), II, 66.
[2] Quoted in Philip Schaff, *History of the Christian Church* (New York: Charles Scribner's Sons, 1888), VI, 211.
[3] *Ibid.,* p. 213.

treme unction, marriage, and ordination. Luther's approach was biblical. Only two of these, he said, were truly sacraments, because only two were to be found in the Scriptures. These were baptism and the Lord's Supper. On the latter the Roman church, contrary to ancient custom, had withdrawn the cup from the laity, who received only the bread. This was scandalous, and Huss had been right in insisting that all the people should receive communion "in both kinds" (that is, both bread and wine to the laity). He hedged on transubstantiation, although he rejected the papal definition of it. That no exclusive miracle happened at the altar Luther was sure. Yet Christ was truly present, not indeed taking the place of the elements but along with them. "Fire and iron, two different substances, are so mingled in red-hot iron, that in every part of it are both fire and iron. Why may not the glorious body of Christ much more be in every part of the substance of the bread?" [4] The sacrifice of the mass incensed him most of all. For this meant that the original sacrifice made by God on Calvary, a gift of God to men, had been reversed and made into a sacrifice by man to God.

In rounding out his great trilogy Luther wrote a little gem of a classic, *On Christian Freedom*. His theme was the paradox expressed in I Corinthians 9:19: "Though I was free from all men, I brought myself under bondage to all, that I might gain the more" (American Standard Version). As Luther phrased it in his Latin: *Omnium dominus est liberrimus, nulli subjectus; omnium servus est officiosissimus, omnibus subjectus.* Man is made free by faith, and by that act is bound wholly to the love of all men through Christ. Faith is primary, not subject to good works. But good works are the fruit of faith. "From faith flow forth love and joy in the Lord; and from love, a cheerful, willing, free spirit, disposed to serve our neighbor voluntarily, without taking any account of gratitude or ingratitude, praise or blame, gain or loss." [5] This tract was about as close as Luther ever came to a nonpolemic work of moderation. In sending it to the pope he typically enclosed a letter so tactless, so argumentative, that all its irenic qualities were lost. "The church of Rome, formerly the most holy of all churches,

[4] *Ibid.,* p. 216.
[5] *Ibid.,* p. 222.

has become the most lawless den of thieves. . . . It is all over with the court of Rome." [6] Quite lost in this invective was the absurd suggestion that Leo himself was "sitting like a lamb in the midst of wolves." This was Luther's last letter to the pope.

Rome finally came to the point of action, however distasteful the prospect was to easygoing Leo X. With great creaking of ecclesiastical machinery in the massive style of pontifical formulas emerged on October 10, 1520, a bull of excommunication. This has been said to be the last such document addressed to the whole of Western Christendom and the first to be widely ignored by a large segment thereof. It began, "Arise, O Lord, and judge thy cause. A wild boar is ravaging in thy vineyard. Arise Peter, Paul, and all the saints to judge this man who, defiant of Mother Church, is tearing asunder the seamless robe of Christ."

Greater, more powerful men than Luther had quailed before a bull from Rome, or even the threat of one. Kings from Lothair to Philip Augustus had thought better of their intentions regarding wives and mistresses. Archbishops and abbots had hastened to avoid the dread consequences following upon publication of a bull. John Lackland had at the end given over his realm of England to become the pope's vassal. How did Luther react? "You would scarcely believe," he wrote, "how pleased I am that enemies rise up against me more than ever. For I am never prouder or bolder than when I dare to displease them. . . . If the word of God were not attacked by them, it would not be God's word." [7] Two months later, at the expiration of the sixty days of grace, Luther, officiating at a little ceremony attended by some professors and students, burned the bull and a copy of the canon law.

2. *Lutheranism.* From the time of the excommunication the case of Martin Luther becomes more and more the case of the Lutherans. This was true at the meeting in 1521 of the imperial diet (assembly) in the Rhenish city of Worms. In this case a secular body sat in judgment over a case that more properly belonged to ecclesiastical authority, such as the church council that condemned John Huss. Of course papal

---

[6] *Ibid.,* p. 225.

[7] Quoted in A. C. McGiffert, *Martin Luther, the Man and His Work* (New York: D. Appleton-Century Co., 1911), p. 187.

legates were present, and secular authority had always taken responsibility for the punishment of heretics. Nonetheless, German nationalism—such as could be said to exist in the sixteenth century—had much to do with what happened at Worms. Present were some who wished to condemn Luther out of hand; also those who stood firmly in his support; and also a group, mainly humanists, who wished to compromise. Compromise was still possible. But, after the diet was over, it was much more difficult. The breach, not yet irreparable, was being deepened and widened.

Luther, in spite of warnings that the imperial safe-conduct might give him no more protection than it had Huss, appeared as required to answer the charges against him. Confronted with a pile of his books, he acknowledged them all to be his. The next day he was required to state whether or not he would maintain the teachings he had set forth, and he replied: "Unless I am convicted by Scripture and plain reason —I do not accept the authority of popes and councils, for they have contradicted each other—my conscience is captive to the Word of God. I cannot and I will not recant anything, for to go against conscience is neither right nor safe. God help me. Amen." [8] He may have added: "Here I stand, I can do no other." Had it not been for the firm support of certain princes, notably Luther's own ruler, the Elector Frederick the Wise, the Saxon reformer might have fared ill. Although the assembly did place him under the ban of the Empire, thus marking him an outlaw, he was permitted to leave Worms peaceably. On the way home he was literally kidnapped—as it turned out, by his friends. He was removed from circulation for a year, until affairs quieted. Friends took him to the castle called the Wartburg. There he busied himself with writing and beginning his famous translation of the Bible into German.

Meanwhile his friends in Wittenberg, especially Carlstadt, sought to carry out the reform as projected, and went, as Luther thought, too far too fast. He favored the reform of the mass, the use of German, the marriage of priests. But when these reforms were accompanied by various combinations of violence and extreme attitudes, iconoclasm

[8] Quoted in Roland H. Bainton, *Here I Stand* (New York and Nashville: Abingdon Press, 1950) , p. 185.

and social egalitarianism, Luther reacted. Breaking out of his retirement, he hurried to Wittenberg to set a middle way of reform. Carlstadt was banished and the enthusiasts rebuffed. Luther had already broken with Rome and was, without planning to do so, founding a new church. But he broke as completely with the radicals, who, having started with him, wished to go further. The Lutheran line would represent, then, a relatively conservative movement in which, although much was changed, much remained. For good order, propriety, and beauty, if a practice were not found contrary to scriptural authority, it might be retained. The result was the *Lutheran Church,* reformed yet traditional, not Romish yet liturgical, orthodox except insofar as Luther had already taken a stand on faith, the sacraments, the priesthood, and papal authority.

About the same time came the separation of Lutherans and humanists, and also the defection of the native agrarian movement. Not until 1524 was Erasmus willing to break openly with Luther. He was loath to part with a man whose purpose was so close to his own. He was appalled at the schism of the church and the threat of violence, but he fixed upon the doctrine of man as a central point. For the spirit of the Renaissance, of which Erasmus partook, tended to exalt man and his freedom of will. Man was not so much fallen from grace as made in the image of God. Man was at least free to make his own destiny. To Luther man was nothing unless raised through the free grace of God. Man was helpless by himself. From this time on Lutheranism went its way, humanism another. Some individuals, notably Philip Melanchthon, succeeded in maintaining bridges to both camps. Melanchthon, Luther's able lieutenant, continued to correspond with Erasmus.

Likewise, in the Peasants' War, Luther broke with the agrarian movement. Sympathetic at first with a group from which he had come, he reacted violently against the call to arms in which peasants rebelled against the constituted authority. *Against the Murderous, Thieving Mob of the Peasants* was one of the most virulent tracts Luther ever wrote. It severed the common bonds that up to this time had worked for alliance between religious and social reform. Most of the peasants either sank back into superstitious Roman Catholicism or went over to the more radical religious movements springing up everywhere.

By 1525 then, the lines were being drawn and fixed: Roman Catholicism still claimed universal spiritual authority over all Christendom as the one true church. Lutheranism steadily crystallized into a visible ecclesiastical organization rejecting the authority of Rome, became firm in its new theological position, and diverged sharply from the sundry movements, religious and otherwise, with which it hitherto had made uneasy association. The one large question was: Is it possible that two different forms of the faith could subsist and survive in the same land? For a thousand years the answer had been negative. Part of the answer at the juncture of the Reformation lay in the person of the Holy Roman Emperor, Charles V.

No one in history has ever been born with the proverbial silver spoon more firmly held in his mouth than Charles. He had four famous grandparents, each of whom left him a large portion of Europe. Never since the almost legendary Charlemagne had a European ruler held sway over more territory. From Ferdinand in 1516 he inherited Aragon and the broad possessions in the Mediterranean including Sicily and the southern part of Italy. From Isabella he inherited Castile and the by now vast claims of Spain in the New World. As king of Spain he ruled over the richest and most powerful of the new national monarchies. From Maximilian he inherited the Hapsburg name, the archduchy of Austria and associated duchies, and from Mary of Burgundy the Netherlands and the Free County. The list of lesser titles was almost endless. And then, in 1519, he was elected to succeed his grandfather Maximilian as Holy Roman emperor.

The world lay at his feet. But it did not stay there long. As against the immeasurable potentialities, Charles labored under some strong limitations. In the first place the work of royal unification in Spain was not complete. He had to struggle against provincial loyalties and medieval customs. In the second place, as holy Roman emperor, he enjoyed little more than honorific authority. The Empire, sunk in medieval senility, showed little sign of regeneration under the impetus of new political forces. It was still divided into over three hundred large and small, more or less independent principalities. The intricacies of imperial power politics were beyond the comprehension of one man, least of all one whose European concerns led far beyond the borders of the Empire.

Beyond internal weakness four possible external threats loomed large. First there was religious strife, both internal and external in nature, sowing discord and dividing subjects into Catholics and Lutherans ready to fly at each other's throats. Second was that ambitious rival, Francis I of France, whose Valois blood boiled at the thought of being surrounded by Hapsburgs. His "most Christian majesty," who hated heretics at home, was not beyond making an alliance with the infidel Turk against "his Catholic majesty" of Spain and Austria. Third was the Moslem Turk, the bogeyman of Europe, whose plans disconcerted Christians of various persuasions. After the stupendous fall of Constantinople in 1453 the Eastern bastion of Christendom collapsed before the advance of the Ottoman Turks. By 1526 they had massacred the Christian nobility of Hungary at the battle of Mohacs and were still advancing up the Danube valley toward Vienna itself. The fourth threat to Charles was the pope. One would expect the papacy to welcome the growing power of so richly endowed a Catholic subject. Such was not the case. As it turned out, at times the papacy seemed almost to welcome the Lutheran power as counteracting the Hapsburg influence in Italian politics. The pope even made overtures to the Turks. And in 1527 an imperial army sacked Rome, although not through the orders of Charles himself.

Such was the complicated and contradictory diplomatic and military situation as Lutherans and Catholics in Germany began to square off. Charles, busy in Spain, was unable to do anything for the time being. After the Diet of Worms the ban against Luther was to be enforced wherever possible. For a while each territory followed its ruler. By 1529 the Diet of Speier decided that where Lutherans were strong, they should have toleration. But Roman Catholic ministers in such lands must be protected, whereas Lutheran ministers in Catholic lands should be suppressed. Lutherans protested against this one-side arrangement, and hence were called "protestants." But they became so because they wanted to "protest"—that is, confess, witness, testify, to their own faith. They were not simply against something; they were *for* something, a faith they regarded as true Christianity. The next year, at the

Diet of Augsburg, they submitted a full statement of their beliefs. This became the famous creed of the Lutheran tradition, the Augsburg Confession. It clearly stated not only the traditional theological formulations drawn from the ancient creeds, but also the evangelical Protestant emphases and corrections of Roman abuses. It was mainly from the pen of Melanchthon.

The following years saw the struggle move from words to swords, varying in intensity and direction according to the various winds blowing from Spain, France, Germany, Italy, and the Turks. At the Diet of Regensburg in 1541, when liberal men of good will spoke for both sides, hope was held for compromise and reunion. That hope was short lived. Although the barrier of justification by faith might have been overcome, the barriers of transubstantiation and papal authority were immovable. Luther died in 1546 in the midst of a struggle that had risen far beyond the issues of his personal career. Finally, when no other solution was possible, the powers agreed on a settlement never before contemplated: bifurcation of the faith on the territorial principle. Henceforth there was to be not one true faith, universal and coterminous with Christendom, but two, each valid in its own sphere. Rest assured, neither side would grant that the other might be true also. But, lacking the means of reunion, division was accepted on the formula *cuius regio, eius religio* ("Of whomsoever is the region, of him is the religion"). This principle, written into the Peace of Augsburg, 1555, provided that each prince or ruler should choose between the two forms of faith for his own territory. All inhabitants were expected to follow the choice of their prince. Within each state one and one faith only should prevail.

The settlement of Augsburg does not seem very generous or liberal to Christians accustomed to the principle of religious freedom. But it is significant as a step, albeit a small one, in the direction of a new attitude, taking form largely in England in the seventeenth century, strengthened from another angle by the Enlightenment of the eighteenth century, and fully expressed only in our own day. Beyond that, the treaty offered a tolerable truce to war-weary antagonists, a truce that lasted, after a fashion, until the last of the great religious wars of modern times, the Thirty Years War, 1618-48.

B. Zwingli and Calvin—The Reformed Churches

The question inevitably appears: If Luther carried through a reform of the church, why reform it any more? Could not all be satisfied, traditionalists in the church of Rome, reformers in the Lutheran? In what direction further reform? And finally, at what point does the process cease? The answers are manifest in history.

In the first place, Luther's effort began a process but did not finish it. Luther was essentially conservative. He did not satisfy humanists, rationalists, social reformers; nor did he complete a satisfactory theological structure. Above all, he did not satisfy any whose native soil was not German. Lutheranism had only limited appeal to people outside Teutonic culture. When Lutheranism spread, it spread largely to areas linguistically, culturally, historically related to Germany. Hence, Scandinavia far more than any other part of Europe absorbed the Lutheran faith and made it her own. There were political and economic reasons for this. For the rest of Europe something more was needed. New directions were given to the Reformation by many leaders, but especially important are two, Huldreich Zwingli and John Calvin.

1. Zwingli. In Huldreich Zwingli we see the fusion of humanistic and theological strains. If the work of Luther centered in Wittenberg, that of Zwingli inevitably is associated with Zurich. In the course of his education at Basel and Bern he was exposed to the new currents of the Renaissance. Unlike Luther, then, Zwingli began his career of reform first in the social category and only later in the theological. One of the most persistent points in the concern of Zwingli was the use of the Swiss as mercenary soldiers in various European armies and especially in that of the papacy. "With right," said he, "do the cardinals wear red hats and cloaks; for, shake their garments, and out fall ducats and crowns; wring them, however, and they drip with the blood of your sons, fathers, and best friends." But his most significant contribution to the Reformation came when he began preaching in 1519 in the cathedral church of Zurich. Ignoring the prescribed lessons for the day, he began a systematic series of exegetical sermons on the book of Matthew, with the Greek New Testament open before him in the pulpit. One Thomas Platter recorded an experience exceedingly rare among people who listen to sermons: Said he, he felt he was being lifted up by the hair of his head! A series of public disputations presided over by the town council led to reform, step by step. The veneration of images was forbidden. Fasts in Lent were abandoned. Priests married. The mass was abolished. Relics were buried. Images and organs were removed from the churches. A degree of reform more radical than that of Luther took form. The real presence of Christ in the Lord's Supper was denied in the sense Luther maintained. Although the sacrament is a channel of grace, there is no miracle and no real presence, only a symbolic recalling of the sacrifice of Christ. Insofar as the participant is moved to repent and become open to the saving grace of the Lord, he benefits. If Luther emphasized, "This is my body," Zwingli preferred, "Do this in memory of me." The service of worship should be chiefly exposition of the Word. Zwingli agreed with Luther on the authority of the Bible, but made a more stringent application of it. Whereas Luther had said practices not in conflict with the Bible might be retained, Zwingli said no practice was valid without specific scriptural authorization.

Unfortunately his career was cut short by the fortunes of war. Although the Reformation spread to several of the Swiss cantons, it by no means took over the whole Confederation. Historically the cantons maintained a proud independence of outside interference and of each other. The old forest cantons especially remained firm in the Catholic faith. A series of incidents involving persecution of Catholics by Protestants and of Protestants by Catholics led to the formation of leagues and, of course, war. Unwilling to see the Protestant cantons taken off piecemeal, Zwingli tried to bring unified effort, not only within Switzerland but among Protestants generally. The most notable effort at agreement, and also the most notable failure, was the Marburg Colloquy, held in 1529, between Zwinglians and Lutherans. The discussions fell apart over the Lord's Supper.

At the Battle of Kappel in 1531, when Zurich found herself virtually alone against the Catholic army, fifteen hundred soldiers were defeated by eight thousand of the enemy. On the field of battle lay twenty-six members of the town council and twenty-five pastors, among them

Zwingli. The ensuing peace was a harbinger of the approaching division of Christendom, but in this case the Catholics were favored.

It is difficult to say what might have happened had Zwingli lived. He had no chance to congeal a church carrying the Zwinglian name. Vigorous and able, his strong personality made its mark on the Reformation and contributed to what has come to be known as the Reformed tradition. As an enemy once said in despair: "He invited the country people to dine with him, talked to them of God, put the devil into their hearts, and his books in their pockets." His successor at Zurich, Henry Bullinger, fed the Zwinglian reform into the Calvinistic reform as the two movements merged in the next generation.

2. *Calvin*. Sometime in the spring of 1534 a young man paid a visit to a very old one. Jacques Lefèvre d'Étaples, crowning decades of devoted scholarship, had just published in final form his French version of the Bible. The young man wanted to talk with him. What they said we do not know. One wishes we did. For the young man was John Calvin, almost twenty-five years old, fresh from advanced study in the University of Orleans. If we knew what took place in that meeting, we might know more about the religious experience of Calvin. We can only guess. But of one thing we may be sure. By this time he was no longer an obedient Roman Catholic, and was going through an unsettling spiritual struggle, the outcome of which was to make him a convinced Protestant. Luther would have talked and written about such an episode for the rest of his life, as would John Wesley. Calvin did not. That was part of the difference between them.

John Calvin was born in 1509 near Paris. He had a good education including a strong regimen of the classics, following the new humanist trends. He studied at the University of Paris, then continued to Orleans to specialize in law. Here is revealed a scholarly, humanistically inclined author with apparently little interest in theology or the Bible. Undoubtedly, however, he knew what was going on in the world of religion, was already asking himself questions. Erasmus' New Testament and Luther's sermons were available in France. The foundations were being laid for a complete change of outlook, which he referred to later as a "sudden conversion." A rectorial address given the next year by his friend Nicholas Cop, although not necessarily written for him by Calvin, probably reflects his ideas in the note of independence and individualism. By 1534 he had gone through a struggle and sought the advice of the aged Lefèvre. That same year he fled France, via Strasbourg, to Basel. Working out his new position with amazing rapidity, he published in 1536, at the age of twenty-seven, the first edition of the *Institutes of the Christian Religion.* This was destined to become a Christian classic of prime importance. (It is discussed later in this chapter.) After certain travels that led him back once to Paris he was on his way to Strasbourg when, on detour, he came to Geneva. This visit marked another about turn.

The little city at the outlet of Lake Geneva was at that time in the throes of reformation under the leadership of a little man with a big voice and a red beard, William Farel. Calvin was caught up in the work, and, as it turned out, with the exception of one short period, remained there until he died in 1565. Having thrown off the political pretensions of the bishop of Geneva and the duke of Savoy, the city was governing itself through a system of councils. Soon after his arrival plans were submitted for further reform and the establishment of discipline. In this case the responsibility for discipline was to rest with the church through the exercise of excommunication. Ordinances for the maintenance of public and private morality were henceforth to come under the surveillance of the church. The council was not sure it accorded with this principle. As a result of conflict Calvin in 1539 was banished. But, as the citizens soon found out, there was just one thing harder than getting along with John Calvin. That was getting along without him. By 1541 he was called back to take up where he had left off and carry through reform as he understood it. He matured during his three years of exile in Strasbourg, and also married, "that I can consecrate myself to the Lord."

In 1556 John Knox, who was to gain fame himself as the leader of the Reformation in Scotland, wrote from exile in Geneva: The city, "I neither fear nor am ashamed to say, is the most perfect school of Christ that ever was in the earth since the days of the Apostles. In other places I confess Christ to be truly preached; but manners and religion

to be so sincerely reformed, I have not yet seen in any other place." [9]
It would never do to regard this community as the kingdom of heaven
on earth. But it was considered by some to be a close approximation.
It was certainly a redeemed society, living under the guidance of God.
The term "theocracy" has been used. In a sense the description is valid.
With no priestly or hierarchical intentions whatsoever, Calvin established control of all aspects of life, civil as well as ecclesiastical. He
never accepted political office, and of course exercised no military authority. His only official position was that of ordained minister. He
did not even become a citizen until 1559. Yet few men have exercised
greater mastery of a city. He spoke for God, revealed through the Holy
Scriptures. Insofar as they lent themselves to the purpose, the books
of the Bible became the law books of the city of Geneva. Church and
council, working together, put the will of God into the form of ordinances. When it was asked, who should interpret the Scriptures, or
what body should act as the supreme court of appeal, the answer was
naturally the ministers, trained in God's word.

They were organized into the Venerable Company, a strictly disciplined body of men. Well educated, thinking rightly, living strin-
gently, the members of the Venerable Company provided guidance in
the scriptural Word of God so sorely needed by the laymen on the
Council. In order that all citizens might live in accordance with God's
will, a Consistory was established, composed of ministers and elders
(laymen). Meeting each Thursday, it undertook the onerous task
of correcting the conduct of everyone. It is easy to portray the work of
the Consistory in purely negative fashion as a "puritanical" device
for intolerable interference in the private lives of citizens. It did indeed
exhibit such tendencies. Men were imprisoned for criticizing the ministers. People were punished for eating fish on Friday and for declaring
there is no devil—and for telling the ministers to go to him. A bride
was censured for ostentation at her own wedding. One hardy soul was
caught writing "all nonsense" in one of Calvin's books. More serious
were the cases of adultery and blasphemy against God. Michael Servetus
serves as the most famous victim of the bitter intolerance by which

---

[9] Quoted in John T. McNeill, *The History and Character of Calvinism* (New York:
Oxford University Press, 1954), p. 178.

Calvin is revealed as a child of his age. In his commentary on Luke 14:23, "And the master said to the servant, 'Go out to the highways and hedges, and compel people to come in, that my house may be filled' " (R.S.V.), Calvin wrote:

At the same time, I do not disapprove of the use which Augustine frequently made of this passage against the Donatists, to prove that godly princes may lawfully issue edicts for compelling obstinate and rebellious persons to worship the true God, and to maintain the unity of the faith; for, though faith is voluntary, yet we see that such methods are useful for subduing the obstinacy of those who will not yield until they are compelled.[10]

And yet all this dismal puritanicalism obscures some real, positive good, a grand design for a better life in accordance with God's will. People were learning to worship God with their whole life, to participate in Christian worship with intelligence and understanding. Evils long rampant were stamped out. It became possible to conceive of a holy commonwealth. Whatever might be happening to the plans of men, God's glory was being attended. And that was the nub of the matter. Man's convenience was of no account, his desires of no importance. All that mattered was that God be acclaimed and his Word proclaimed. That was done in Geneva with a vengeance! Such was the beginning of the *Reformed Church* in Switzerland.

3. Calvinism and the Reformed Churches. Quite apart from other considerations, Calvinism may be distinguished from Lutheranism by its amazing adaptability and expansion. Whereas the ecclesiastical system of Luther remained largely in Germany and Scandinavia, close always to the German tongue and Teutonic environment, Calvinism became truly international. Geneva was the active center for education in an active faith. From Geneva converted missionaries went forth to all corners of Europe. Calvinism spread successfully almost everywhere except in Latin Europe, where all forms of Protestantism tended to wither on the vine for lack of spiritual sustenance. But especially it

[10] John Calvin, *Commentary on a Harmony of the Evangelists* (Edinburgh: Calvin Translation Society, 1845), II, 170 ff.

spread to France, the Netherlands, and Scotland. For briefer periods and to less extent it also spread to Poland, Bohemia, and Hungary.

Francis I of France loved his sister Marguerite, and his sister loved him. For that reason he indulged her predilection for liberal and literary Frenchmen whose religious ideas were not altogether orthodox, although they could not be called heretical. There were some poets, and some philosophers, and a few churchmen. Some of them were said to have been reading Luther's books. Lefèvre d'Étaples brought out a French New Testament. The bishop of Meaux was friendly to the new currents. But enough was enough. When word came to Francis that some of these litterateurs and humanists were infected with Lutheranism, he reacted and called a halt to the spread of dangerous doctrines. In this he was ably seconded by the theologians and the universities. Nevertheless, throughout his reign Protestant ideas seeped into France, enough at least to turn the mind and heart of one student, John Calvin. There were a few executions.

But when Francis died and was followed by Henry II, persecution of Protestants began in earnest. Yet the curious fact is, the more he persecuted, the larger and stronger grew the new teaching. Indeed, his reign saw the formation of the *French Reformed Church,* complete with synodical organization. The Protestants became not only a religious group but also an identifiable political faction, known as Huguenots. This movement was wholly Calvinistic after the publication of the *Institutes* and the rise of Calvin in Geneva. From the 1560's on, France was plunged into civil war over the confused issues involving both politics and religion. Three parties emerged: the Huguenots, Protestant, led by the famous Admiral Coligny; the arch-Catholics, led by the house of Guise; and the nationalists, or moderates, exemplified by Catherine de Medici, queen of one monarch and queen mother of three others, one of the most influential persons of the time. The climax of religious tumult came with the Massacre of St. Bartholomew, 1572, when thousands of Huguenots, first in Paris, then throughout the realm, were bloodily exterminated. Coligny and other leaders were lost. One young Protestant, Henry of Navarre, of royal blood, escaped. He became one of the three in the War of the Three Henries. The others were King Henry III and Henry, Duke of Guise. The issue of this three-cornered war was achieved not so much by battle as by assassination. Two of the Henries were eliminated, leaving only Henry of Navarre, who claimed the throne. He along with most of France was weary of civil war. To avoid a long-drawn-out struggle of uncertain issue, he agreed to accept the Roman Catholic faith of the majority of his subjects and entered Paris as Henry IV. He made sure of the safety of his erstwhile comrades with the Edict of Nantes, 1598, by which the Huguenots were given not only civil and religious liberty, but also special political and military rights to guarantee performance. This edict remained in effect, with later elimination of special rights, until its revocation by Louis XIV in 1685.

In the Netherlands, which covered roughly the area now occupied by Belgium and Holland, the situation was different from that in France, because these provinces were not independent, but rather were under the control of the Emperor Charles V, who had inherited them from his paternal grandmother, Mary of Burgundy. When he retired in 1555, these lands passed into the hands of his son, Philip II, who became king of Spain but not holy Roman emperor. All this will help explain why, in the year 1567, an army of nine thousand men descended upon the Low Countries, having made its way from Spain via Italy over the Mt. Cenis Pass. Its commander, the Duke of Alva, had orders to show the meaning of submission to constituted authority to the rebellious inhabitants of these provinces of Spain. All efforts at negotiation had failed, and Marguerite of Parma, the regent, was letting things get out of hand. The time had come to teach these boorish Dutchmen a lesson. The troubles were, as is so frequently the case, a compound of religion and politics. On the one hand Lutheranism, and then Calvinism, had penetrated the country. On the other hand the Netherlanders, who had got along rather well with Charles V, always sympathetic to Burgundian interests, were not at all happy with the "Spanish" king, Philip, who knew little and cared less about the interests of his Dutch subjects.

The groundwork for religious change had been laid long before the sermons of Luther found their way into the Dutch provinces and language. This area had been the scene of vigorous mystical movements of the late Middle Ages. The work of Gerhard Groote, the Deventer

[61]

school, and the Brethren of the Common Life had great influence on the religious character of the Dutch people. When Luther's writings began to appear quite early, they were avidly read in spite of efforts to suppress them. Likewise quite early various left-wing movements appeared. Religious unity was already cracked, then, when the teachings of Calvin entered to complete the disintegration. Some refugees from persecution went to Geneva, where they learned of Calvinism. Others fled to England, where they found freedom not even granted to Englishmen. John Lasco, the Polish reformer, influenced Netherlanders in both England and East Friesland. The result was amazing spread of Calvinism in the Low Countries, especially among the merchant groups. By 1568 a general synod of the *Dutch Reformed Church* met at Wesel, and soon a national church was in being. All of this took place while Philip, from Spain, was bending every effort to extirpate heresy in his recalcitrant Burgundian possessions.

Through most of the rest of the century the country was devastated by war. Alva sought by various means to subdue the fighting spirit. He by subterfuge arrested certain of the potential leaders of opposition, all except William, Prince of Orange, who became the center of national Protestant resistance against Spanish Catholicism. Rough mercenary troops were quartered on helpless householders. The Council of Troubles, established by Alva to deal specifically with cases of heresy-treason soon earned the nickname "Council of Blood." But all these measures failed to reduce the Netherlanders to acceptance of foreign rule and the Catholic faith. What finally drove them to violent revolution was the imposition of heavy taxes for maintenance of the army of occupation. Alva besieged city after city, threatening uncontrolled sack. Malines fell, Zutphen, Haarlem—on to Alkmaar, which was invested but did not fall. Alva's bludgeon had failed. He requested his own recall.

Finally, after bitter struggle culminating in the siege of Leyden, which was relieved only by the cutting of the dikes, a new governor, Alexander Farnese, Duke of Parma, succeeded after a fashion where Alva had failed. He conquered by dividing. Taking advantage of the linguistic, political, economic, and religious differences between the south and the north, he drew away the southern provinces. Spain was unable to restore control over the north, which by the end of the century was, in fact, independent. Not until the Treaty of Westphalia, 1648, was Holland granted independence *de jure* as the Kingdom of the Netherlands. While the Spaniards were thus being thwarted, the canny Dutch were busy quietly taking over the carrying trade in Europe and overseas, even that of Spain itself, enriching themselves at the expense of the subjects of Philip II.

In the midst of the war the Dutch Calvinists found time to quarrel among themselves. Two groups arose, the *Rekellijken* or indulgent thinkers, and the *Preciesen* or strict Calvinists. The most controverted issue had to do with the doctrine of election, whether it was supralapsarian—that is, before the fall of man—or infralapsarian, after the fall. Jacob Arminius, although a convinced Calvinist, could not accept supralapsarianism, and developed the teaching that man could "cooperate" in the work of salvation. The saving work of Christ is sufficient for all, and election pertains to those who repent, while condemnation is reserved only for the impenitent. Arminian doctrines, held by the Remonstrants, were rejected at the Synod of Dort, 1618. The synod outdid Calvin himself in stating with unsparing vigor the principles of Calvinism: unconditional election, limited atonement, total depravity, irresistible grace, perseverance of the saints.

Of all the missionaries who went forth from Geneva, the most spectacular was John Knox, builder of the *Kirk of Scotland* and organizer of Presbyterian polity and forms of worship. He was not the destroyer of the Roman Catholic Church in that country, for it had already fallen apart before he even began preaching. Scotland lay in the backwash of European culture. Politically, economically, culturally, religiously, the land was almost barbaric, compared with the enlightened regions of the Continent. Traditionally the clans quarreled among themselves, united only for the purpose of raiding the common enemy, England. At the beginning of modern times Scotland suffered heavy defeats at the hands of the English. Since France in the late Middle Ages was at war with England in the Hundred Years War, an alliance between France and Scotland was natural. By marriage the Scottish line was connected with both England and France.

Some of Luther's works found their way to Scotland. But not until the 1540's is any real effort at reform apparent. David Beaton was already, since 1539, the worldly archbishop of St. Andrews. Presently, upon the death of James V, his daughter, six-day-old Mary Stuart, succeeded to the throne. This meant that his widow and the baby's mother, Mary of Guise, of the noted French Roman Catholic family, took over as regent. Under these conditions circumstances were not propitious for an immediate reformation. This explains why the heroic Zwinglian George Wishart came to a martyr's death in 1546. Then for the part he had in Wishart's execution Cardinal Beaton was murdered by a band of nobles.

A year later, when these leaders, together with some Protestants, were captured as they defended the castle of St. Andrews, one of the captives was John Knox. He spent nineteen months condemned to the French galleys. Then he escaped to England, where he spent five profitable years until Queen Mary (Tudor) forced his departure.

First at Frankfurt, then in Geneva, he came to a place of leadership among English-speaking Calvinists. In 1559 he returned to Scotland for good, having just insulted the new Queen Elizabeth of England with his book, *First Blast of the Trumpet Against the Monstrous Regiment of Women*. The volume, however, was really directed against Mary of Guise and Mary Tudor.

When John Knox took hold in Scotland, the lukewarm reformation became white hot. Within one year the Scots repudiated finally both the Roman Catholic faith and the French alliance. By the Treaty of Edinburgh, 1560, both French and English troops left Scotland, and the land was at last free to determine its destiny. That destiny had been worked out by Knox.

Following precedent, the religious reform was carried out by act of Parliament, though of course Knox and the Calvinist ministers had a determining voice in the work of preparation. The "First Scottish Confession" put in plain form a strong but not extreme Calvinism. The true Church is invisible because "God alone knows whom he has chosen"; but it may be distinguished clearly from the false church, which does not possess the proper "notes": true preaching of the Word, right administration of the sacraments, application of ecclesiastical discipline.

As to the political situation, Mary Stuart was presently welcomed back home from France. Knox's opinion of this event is recorded in his sharp *History of the Reformation in Scotland:*

The very face of heaven, the time of her arrival, did manifestly speak what comfort was brought unto this country with her, to wit, sorrow, dolour, darkness, and all impiety. For, in the memory of man, that day of the year was never seen a more dolorous face of the heaven than was at her arrival, which two days later did so continue; for besides the surface wet, and corruption of the air, the mist was so thick and so dark that scarce might any man espy another the length of two pair of boots. The sun was not seen to shine two days before, nor two days after. That fore-warning gave God unto us; but alas, the most part were blind.[11]

Trouble began almost immediately when Mary had mass celebrated the first Sunday. In answer Knox preached openly against the episode. Had a gentler personality stood in the place of Knox, the fate of Mary Stuart might not have been so tragic. Given her flighty character, however, and his unbending one, the result was almost inevitable. After considerable struggle and direct debate, Mary assured her own downfall by unwise marital adventures. She ended her romantic career on a scaffold reluctantly provided by Queen Elizabeth, whose throne she claimed. By the time of Knox's death, 1572, the Reformation in Scotland was well rounded out.

Calvinism also spread through central and eastern Europe, taking hold in Poland, Bohemia, and Hungary. Although checked in these areas by the Counter Reformation, it remained vigorous, except in Poland.

4. The Protestant Faith. The publication of Calvin's *Institutes* gives occasion for pause before continuing the narrative. The main ingredients of historical Protestantism are embodied in this majestic work, more systematically and more completely than in any previous production. And yet it cannot be said that Calvin first formulated the Protestant position. Luther and Zwingli had contributed much. His-

[11] John Knox, *History of the Reformation in Scotland* (New York: Philosophical Library, 1950), II, 7.

toric Protestantism in the context of the Reformation is an amalgam of all three. All were agreed on some major premises.

Of these the first is justification by faith. Luther began with this and made it the keystone. Zwingli and Calvin went along, although not giving it such central importance. Man is saved by faith freely given by God. The redemptive work of Christ has made this possible, even though man is sinful and in justice deserves nothing. Good works are unavailing in obtaining the saving grace. It is the other way around. A man justified by faith will then be able for the first time to bring forth the fruits of the Spirit, live a life in accordance with God's will.

A further principle, the full implications of which were not yet apparent, was also set forth by Luther and accepted in one form or another by the others: the priesthood of all believers. Each man is his own priest and a priest for others—that is, in the last resort needs no priestly office, no sacramentally mediated grace, but stands directly before the judgment of God, carries responsibility for individual decision in matters of religion. This principle might well have led to atomistic individualism were it not for a third principle, common to all the great reformers: the final authority of the Bible as a standard of faith. The Scriptures stand for the Word of God. By use of the native intelligence with which we are endowed by God, guided by the Holy Spirit, we may discover the basic principles of life and redemption. For the Bible alone is sufficient. No man may claim the sole right to interpret the Word for all. Each runs his own spiritual race.

Let it clearly be understood: This new expression of Christian faith was not an invention, made up by the leaders of the Reformation. This is rather the gospel itself, rediscovered and regenerated. None of these men was conscious of departure from the Christian tradition of wandering into unknown and untried paths. Rather all were convinced that Christianity was being brought back onto the right road and that the gospel, or good news, was once again truly proclaimed. This was renewal, not innovation; regeneration, not aberration; revival, not corruption. One of the strong elements of the Reformation was the conscious recovery of the Christian faith and life of the primitive church of the Apostles. In this sense the Protestant faith did not begin with the sixteenth century and did not represent a departure from Christian tradition and the heritage of the ages. Rather it was the recovery of that true tradition and the renewal of that heritage. Behind Luther, Zwingli, and Calvin stood Augustine, Paul, the apostolic Christians, and the saints of all centuries. Rome, all were agreed, had long since departed from the true faith and corrupted it.

Zwingli went beyond Luther in some respects, although holding fast to these central Protestant affirmations. Detailed differences between them, as for example their interpretations of the Lord's Supper, are illustrations of the fundamental difference of approach, Zwingli's being more intellectual and moral than Luther's. He also took a more extreme view of scriptural authority, resulting in more radical surgery on traditional forms.

Calvin did for the Protestant heritage something neither of the others could have done. Luther was too bellicose and unsystematic. Zwingli lacked the intellectual acumen of Calvin, and died too soon. In the *Institutes* Calvin provided a comprehensive, systematic work on theology on Protestant principles. It was both an apology *for* Protestantism and a summary *of* it. In later editions the latter feature became more and more prominent. The significance of the work lies in more than any one doctrine, even that of the absolute sovereignty of God. The whole Word of God, in its utter simplicity along with its profound complexity, is the subject. The conviction is inescapable, however, that the sovereignty of God is the central fact underlying and justifying other and more "Calvinistic" teachings. No more than any other work of theology is it completely logical. The human mind, as always, finally contemplates the mystery of God. The author did not rejoice, however, in paradoxes and careless exaggerations. There is always the recurrent emphasis on the sovereignty of God. From the crass rocks of the earth and sinful man to the ends of the universe, all creation sings of the greater glory of the Creator and Sustainer, as well as Redeemer. Truly the chief end of man is to glorify God and enjoy him forever. All of the ancient and orthodox doctrines of the Christian faith find their place in the frame of the *Institutes*: the Trinity, the twofold nature of Christ, man created in the image of God but fallen and sinful, Christ the Redeemer, the Holy Spirit as comforter and guide, the Church visible and invisible, communion of saints, life everlasting. Here too are Lutheran doctrines and something of Zwingli. It can be appreciated fully only if contemplated in its entirety.

The first edition of 1536 was relatively simple, with its six chapters dealing with law, faith, prayer, sacraments, Romish sacraments, and Christian liberty. Luther's catechetical writings had made much the same approach. The second edition of 1539 showed a maturing of thought through the study of Paul and the ancient church writers, especially Augustine. By 1559, the year of the last edition presided over by Calvin himself, the original six chapters had expanded to eighty-one, organized into four extensive books: God the Creator, God the Redeemer, God the Holy Spirit, and the Church. The majesty of God, Providence, the Law and Gospel, sin and repentance, the grace of God general and special—all are here, ready to mark the thought of Christians down to this day. Deep in the vast work may be found those "horrible decrees," included in the doctrine of predestination. Each man is predestined either to heaven or to hell. Those whom God has elected cannot resist his grace, nor can they fall from it. If men on that account charge God with injustice, this is evidence not of God's obliquity but of man's ignorance and sinful pride. God's is all the glory. The ultimate important might be the apostolic dictum: "We are not our own, but we are God's."

Although the Reformation was delineated in its main lines by Luther, Zwingli, and Calvin, further expressions are to be found in the left-wing movement on the one hand and the English Reformation on the other. They stand almost at opposite poles, the one radical, the other conservative; the one rejecting any connection with political authority, the other closely related. These further developments are described in the following sections.

C. The Left Wing of the Reformation

Then came confusion. Balthasar Hübmaier baptized three hundred people with water carried in a plain pail. Elsewhere grown men and women were baptized, even though they had already been baptized as infants. Hans Hut proclaimed the second coming of Christ for May 15, 1527. Melchior Hoffmann said the great event would occur in Strasbourg in 1533, at which time he and all other prisoners for Christ's sake would be freed. He never left prison. Others began to wash the feet of the brethren. Then some in Holland began to parade naked, saying Isaiah had done so. Presently one said he was Enoch reincarnated. Then another said he was David, another Elijah. New Jerusalems sprang up.

What was happening? The Word appeared to have gone wild. So indeed thought many sober Christians, Catholic and Protestant alike. These exuberant manifestations were aspects of a movement inchoate yet purposeful, diverse yet united in a common effort to recover the faith of the apostolic church. Generally all the groups have been lumped together and called "Anabaptists," or re-baptizers. The term is not suitable, because they claimed the only valid baptism was the one they administered, because not all of them rebaptized, and because that teaching was by no means the most important. Time, however, has fixed its usage. The left wing developed from the conviction that Luther, Zwingli, and Calvin had not carried the reformation far enough. In fact, Luther was the prime source of the movement. Other influences were Erasmus and humanism, the late medieval mystics, the illuminations of Joachim of Floris and others, and, with some, the Taborite group within Hussitism. If one characteristic is dominant, it is diversity. There were all kinds—different types of leadership, different geographical areas, different forms of biblical interpretation, different applications of social ethics. Through all, however, certain ideas were commonly held: restitution of the ancient church, understood in terms of biblical primitivism; the Church as the community of the saints, reborn and saved; separation of church and state insofar as the general community contains sinners as well as saints; baptism important as a sign of rebirth, generally performed in adulthood; biblical literalism; and millennialism. In addition many, although not all, believed in pacifism and communism as characteristics of apostolic Christianity. This communism was a simple form of radical sharing, such as found in the book of Acts. Of all the Christians of the sixteenth century they came closest to a belief in religious toleration for all. Of course they had everything to gain and nothing to lose.

[69]

The Anabaptists brought the anger of the "orthodox" Christians—Lutheran, Catholic, Zwinglian, Calvinist—to white heat. They were heretics of the worst kind. In addition to the well-attested charges many violent and ugly beliefs were falsely attributed to them. Pursued from one end of Europe to the other, they literally had not where to lay their heads. Their enemies said, if they want to be baptized, let them be baptized—permanently. Sometimes they were bound together in bundles and thrown into the river. They became a distraught and miserable accumulation of refugees, attacked in Switzerland, Moravia, the Netherlands, the Rhineland, driven from one place to another as persecution waxed and waned. And still they survived, survived to continue their testimony of peaceful, quiet, wholehearted faith, *die Stille im Lande.*

The earliest of the left-wing leaders were capable, responsible, and relatively moderate men, like Conrad Grebel and Felix Manz in Switzerland, Balthasar Hübmaier and Hans Denck in Germany. But these died or were ruthlessly killed off by intolerant opponents. Then the wilder, more illiterate spirits came forward to take over leadership: Melchior Hoffmann with his eschatological prophecies, Hans Hut with his biblically justified sword to be used by the regenerate against the worldly degenerate, John of Leiden following the lead of Old Testament worthies in polygamy, David Joris with his mystical individualism and Messianism. Especially obnoxious was the episode of Münster, in Westphalia, where for a brief spell the saints seized control of the whole community. They drove out both Roman Catholics and Lutherans, and turned the city into a New Jerusalem. They practiced communism and polygamy, both on biblical grounds. With millenarian enthusiasm they proclaimed John of Leiden "King David." Although it was short-lived, exceptional, and not representative, the infamy of Münster gave the movement in general a bad name. Most of the information concerning these radicals has come down from the pens of opponents.

By the middle of the century a more moderate and peaceful trend arose, associated with Menno Simons (d. 1561), founder of the *Mennonite Church.* This is one of the few groups within the left wing to survive to our day. The *Amish* date from seventeenth-century dis-

ciples of Jacob Ammann, who thought the Mennonites were depart-
ing from their original discipline. Also surviving are the *Schwenckfelders,* followers of Kaspar Schwenckfeld, and the *Hutterites,* or Hut-
terian Brethren, followers of Jacob Hutter. The former are still found
in Pennsylvania, the latter in North Dakota. Other groups have been
strongly influenced by the Anabaptist tradition, especially the *Church
of the Brethren.*

The glory as well as the terror of their experience is reflected in an
old Anabaptist hymn:

> Sheep without shepherd running blind
> Are scattered into flight.
> Our house and home are left behind,
> Like birds we fly by night,
> And like the birds, naught overhead
> Save wind and rain and weather,
> In rocks and caves our bed.
>
> We creep for refuge under trees.
> They hunt us with the bloodhound.
> Like lambs they take us as they please
> And hold us roped and strong-bound.
> They show us off to everyone
> As if the peace we'd broken,
> As sheep for slaughter looked upon,
> As heretics bespoken.
>
> Some in heavy chains have lain
> And rotting there have stayed.
> Some upon the trees were slain,
> Choked and hacked and flayed.
> Drownings by stealth and drownings plain
> For matron and for maid.
> Fearlessly the truth they spoke
> And were not ashamed.
> Christ is the way and Christ the life
> Was the word proclaimed.
> Precious in Thy sight, O God,
> The dying of a saint.

> Our comfort this beneath the rod
> Whenever we are faint,
> In Thee, O God, in Thee alone
> Are earthly peace and rest.
> Who hope on Thee, eternally
> Are sustained and blessed.[12]

D. The Reformation in England

Following a path of its own, more significant for ecclesiastical than for doctrinal formulations, the English Reformation is closely associated with the reigns of the Tudor monarchs who dominated the sixteenth-century history of the island kingdom. Further, the movement for reformation was not spent in the sixteenth century, in fact reached its full expression only in the Puritanism of the seventeenth.

1. Henry VIII (1509-47). The second in the new English dynasty of the Tudors was Henry VIII. His reign was crucial for the prospects of the family, for the development of English political and religious institutions, and for the very survival of the little kingdom itself. A favorite historical guessing game is concerned with the motivation for the "divorce" of Henry VIII. Did he put away Catherine of Aragon because he was in love with Anne Boleyn, or because he needed a male heir to the throne, or because he had a conscience smitten with the Levitical law? Undoubtedly he had a conscience, although he managed to keep it very well concealed. He was certainly aware of the regulation in Leviticus 20:21: "If a man shall take his brother's wife, it is an unclean thing: he hath uncovered his brother's nakedness." What really gave him pause was the dire prophecy that followed: "They shall die childless." Henry had married his brother's wife. Catherine had come to England first as the bride of his brother Arthur, who had died, and Henry had married her. And they were childless! That is, it amounted to the same thing, for there had been born only one surviving child, a girl baby, Mary. Perhaps more directly in Henry's thought was the knowledge that there would be no more children of this marriage, boys or girls. The prospect of passing the Tudor

---

[12] Quoted in Roland H. Bainton, *The Reformation of the Sixteenth Century* (Boston: Beacon Press, 1952), p. 104. Used by permission of the publishers.

crown, only two generations old, to a woman was unthinkable—in a world of raiding Scots, rapacious French, aspiring Hapsburgs, to say nothing of jealous Englishmen. Only a few years before, the elder Henry Tudor had won his crown on the field of battle, to become Henry VII. Too many people in England remembered a different day and a different ruling house. What was needed was the strong man's hand. It is one of the ironies of history that the strongest Tudor hand of all turned out to be that of a woman, Elizabeth, and that, of the three reigning descendants and heirs of Henry VIII, the only man's hand was that of a sickly boy too young to rule, too weak to live. And then, of course, there was Anne Boleyn, tantalizing in her proximity as a lady-in-waiting at court. That Henry was entranced after the manner of the flesh is indubitable.

However weighty each of these factors was in the mind of Henry, the English Reformation was a by-product, in the first instance of the case of annulment of the marriage with Catherine. Now Henry was willing to sacrifice this union, but Catherine was not. She, of unbending Aragonese virtue, was unco-operative. That made all the more difficult the task of Thomas Wolsey, archbishop of York, lord chancellor of England, papal legate, cardinal, minister and diplomat extraordinary. A self-made man, wealthy and powerful through the support of the king, he ignored his clerical brothers, spurned the established aristocrats, disdained the commoners from whom he sprang. Upon him fell the responsibility of carrying on the suit with Rome. Briefly, he failed. He failed in part because of a factor neither he nor his royal master could control: Catherine had a nephew named Charles. He happened to be holy Roman emperor and king of Spain. At this particular time Charles V held the papacy in thrall. Even if the pope had wished to accommodate for a price his English son—the "Defender of the Faith," as he had dubbed him—it was impossible. The suit failed and Wolsey fell. Great was the fall thereof. He was under arrest and on his way to trial, degradation, and death, when he died, reputedly commenting: "Had I served my God as diligently as I have served my king, he would not have given me over in my gray hairs."

About this time appeared Thomas Cranmer, an able churchman who, when the old archbishop of Canterbury died, was appointed to this place of primacy. Cranmer was to be the central figure in three reigns in the formulation of the doctrine, ritual, and polity of the *Church of England*. Foiled, Henry turned to Parliament, the clergy of England, and the universities of Oxford and Cambridge, craving their advice on the marriage. They returned the advice sought, and the marriage was annulled without benefit of the pope. Since Anne was already pregnant, a secret marriage followed. Presently there was born another heir to the throne—a girl baby! This was Elizabeth.

Henry had other matrimonial adventures, only two of which need detain us. When Anne was tried and executed for adultery, Henry obtained on the day of her execution a license to marry Jane Seymour. Finally, she gave Henry what he so desperately wanted, a boy, Edward. Great was the rejoicing, for it was not yet known in what precarious health the little child would live, nor did the unhappy death of Jane as a result of childbirth bring more than a momentary pause in the festivities. Since by this time (see below) the English church had broken with Rome, the diplomatic situation called for a Protestant alliance. If the Catholic powers should unite against an isolated England, the peril would be overwhelming. Hence Henry's new lieutenant, Thomas Cromwell, cast about for a proper alliance to be cemented, after the custom, with a marriage. The result was the project of marriage with Anne of Cleves, eligibly Protestant. Henry went down to the port to meet her. In spite of the fact that she was not what he had hoped for, Henry went through with the diplomatic marriage. Anne, being a sensible girl, presently acquiesced in the dissolution of this match by common agreement and financial settlement.

Now, to return to the religious issue, when Henry forced through the annulment of the marriage with Catherine, the pope naturally resented the action and excommunicated Henry. The king reacted by having a series of statutes passed removing the English church from the control of the pope. Of these the most important was the Act of Supremacy, 1534, by which Henry became "supreme head on earth of the English church." A few Roman Catholic leaders, among them John Fisher, bishop of Rochester, and Thomas More, former lord chancellor and noted humanist, refused to acknowledge this extension of royal authority and paid with their lives. Henry balanced the records by executing some equally recalcitrant Protestants. The Ten Acts and the Six Acts, both of Henry's reign, attempted, with no notable success, to define the doctrinal position of the English church. The position was quite conservative, not far removed from the Roman interpretation. And the later Six Acts were even less Protestant than the Ten Acts. Henry was certainly not motivated by a zeal for Protestantism.

Only one other aspect of the religious development calls for attention: the dissolution of the monasteries. As ever in Europe, the old monastic establishments had gathered over the centuries much treasure into their barns. The bulk of earthly treasure seemed to be crowding out the spiritual. Aware of this, and in chronic need of funds, Henry had an ecclesiastical commission investigate conditions in the monasteries. On the basis of these findings, in the late 1530's, the monasteries were dissolved and their assets added to the royal coffers. This meant that one sixth of the land of England changed owners. Much of the income was used for valid ecclesiastical and educational services; but too much went into the hands of favorites. Little else of reform is seen while Henry was on the throne, except the growing interest in the use of the English Bible. The work of William Tyndale illegally and of Miles Coverdale legally belongs to this period. The Great Bible, revision of an earlier version, was authorized to be read in all the churches. In 1547, old and sick and weary, Henry gave up the ghost.

2. *Edward VI (1547-53) and Mary (1553-58)*. Before he died, Henry made a will that was enacted as a statute of the realm, providing for the Tudor succession. His son should be first in line, and after him, barring direct descendants, Mary, and finally Elizabeth.

What Edward lacked in body he made up in mind, being precocious for his age, nine years. Since he was a minor, a council of regency was established, with Edward Seymour, duke of Somerset, as the first lord protector. He was a man of moderate Protestant sympathies, responsible and sincere. During this reign the church moved to its most Protestant position. The Six Acts were repealed, together with other restrictive laws. Continental influences came from various quarters. Humanism, Zwinglianism, and Calvinism were more important than Lutheranism. Refugees of Calvinist persuasion poured in, including intellectual

[75]

leaders like Peter Martyr, Bernardino Ochino, John Lasco. A corporative charter was issued for the London Dutch Church of Austin Friars. Besides the Dutch there were several congregations of French refugees. Archbishop Cranmer, following upon an Act of Uniformity requiring a book of common prayer, prepared the First Prayer Book of Edward VI. This work has become not only the foundation for the Anglican form of worship but a classic of devotional appeal to all Christians as well. The Second Prayer Book was even more radically Protestant. The altar became a table, the priest a minister. Doctrinally the standard was set in the Forty-two Articles, again largely the work of Cranmer. These, however, were never published, although the larger part were incorporated in the Thirty-nine Articles established under Elizabeth.

When at the age of sixteen Edward died, Mary, daughter of Catherine of Aragon, succeeded. An attempt engineered by the self-seeking Duke of Northumberland, second lord Protector, to stave off personal disaster by overthrowing Mary in favor of a Protestant queen, Lady Jane Grey, failed. Both Northumberland and his relatively innocent claimant suffered for treason. Mary, loyal to the memory of her mother, had a strong emotional attachment to Roman Catholicism. Soon she put into operation a program intended to bring England back to the fold. The thousands of foreign refugees, seeing the trend, left the shores of England to seek refuge in Switzerland, Germany, and, unsuccessfully, Denmark. Along with them now went English Protestants, who in considerable number settled in Frankfurt, Zürich, Geneva, and elsewhere. Deeply they drank from the fountain of the Reformed religion, prepared themselves for a return to their native land.

In England the return to Rome proceeded apace. Catholic-minded bishops like Stephen Gardiner, set aside under Edward, were now returned to their sees. The Edwardian religious arrangements were repealed, and by 1554 the English nation was finally absolved and received back into the fold. The remainder of the reign saw continued efforts, after the fashion of the sixteenth century, to stamp out heresy. The results were numerous executions, preserved as a record of infamy in John Foxe's *Book of Martyrs*. Bishops Latimer and Ridley were among the victims burned at the stake. The former, aged and long since done with his active years, encouraged the more youthful Ridley with words incased in tradition: "Be of good comfort, Master Ridley, we shall this day light such a candle by God's grace in England as, I trust, shall never be put out."

Archbishop Cranmer faced a doubly difficult problem. Over the years he had supported the royal establishment according to the Act of Supremacy. But now a Roman Catholic was monarch. Two loyalties besieged him as he lay in prison. After a brief submission, he repented and gave his final loyalty to his heavenly King, died at the stake like Latimer and Ridley.

Unhappily married to Philip II of Spain, unwell, and increasingly remote from her subjects, Mary died in 1558.

3. Elizabeth (1558-1603).

And further be it enacted by the queen's highness, with the assent of the Lords and Commons in this present Parliament assembled, and by the authority of the same, that all and singular ministers in any cathedral or parish church, or other place within this realm of England, Wales, and the marches of the same, or other the queen's dominions, shall from and after the feast of the Nativity of St. John Baptist next coming be bounden to say and use the Matins, Evensong, celebration of the Lord's Supper and administration of each of the sacraments, and all their common and open prayer, in such order and form as is mentioned in the said book [the Book of Common Prayer], so authorized by Parliament in the said fifth and sixth years of the reign of King Edward VI.[13]

So ran the Act of Uniformity, 1559, following directly upon the Act of Supremacy that made Elizabeth "the only supreme governor of this realm . . . as well in all spiritual or ecclesiastical things or causes, as temporal." These documents laid the religious foundations for the reign of the peerless queen who personifies modern England at its best. The Elizabethan Age was a golden age, when the English navy had its baptism by fire against the Great Armada, when Shakespeare dominated a collection of literary masters each of whom would have been world-famous had he not been a contemporary of the bard of Stratford, when English ships on the seaways of the world were

---

[13] Act of Uniformity, 1559. Henry Bettenson, ed., *Documents of the Christian Church* (New York: Oxford University Press, 1947), p. 334.

harbingers of great days to come. But especially this was an age in which some permanent institutions, ranging from royal authority to the Book of Common Prayer, were established. The religious settlement was purposely framed as broadly as possible, with a view to providing room for various predilections. Excluding Roman Catholicism on the one hand and radical sectaries on the other, the ambiguous formulas gave ample opportunity for wide variations in interpretation. The stage was set for the interminable debates over just what the Church of England really stood for. A revised form of the Second Edwardian Prayer Book was prescribed. Matthew Parker was made archbishop of Canterbury. The Thirty-nine Articles were formulated to define the belief and polity of the church, and all clergymen were required to subscribe. The most famous classic defending the Anglican position against Roman Catholics and Puritans alike was Richard Hooker's *Of the Laws of Ecclesiastical Polity*, 1600.

During the reign of Elizabeth, Roman Catholics were suppressed. This is not surprising in view of the fact that the pope completely rejected the Elizabethan Settlement and excommunicated Elizabeth. "Moreover," said the pope in the bull *Regnans in excelsis,* "we declare her to be deprived of her pretended right to the aforesaid realm, and from all dominion, dignity and privilege whatsoever." And all her subjects were absolved from their oaths of allegiance. Hence, to be a Roman Catholic was to be suspect of treason. Nevertheless, the Roman faith in England survived and even revived. On the other hand, Puritanism began to appear. This is discussed in the following chapter.

E. The Catholic Reformation

That part of Christendom that remained firmly attached to Rome during the upheavals of the Reformation was not untouched. A "reformation" was accomplished within the body of Roman Catholicism. The term "Counter Reformation" is sometimes used, and it has merit as describing one aspect of the movement—but only one. The Catholic Reformation was not an entirely negative reaction against Protestantism. Four major aspects may be discerned.

The first aspect, upon which the others depended, was the reformation of the papacy. Paul III and Paul IV were different men from

Julius II and Leo X. Considering the vulnerability of the papacy under the attacks of the Protestants, reform here was a long time coming. Clement VII was in part responsible for the delay. Preserved Smith has quoted a description of his pontificate as "one of scruples, considerations and discords, of buts and ifs and thens and moreovers, and plenty of words without effect." [14] Of easygoing and dilatory temperament, Clement avoided year after year the task of calling together a council of the church to carry out the program of reform unsuccessfully attempted a hundred years before in the "reforming" councils of the fifteenth century. Fearing the repercussions of such a long-deferred council on the papacy itself, he never got around to it. But the demands increased over the years.

When Paul III became pope in 1534, the dam holding back the flood broke. His pontificate saw the calling of the Council of Trent, the establishment of the Society of Jesus, and the reorganization of the Inquisition and Index—all major elements of the Catholic Reformation. Besides this he made a number of excellent appointments to high ecclesiastical positions, including Caraffa, who was his successor as Paul IV, and Contarini, broad-minded ecclesiastical statesman. Whatever may be said of the popes after Paul III, they were not lackadaisical humanists, nor were they incompetent or despicable. Many of them were stern advocates of reform and ecclesiastical discipline. Such men as these would probably have dealt quite differently with Martin Luther.

When Paul III published a call for a general council, he had in mind certain previous councils that had begun reform by deposing popes. He also had in mind that a council was just what Luther had earlier clamored for. He also realized that political factors might defeat the best of intentions. He made sure that the system of representation and the right of legislative initiative would remain under papal control. He was correct in apprehending political interference. The Council of Trent met intermittently from 1545 to 1563, in the shadow of the Italian Alps. The results were notable. The canons of this council defined the position of the Roman Catholic Church down to our day.

The first task was the redefinition of the Catholic position as against

[14] *The Age of the Reformation* (New York: Henry Holt & Co., 1920), p. 381.

those taken by the Lutherans and, later, the Calvinists. The question of final authority in matters of faith was solved by the formula of Bible *and* tradition. That is, the Scriptures are the standard of authority as understood and interpreted by the tradition and teaching of the church. As against Luther's justification by faith alone, the Council settled on justification by faith *and* works. Many were the stormy debates, however, on this thorny question. The sacraments were maintained to the number seven, and transubstantiation was reaffirmed. In this way a clear line was drawn between Catholicism and Protestantism. The chasm was getting deep, and would get deeper with the passage of years and the multiplication of Catholic dogma. From the Council of Trent to the promulgation in 1950 of the dogma of the Assumption of the Virgin, every dogmatic definition has dug deeper and wider this great gulf.

After Trent hopes of reunification of Christendom went glimmering. On the other hand this same council succeeded in carrying out a series of reforms, the import of which was the elimination of most of the abuses against which Luther had originally protested. Clergy were directed to dwell in their own parishes and do the work of the Lord therein. Preaching could be heard in the native tongue under certain conditions. Seminaries were ordered established for the better preparation of priests. These reform decrees were by no means universally accepted in Catholic countries. Spain, for example, gave assent "saving the royal authority." France was willing to accept the dogmatic canons but not the reform decrees. Nevertheless, great strides had been made toward cleaning up the church and rooting out sin.

Now we come to another powerful move of Rome. The church was interested not only in rooting out sin but also in rooting out heresy. At this very time, ripe for the opportunity, appeared a new monastic movement tailor-made to the task. The members of the Society of Jesus became the shock troops of the Counter Reformation. The founder of this order of "Jesuits" was Ignatius Loyola, a Basque of northern Spain who began his career as a soldier. A crippling injury at the age of twenty-eight ended that career. The painful process of recovery led his thoughts to religion and his body to a pilgrimage to Jerusalem. After a determined program of education, in the course of which his ascetic rigor twice came under the suspicious eye of the Inquisition, he gathered about him a small following. Among these was Francis Xavier, who later became famous as a Jesuit missionary in the Far East. For the spiritual training of candidates he prepared the *Spiritual Exercises,* a spiritual daily dozen for discipline and preparation through prayer and meditation. With the formal establishment of the new order in 1540, a constitution provided the framework for one of the most totalitarian institutions ever conceived. Members were directed to serve the Lord alone and the pope, his vicar. Absolute obedience became a mark of the Order. As the constitution put it:

Let us with the utmost pains strain every nerve of our strength to exhibit this virtue of obedience, firstly to the Highest Pontiff, then to the Superiors of the Society; so that in all things, to which obedience can be extended with charity, we may be most ready to obey his voice, just as if it issued from Christ our Lord . . . ; by directing to this goal all our strength and intention in the Lord, that holy obedience may be made perfect in us in every respect, in performance, in will, in intellect; by submitting to whatever may be enjoined on us with great readiness, with spiritual joy and perseverance; by persuading ourselves that all things [commanded] are just; by rejecting with a kind of blind obedience all opposing opinion or judgment of our own; and that in all things which are ordained by the Superior where it cannot be clearly held that any kind of sin intervenes. And let each one persuade himself that they that live under obedience ought to allow themselves to be borne and ruled by divine providence working through their Superiors exactly as if they were a corpse which suffers itself to be borne and handled in any way whatsoever; or just as an old man's stick which serves him who holds it in his hand wherever and for whatever purpose he wish to use it.[15]

In the course of a long and, in some respects, glorious history the Jesuits became famous for recovery of Protestant lands for Rome. They were the epitome of counter-reformation. They began to make a name for themselves in the fields of education and scholarship. And above all they carried the Christian message in the work of foreign missions. This is a story told in a later chapter.

[15] Bettenson, *Documents of the Christian Church,* p. 366. Used by permission of the publishers, Oxford University Press. Taken from C. Mirbt, *Quellen zur Geschichte des Papsttums und des Römischen Katholizismus* (Tübingen: J. C. B. Mohr, 1934), p. 276.

Along with the Jesuit Order came a revival of discipline throughout the church. This is exemplified in the organization of the Roman Inquisition and the establishment of an Index of prohibited books. In Spain an efficient inquisition had been in operation since 1480. Diligent inquisitors like Torquemada rendered the name terrible as Judaizers, former Moslems, and, later, a few Protestants, were ferreted out and punished. By 1540 some twenty thousand persons had been burned at the stake, and ten times that number languished in prison or slaved in the galleys. The Roman Inquisition, an attempt to extend the system to all Christendom in theory, was never so efficient or effective, even in Italy.

Together with inquisitorial methods went the censorship of reading. From lists previously worked out by the University of Louvain the Council of Trent established a fundamental Index of prohibited reading. The purpose of this censorship was not moral but rather doctrinal and ecclesiastical.

In these various ways the Roman Catholic Church sought to defend itself against further encroachment, to recover its inner spiritual strength and vitality, and to advance into the new world appearing on all sides and in all aspects of life. In part it succeeded. But in doing so it congealed into more and more rigid forms as an institution that remained essentially medieval.

F. Christianity and Society

That the Reformation involved political and social factors as well as religious should be apparent. Undoubtedly the political forces of the Empire, France, Spain, England, the Papal States, and even the Turks, had much to do with the success or failure of the spiritual movements engendered by the reformers. One side of the story is concerned with these environmental factors in the history of Christianity. That is not, however, the chief concern of this section. If the course of the Reformation was influenced by social factors, so also was society influenced by the released religious forces. This influence was felt in three ways.

In the first place, all the churches, new and old, were institutions *in* society. Especially the Roman Catholic Church had large political and economic interests simply as an institution. One example is seen in the relation of the papacy to the history of modern banking. Some of the largest transactions of the Medici and the Fugger were ecclesiastical in nature.

In the second place, the Reformation made a broad impact on society through the teachings of the leaders. Luther and Calvin had definite ideas about the political and economic order, and expressed their ideas clearly.

In the third place, a further, less tangible, but perhaps more important influence is seen in the social implications of the faith itself. Luther's reliance on justification by faith and the priesthood of all believers had ultimately more effect on the Christian world outlook than did the specific teachings, attitudes, and prejudices of Luther himself. Calvin's doctrine of the absolute sovereignty of God and its corollaries of election and the end of man played a much larger part in molding the political and economic outlook of Calvinists than did the personal opinions of the founder. This is simply to say that theology bears on life, ethics, and conduct. The psychological effects of faith are imponderable but immense.

The distinction between the actual teachings of the reformers and the actual effects of their religious doctrines will help to explain why Calvin could have taken so conservative a position on the issues of the day, could have built so rigid a theocratic regime in Geneva, and yet could have set in motion forces that provided one of the chief roots, if not the taproot, of modern democracy and economic independence.

1. Political Theory. None of the reformers had a truly modern idea of the state. In general they all accepted the interpretation that had evolved during the Middle Ages, that society in all its aspects is an organic unity. The problem was not simply one between the individual and the state, but rather one involving the individual and the state as both were related to the will of God. The authority of the state as separate from the will of God was inconceivable. Whether the outlook was pessimistic, as with Luther, or relatively optimistic, as with Calvin, the state always stands under the judgment of God, as does the individual. All the reformers had profound respect for political authority as representing, however imperfectly, the will of God. This is quite clear in Luther. In 1523 he published a tract "Of Temporal Power, in How Far One Should Obey It." Here the classic scriptural quotations from Romans 13:1 and I Peter 2:13 are emphasized: "Let every person be subject to the governing authorities. For there is no authority except from God, and those that exist have been instituted by God"; "be subject for the Lord's sake to every human institution, whether it be to the emperor as supreme, or to governors as sent by him to punish those who do wrong and to praise those who do right" (R.S.V.). The individual Christian is under obligation to submit to the constituted authority. True, Christians within the circle of fellowship should rely only on the force of love. In the world, however, the authority of the magistrate is necessary for the preservation of order, and to this end he has been endowed by God with the sword. Since Christians live in the world, participation in public life is not only permitted but required. The Christian magistrate has a high calling. Hence public responsibility involves the taking of oaths, the execution of the law, defense of the realm by military might. In this sense Luther, following Augustine, has a double ethic, one for the individual Christian, the other for the public servant. The individual must submit, may not resist authority with force. The magistrate, on the other hand, is obligated to use force in the maintenance of order. Even the public executioner can be a good Christian!

Are there no limits? There are. Luther recognized that political power corrupts and that it may not follow the will of God. In such cases, where authority is clearly counter to the faith, the Christian must refuse to obey, may never defy God's will. This would follow Acts 5:29: "We must obey God rather than men" (R.S.V.). The Christian must refuse to obey—and take the consequences. Never is the individual justified in revolution, even against a tyrant. As Luther put it in his *Address to the Christian Nobility,* "I will always side with him, however unjust, who endures rebellion and against him who rebels, however justly." The Christian's testimony must in this case be like that of the Anabaptists, who suffered gladly for the Lord. The magistrate, however, is in a different position. Endowed with authority of divine origin, he has the responsibility for order and defense. One magistrate may well, therefore, defend the true faith against a tyrant. This teaching, which appeared more clearly later, justified Luther in supporting the resistance of the princes against the attempts of Charles V to impose religious conformity. As to war, Luther accepted the traditional Augustinian position. He discussed the position of the soldier in his *Whether Soldiers Can Be Christian,* in 1526. His conclusion was that soldiering was just another profession, and a respectable one. The Christian soldier is of course never hateful and vindictive, but simply follows orders in killing the enemy. Luther was no pacifist as regards public responsibility. He was a pacifist insofar as he forbade the individual Christian to take arms in his own right. Passive resistance to tyranny, however, is an obligation.

It may well be that later Lutheranism, which accepted with fewer qualifications the leadership of the secular power, prepared the ground for that respect for authority and acceptance of command that made possible the rise of Hitler and Nazism. But there is very little in the teaching of Luther or in the effect of Lutheran doctrine to justify the assertion that Luther led the way to Hitler. "German Christians" were not the spiritual descendants of Luther. In fact, the emphasis on the individual experience of justification by faith, the reliance on the authority of the Bible as over against the organized church, and especially the priesthood of all believers, had large political implications that worked against, rather than for, the absolute state. In its practical effect, however, through the continuing influence of the territorial prince in the history and locale of Lutheranism, the Lutheran tradition may be said, in contrast to later Calvinism and the free-church principle, to have contributed to the support of the absolute state. In this sense it belongs with Roman Catholicism and, with qualifications, Anglicanism. In that same tradition, at least insofar as the rights of the individual as over against political authority are concerned, stands the theocracy of Geneva.

The story of what happened under Calvinist influence in Switzerland, Holland, Scotland, England, and New England is quite different. In spite of the conservatism of Calvin himself, the world view of Calvinism fostered strong lines of political individualism. Not only the mere limitation of governmental authority, but also the principles of modern democracy, are rooted, however indirectly, in this religious tradition. Other roots are to be recognized from the ancient Greek and Roman tradition, from English history quite apart from religion, and especially from the Enlightenment of the eighteenth century. And one must recognize at the outset that the sixteenth century saw no real democracy, in the modern sense, anywhere. But in the outworkings of Calvinism may be found the taproot. Other grounds provide reasonable and pragmatic support. But here individual freedom becomes part of the quintessence of faith. No one would have been more surprised at this outcome than Calvin.

Calvin's holy experiment at Geneva has already been discussed. Clearly he was no democrat, had little regard for individual freedom as over against governmental authority. Some of the inhabitants of the town came to think of the regime as intolerable tyranny. Geneva does illustrate one point clearly: All of life, public as well as private, is under the sovereignty of God. Government is in the sphere of common grace, the church in that of special grace. Both are parts of God's creative work and subject to his continuing control. This concept conflicts sharply with that of Machiavelli, for, if God is the source of political power, then justice must be the measure of its excellence. Right makes might. Geneva further provides an edifying contrast to the common standard of government in the sixteenth century. Interference in the private affairs of the people was a common feature of governments all over Europe. The busy little business of the Privy Council in England will illustrate. Geneva was purified of age-old vices, enjoyed an efficient and honest administration, ordered her affairs under law, and dreamed a great dream, glorifying God. Moreover, the church did not become, as too frequently in Lutheran, Zwinglian, and Catholic circles, the minion of the state. And yet one finds in Calvin little more support than in Luther for revolution against despotism. The principle is enunciated in the Preface to the *Institutes* that royal violation of the law of nature releases subjects from allegiance. But this is not an invitation to revolution. The most that it would maintain is the ultimate divine limitation on political power. As Calvin put it in another place:

[86]

For the condition of the people most to be desired is that in which they create their shepherds by general vote. For when anyone by force usurps the supreme power, that is tyranny. Also where men are born to kingship, this does not seem to be in accordance with liberty. Hence the prophet says: we shall set up princes for ourselves; that is, the Lord will not only give to the church freedom to breathe, but also institute a definite and well-ordered government, and establish this upon the common suffrages of all.[16]

Implied in Calvinism was not only limitation of the sphere of government, but also the sovereignty of the people, under God. Many factors lay behind this development. One factor hard to measure is the Presbyterian form of government within the church, based on the consent of the governed. Another, more important, is the doctrine of the absolute sovereignty of God, to which the state is as subject as the individual. Another is the doctrine of man as sinner. The most exalted ruler thus stands before God on the same plane as the most humble citizen. Sin is a mighty leveler. The doctrine of election works in the same way, tending toward democratic equality as all other distinctions disappear in the face of the all-important distinction between the saved and the lost, and tending toward aristocratic inequality as the common-born saint gains prestige over the most blue-blooded sinner. The doctrine of the calling gives to every man a valued place in the workaday world, insomuch as each may glorify God in his own calling. And finally the exercise of Calvinist discipline prepared the character of the individual for the heady wine of freedom. Only men living under the discipline of God's will can live in the atmosphere of democratic freedom. Only as we are bound to God are we ready to be freed from the restraints of men. In this way we return to the fundamental principle of the sovereignty of God.

Out of Calvinism, then, and especially out of its expression in England, France, New England, and Holland, have come two strains of political theory, the one relatively conservative, the other relatively radical. Religiously the one found expression in Presbyterianism, the other in radical Puritanism, nonconformity. In England the distinction is seen in the Presbyterians and the Independents, in New England be-

---

[16] Quoted in John T. McNeill, "The Democratic Element in Calvin's Thought," *Church History*, XVIII (1949), 165.

tween Massachusetts Bay Colony and Rhode Island. The two strains led respectively to conservative-authoritarian and radical-individualist interpretations of the ideas of the church, the covenant with God, the work of the Holy Spirit, the interpretation of the Bible, and the relation of church and state. Most of these tendencies belong to the later period, especially the seventeenth century. But the roots are to be found in the sixteenth, when already we note the full development of the essential concept of the covenant, as found in II Kings 11:17: "And Jehoiada made a covenant between the Lord and the king and the people, that they should be the Lord's people; between the king also and the people." A fine example of the way in which this was interpreted is found in the *Vindication Against Tyrants*, 1579. In this work the idea of the covenant as double, between God and the king and between God and the people, is developed. The ruler is obligated to judge the people in the name of God. But the people are also obligated to punish the ruler who rebels against God. The real rebel is he who departs from the will of God, not he who rejects the authority of an ungodly king. There is, then, one thing worse than rebellion of subjects against rulers: That is rebellion of the ruler against God.

Quite apart from political theory, but yet a manifestation of it, were the religious wars. We have already described the major conflicts of the sixteenth century: the struggle between the Lutherans and the Catholics in the Empire, ending in the Peace of Augsburg, 1555; the civil wars in France between Calvinists and Catholics, culminating in the War of the Three Henries, from which Henry of Navarre emerged as Henry IV; and the war for independence in the Netherlands. All these conflicts were motivated by religion. Although political and economic factors were present, the cause and course cannot be understood without first consideration of the religious factors. Wars have varied in quality as well as quantity over the ages. In the medieval period most struggles were feudal in nature, between the liege vassals of powerful suzerains, involving relatively few people. In the sixteenth century wars were primarily religious, although here also are to be found exceptions, for example the conflict between France and Spain over Italy, which began before the Reformation. With the seventeenth century a great change can be observed in the course of the Thirty Years' War, which began as a religious struggle and ended as a dynastic one. For over a century wars were concerned with dynasties, as even the names of some indicate: the War of the Spanish Succession, the War of the Austrian Succession. Bourbons against Hapsburgs against Hohenzollerns against Romanovs—that is the story. In the nineteenth century wars achieved the national character that led to the terrible Napoleonic conflicts, Bismarckian wars of unification, finally the debacle of World War I. With the twentieth century the world was submerged in the global, or total, war, in which practically all "civilized" members of the human race were involved.

The era of religious wars came to a conclusion with the extended Thirty Years' War, 1618-48. It came at a time when the Catholic Reformation was being consolidated and when Protestants were still hoping to win all Europe. Although many factors contributed to hostility, one of the causes was the Peace of Augsburg. The principle *cuius regio, eius religio* had proved difficult to administer. Both sides were willing to ignore the treaty when it served their interests. Over several decades ill feeling was exacerbated, until in 1618 open war came. The occasion was the Defenestration of Prague, when two Hapsburg counselors were thrown out of a high window in Prague by some Protestant leaders. At first the sides were drawn along strictly religious lines. Catholic forces under the Duke of Bavaria went into battle crying, "For the Virgin Mary!" During the early periods of this desultory but destructive war the Protestants were generally defeated. Count Palatine Frederick was beaten and his palatinate devastated. The Lutheran king of Denmark was driven out of the Danish peninsula. Not until the king of Sweden, Gustavus Adolphus, brought his military skill to the Protestant side was there any hope of victory. But then King Gustavus was killed in battle, and another stalemate developed. When it seemed the war was over, France entered—but not on the Catholic side. The amazing shift that led Catholic France into the Thirty Years' War on the side of the Protestants can be attributed to the power of the great Cardinal Richelieu (d. 1642), chief minister of King Louis XIII. This master of the involved diplomatic maze of seventeenth-century power politics was a Roman Catholic churchman who succeeded in reducing Protestant influence in France without actual persecution and without the purpose of extirpating heresy. The special political and military privileges granted under the Edict of Nantes were removed. His zeal was not so much for the advance of Roman Catholicism as for the dominance of royal France. In like manner he approached the diplomatic problem of the Thirty Years' War not from religious but from political considerations. To be more specific, he sought from the conflict a victory for the French Bourbons against the Austrian Hapsburgs. That the largely Catholic French army should be fighting alongside the Protestant forces of Scandinavia and Germany did not scandalize him at all. The whole character of the war was altered, and this may be taken as a symbol of the end of the religious wars. Men would still fight and kill, but henceforth not primarily for religious reasons.

By 1648 all the powers were weary. Germany was devastated in great swaths as armies marched and countermarched. The Peace of Westphalia, one of the landmark treaties of European history, was a compromise in that neither religious party was able to impose uniformity of faith on the other, nor was either dynastic power able to vanquish the other. France, however, emerged as a powerful Bourbon kingdom being forged into an absolute monarchy, and Brandenburg set out on its way to future power as the German Empire. The principle of *cuius regio, eius religio* was continued in the Holy Roman Empire, with the addition of Calvinism to the number of choices. In this way religion contributed to continuation of decentralization of the German-speaking peoples of central Europe.

2. Economic Theory. Luther shared an age-old suspicion of the merchant, a suspicion that has not disappeared to this day. The Bible tells us, said Luther, "how evil are the world's works." "Therefore some of the merchants too have been awakened, and have become aware that in their trading many a wicked trick and hurtful financial practice is in use, and it must be feared that the word of Ecclesiasticus applies here, and that 'merchants can hardly be without sin.' " [17] This is sufficient indication that Luther brought in no startling new economic attitude. Indeed, the religious leaders of the sixteenth century

[17] *Works of Martin Luther* (Philadelphia: A. J. Holman Co., 1915), IV, 12.

as a whole did not envisage any radical departure from the traditional fixtures of economic life. This was an age when the medieval non-capitalistic outlook was still strong, when the authority of the guild was by no means at an end, when the concepts of the just price and sub-sistence income were still influential. This was also an age in which the new forces of financial and commercial capitalism were beginning to break down the old barriers to untrammeled trade. The most impor-tant issue, therefore, is the relation of the churches to nascent capital-ism.

In the first place, there had always been capitalism, from ancient times on. The significant variable is the relative *number* of capitalists. They were few and far between in early and medieval times, but with the dawn of the modern age they multiplied. They multiplied long before Luther and Calvin came on the scene. Their first relations with the church were with the papacy of the fourteenth and fifteenth cen-turies. An important chapter in the history of banking and the develop-ment of instruments of credit has to do with the financial operations of the papacy and the Italian bankers, such as the Frescobaldi, Bardi, Medici. Capitalism preceded the Reformation. Moreover, the early reformers were uniformly conservative in their economic outlook, whether Luther with his agrarian background or Calvin with his urban environment. Neither had a good word for the ambitious worldly capitalist. Their attitude on the issue of usury is illustrative. Luther thought that as an ideal all interest ought to be prohibited, although he recognized in practice a limited necessity. His important treatise *On Trading and Usury*, 1524, clearly rejects the principle of free trade and financial negotiation. Usury is one of five kinds of theft. If both parties benefit, however, interest may be charged on a loan. Actually Luther was not deeply interested in the problems of the business world, and did not depart widely from the formulations of St. Thomas.

On the positive side Luther did make some real contributions to a reappraisal of work. The stigma on work as a punishment for original sin is removed, and industriousness is commended as a Christian virtue. Idleness is denounced. Beyond this daily work came into a new religious significance through the doctrine of the calling, *vocatio*. The original *vocatio* to come out from life into the cloister was transferred by Luther

—and even more by Calvin—to all decent "callings" or vocations. All callings are religious callings in the sense that a man may properly serve God in his daily work, through diligence, sobriety, skill, discipline. The doctrine of the priesthood of all believers contributed mightily to this new emphasis.

Where Luther began, Calvin carried further. He too was conservative in his economic outlook, although he belonged to an urban world. But his teaching and influence took on great significance through the thesis that the Calvinist ethic contributed to the development of the spirit of capitalism. This thesis was set forth by Max Weber in his essay on *The Protestant Ethic and the Spirit of Capitalism.* His theory was that Calvinist discipline created a new type of businessman, obsessed with a demonic drive to work without regard to personal comfort or propriety, by furious labor to build his business bigger and bigger, to accumulate capital for investment rather than to squander profits in riotous living—in short, to become an ambitious capitalist free from medieval restraints and ordinary human weaknesses. The necessity of being counted among the elect was said to have contributed to this tremendous drive. The conviction that one glorified God through diligent effort in daily work added fuel. And the practice of the disciplined life inevitably led to economic success. Weber's theory has been much criticized, sometimes unfairly. Undoubtedly he erred in his efforts to build too good a case. He failed to distinguish between early and late Calvinism, and exaggerated such elements as asceticism and the importance of election. The facts remain, however, that capitalism did develop most fully in those countries that were under the greatest influence of Calvinism—England, Scotland, the Netherlands. And undoubtedly the spirit of Puritan Calvinism led to the development of a type of character perfectly adapted to the new capitalist world.

Calvin himself was no more sympathetic with capitalism than were Luther and the medieval church. Here again one must distinguish between the actual teaching and attitude of a leader and the ultimate effects of his whole doctrine. Just as religious individualism had correlative applications in the direction of political democracy, so also in the direction of economic freedom. Calvin's blessing was on the glorification of God through the disciplined life in one's calling, not on the riches that resulted. A similar phenomenon is seen in the Wesleyan revival of the eighteenth century, and also in the history of the Quakers. Truly they all stood in the succession of Joseph, of whom it is written in Genesis 39:2: "The Lord was with Joseph, and he became a successful man" (R.S.V.).

For Further Reading

GENERAL

Bainton, Roland H. *Bibliography of the Continental Reformation*. Chicago: American Society of Church History, 1935, 54 p. Materials in English.

Kidd, B. J., ed. *Documents Illustrative of the Continental Reformation*. New York: Oxford University Press, 1911, 742 p. Most materials are in original language.

Bainton, Roland. *The Reformation of the 16th Century*. Boston: Beacon Press, 1952, 276 p.

Grimm, Harold J. *The Reformation Era. 1500-1650*. New York: The Macmillan Co., 1954, 675 p.

Smith, Preserved. *The Age of the Reformation*. New York: Henry Holt & Co., 1920, 861 p.

Lindsay, Thomas M. *A History of the Reformation*. New York: Charles Scribner's Sons, 1906, 2 vols. Old but sound.

Moreau, E. de, *et al. La crise religieuse du xvie siècle*. Paris: Bloud & Gay, 1950, 461 p. *Histoire de l'Eglise*, XVI.

Bainton, Roland H. *The Travail of Religious Liberty: Nine Biographical Studies*. Philadelphia: Westminster Press, 1951, 272 p.

Dillenberger, John and Claude Welch. *Protestant Christianity Interpreted through Its Development*. New York: Charles Scribner's Sons, 1954, 340 p.

Jordan, W. K. *The Development of Religious Toleration in England*. Cambridge: Harvard University Press, 1932, 490 p. Tudor period, first of a 4-vol. series.

Wilbur, Earl M. *A History of Unitarianism: Socinianism and Its Antecedents*. Cambridge: Harvard University Press, 1945, 617 p.

———. *A History of Unitarianism in Transylvania, England, and America*. Cambridge: Harvard University Press, 1952, 518 p.

LUTHER AND LUTHERANISM

Bainton, Roland H. *Here I Stand: A Life of Martin Luther*. New York and Nashville: Abingdon Press, 1950, 422 p.

———. "Luther's Struggle for Faith," *Church History*, XVII (1948), 193-206. Moving appreciation.

Boehmer, Heinrich. *Road to Reformation*. Philadelphia: Muhlenberg Press, 1946, 449 p. Luther's early career.

McGiffert, Arthur C. *Martin Luther, The Man and His Work*. New York: The Century Co., 1911, 397 p.

Rupp, Ernest G. *Luther's Progress to the Diet of Worms*. Chicago: The Wilcox & Follett Co., 1951, 109 p.

Schwiebert, E. G. *Luther and His Times*. St. Louis: Concordia Publishing House, 1950, 892 p.

Richard, J. W. *Philip Melanchthon*. New York: G. P. Putnam's Sons, 1898, 399 p.

ZWINGLI AND CALVIN

McNeill, John T. *The History and Character of Calvinism.* New York: Oxford University Press, 1954, 466 p.

Mackinnon, James. *Calvin and the Reformation.* New York: Longmans Green & Co., 1936, 302 p.

Toth, William. "Highlights of the Hungarian Reformation," *Church History,* IX (1940), 141-56.

Harkness, Georgia. *John Calvin, the Man and His Ethics.* New York: Henry Holt & Co., 1931, 266 p.

Hunt, R. N. C. *Calvin.* London: Geoffrey Bles, Ltd., 1933, 335 p.

Reyburn, H. G. *John Calvin, His Life, Letters and Work.* London: Hodder & Stoughton, 1914, 376 p.

Baird, H. M. *Theodore Beza, the Counsellor of the French Reformation.* New York: G. P. Putnam's Sons, 1899. 376 p.

Eells, Hastings. *Martin Bucer.* New Haven: Yale University Press, 1931, 539 p.

Percy, Eustace. *John Knox.* London: Hodder & Stoughton, 1937, 438 p.

Bainton, Roland H. *Hunted Heretic: The Life and Death of Michael Servetus.* Boston: Beacon Press, 1953, 270 p.

Jackson. S. *Huldreich Zwingli.* New York: G. P. Putnam's Sons, 1901, 519 p.

LEFT WING

Bax, E. B. *Rise and Fall of the Anabaptists.* New York: The Macmillan Co., 1903, 407 p.

Friedmann, Robert. *Mennonite Piety Through the Centuries: Its Genius and Its Literature.* Goshen, Ind.: Mennonite Historical Society, 1949, 287 p.

Smith, C. Henry. *The Story of the Mennonites.* Berne, Ind.: Mennonite Book Concern, 1941, 823 p.

Bender, Harold S. *Life and Letters of Conrad Grebel.* Goshen, Ind.: Mennonite Historical Society, 1950, 326 p.

————. *Menno Simons' Life and Writings.* Scottdale, Pa.: Mennonite Publishing House, 1936, 110 p.

Dosker, H. E. *The Dutch Anabaptists.* Philadelphia: Westminster Press, 1921, 310 p.

Littell, Franklin. *The Anabaptist View of the Church.* Philadelphia: American Society of Church History, 1952, 148 p.

Vedder, H. C. *Balthasar Hubmaier.* New York: G. P. Putnam's Sons, 1905, 333 p.

See also immense material in *Mennonite Quarterly Review.*

ENGLAND

Moorman, John. *A History of the Church in England.* New York: Morehouse-Gorham Co., 1954, 460 p.

Hutchinson, F. E. *Cranmer and the English Reformation.* New York: The Macmillan Co., 1951, 188 p. "Teach Yourself History" series.

Pollard, Albert F. *Thomas Cranmer and the English Reformation.* New York: G. P. Putnam's Sons, 1904, 399 p. Solid and sympathetic.

Hughes, Philip. *The Reformation in England.* New York: The Macmillan Co., 1951-54, 3 vols. Scholarly, by a Roman Catholic.

Powicke, F. M. *The Reformation in England.* London: Oxford University Press, 1941, 137 p.

Smith, H. M. *Henry VIII and the Reformation.* New York: The Macmillan Co., 1948, 480 p.

Knappen, M. M. *Tudor Puritanism*. Chicago: University of Chicago Press, 1939, 555 p.

Smith, Lacey Baldwin. *Tudor Prelates and Politics*. Princeton: Princeton University Press, 1953, 333 p.

Hackett, Francis. *Henry the Eighth*. New York: Liveright Publishing Corporation, 1929, 452 p. Flamboyant.

Pollard, Albert F. *Henry VIII*. New York: Longmans, Green & Co., 1906.

Prescott, H. F. M. *Mary Tudor*. London: Eyre & Spottiswoode, Ltd., 1953, 434 p.

Darby, Harold S. *Hugh Latimer*. London: Epworth Press, 1953, 262 p.

Hollis, Christopher. *Thomas More*. Milwaukee: Bruce Publishing Co., 1934, 256 p. By a Catholic, fair.

Dawley, Powel Mills. *John Whitgift and the English Reformation*. New York: Charles Scribner's Sons, 1954, 254 p.

Pollard, Albert F. *Wolsey*. New York: Longmans, Green & Co., 1929, 393 p.

Loane, Marcus L. *Masters of the English Reformation*. London: Church Book Room Press, 1954, 247 p. Bilney, Tyndale, Latimer, Ridley, Cranmer.

CATHOLIC REFORMATION

Cristiani, L. *L'Eglise a l'époque du concile de Trente*. Paris: Bloud & Gay, 1948, 494 p. *Histoire de l'Eglise*, XVII.

Janelle, P. *The Catholic Reformation*. Milwaukee: Bruce Publishing Co., 1949, 397 p.

Kidd, Beresford J. *The Counter-Reformation, 1550-1600*. New York: The Macmillan Co., 1933, 271 p.

Lea, H. C. *A History of the Inquisition of Spain*. New York: The Macmillan Co., 1906, 4 vols.

Brodrick, James. *The Origin of the Jesuits*. New York: Longmans, Green & Co., 1947, 274 p.

————. *The Progress of the Jesuits*. New York: Longmans, Green & Co., 1947, 337 p. 1556-79, sequel to *Origin*.

Hanke, Lewis: *Bartolomé de las Casas: An Interpretation of His Life and Writings*. The Hague, 1951, 102 p.

Van Dyke, Paul. *Ignatius Loyola, Founder of the Jesuits*. New York: Charles Scribner's Sons, 1926, 381 p.

Sedgwick, H. D. *Ignatius Loyola*. New York: The Macmillan Co., 1923, 399 p.

Brodrick, James. *Saint Francis Xavier* (1506-1552). New York: Pellegrini & Cudahy, 1952, 548 p.

CHRISTIANITY AND SOCIETY

Grimm, Harold J. "Luther's Conception of Territorial and National Loyalty," *Church History*, XVII (1948), 79-94.

Mueller, William A. *Church and State in Luther and Calvin*. Nashville: Broadman Press, 1954, 183 p.

Baron, Hans. "Calvinist Republicanism and Its Historical Roots," *Church History*, VIII (1939), 30-42.

McNeill, John T. "The Democratic Element in Calvin's Thought," *Church History*, XVIII (1949), 153-71.

Tawney, R. H. *Religion and the Rise of Capitalism*. New York: Harcourt, Brace & Co., 1926, 339 p.

Read, Conyers. *Social and Political Forces in the English Reformation*. Houston, Tex.: Elsevier Press, 1953, 87 p.

FAMOUS BOOKS

Huldreich Zwingli (d. 1531). *An Exposition of the Faith.*

Desiderius Erasmus (d. 1536). *Education of a Christian Prince; Enchiridion; Praise of Folly.*

Martin Luther (d. 1546). *Address to the German Nobility; On Christian Freedom; On the Babylonian Captivity; Lectures on Romans* and *Commentary on Galatians.*

Thomas Cranmer (d. 1556). *Book of Common Prayer.*

John Calvin (d. 1564). *Institutes of the Christian Religion; Treatises; Commentaries.*

John Jewel (d. 1571). *Apology for the Anglican Church.*

John Knox (d. 1572). *History of the Reformation in Scotland.*

Henry Bullinger (d. 1575). *Decades.*

Richard Hooker (d. 1600). *Of the Laws of Ecclesiastical Polity.*

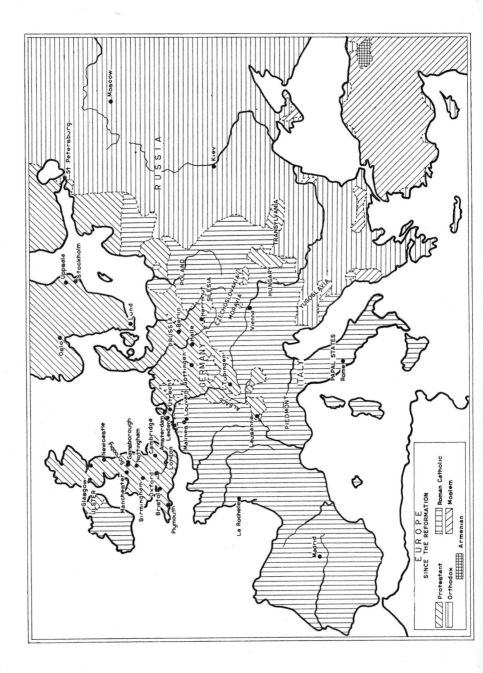

EUROPE
SINCE THE REFORMATION

Protestant   Roman Catholic   Moslem

Orthodox   Armenian

RUSSIA

Moscow

Kiev

St Petersburg

Uppsala
Stockholm
Lund

Oslo

POLAND
SILESIA
CZECHOSLOVAKIA
MORAVIA
TRANSYLVANIA
HUNGARY
YUGOSLAVIA

Herrnhut
Berlin
Halle
RUSSIA
GERMANY
Göttingen
Tübingen
Vienna
ALSACE

Newcastle
Gainsborough
Glasgow
Nottingham
Manchester
Cambridge
ULSTER
Birmingham
Oxford
Amsterdam
Bristol
London
Leiden
Plymouth
Utrecht
Malines
Louvain
ITALY

PIEDMONT
PAPAL STATES
Rome
Lausanne
La Rochelle

Madrid

CHAPTER III

The Age of Enlightenment
[1603-1815]

A. Stuart England and Roman Catholic Europe

THE REFORMATION WAS THE BEGINNING OF REFORMATION. THAT IS to say, the movement associated with Luther and Calvin in the sixteenth century gave rise to many forces that continued to change the face of Christianity. If the ideal of Catholicism has been dogmatic stability, that of Protestantism has been dynamic development. This means that the significance of the Reformation cannot be measured solely in terms of the sixteenth century. The evolution of its implications carries far, down to our own day. The impact of Calvinism has been far greater than the force of Calvin's own teaching. The Genevan master would have been amazed could he have foreseen the outworking of his authoritarian theology. The full force of "A Mighty Fortress Is Our God" is seen in the face of Bishop Berggrav as he peers through the fence of a Nazi concentration camp.

Thus, the dissenting churches of the seventeenth-century English tradition, the Wesleyan revival of the eighteenth century, and the Great Awakening in America represent the continuation of the Reformation. John Bunyan, Roger Williams, Jonathan Edwards, John Wesley, Francis Asbury, are part and parcel of the Reformation.

1. The Established Church—Puritanism. The historic unity of the Protestant tradition from the sixteenth century on is clearly evident in the case of England. One might even say that the true English Reformation occurred in the seventeenth century. Certainly the Thirty-nine Articles of the Elizabethan period did not represent the final word for English religion.

The Church of England, the Anglican church, settled down to an amorphous compromise after the violent reactions attendant upon the Tudor succession. During the long reign of Queen Elizabeth (1558-1603) the formula was conformity within broad limits. One of the prime requisites was a new interpretation of the church in England as related to the Church of God. The Anglicans were not at all willing to sever the ties with historic Christianity. The doctrines of apostolic succession, the historic episcopate, sacramental liturgics, appealed strongly to such men as Bishop John Jewel, who wrote an anti-Roman *Apology for the Anglican Church* (1562), and Richard Hooker (d. 1600), whose *Laws of Ecclesiastical Polity* stands as a classic of Christian literature beyond its importance as a double-bladed defense of the Anglican church against the Roman Catholics on the one hand and the Puritan Presbyterians on the other. It was widely held that the commodious vessel of the Thirty-nine Articles offered abundant space for respectable Christians of many persuasions. Only, don't rock the boat! Unfortunately, the storms of reform were not over, especially in England.

Ever since the days of Edward a non-Anglican Protestantism had been present in England. Fostered by visitors and refugees like Martin Bucer, Peter Martyr, John Lasco, and Jan Utenhove, and greatly strengthened by the Marian exile, in the reign of Elizabeth it took the form of *Puritanism*. Historically the term refers to the effort to purify the Church of England, to expunge nonscriptural or Roman practices. Like all such movements, it went through various stages. At first it took a negative form, as protest against certain customs, particularly the use of clerical vestments, kneeling at the Lord's Supper, the ring in marriage, the sign of the cross in baptism. All such practices were said to be forbidden because no scriptural sanction could be found for them.

A second stage, noticeable already in Elizabethan times, was a more positive demand for reform. Thomas Cartwright (died the same year as Elizabeth), strongly influenced by the Genevan Calvinists, spoke from his position as professor of divinity at Cambridge University in favor of a thoroughgoing reform along Presbyterian lines. For his pains he was deprived of his professorship in 1570. But two years later a first presbytery was formed. The third stage in the development of Puritanism, the effort to purify the church of all unscriptural elements, came in the early seventeenth century. It was closely associated with the political disturbances following the accession of the Stuarts.

When Queen Elizabeth I died, the line of Tudor succession provided by the will of Henry VIII was at an end. The claimant by heredi-

11655
tary right was James VI, already king of Scotland, who now became also James I of England. To that extent—but only so far—the two British kingdoms were united in 1603. James, who had been raised in the environment of Scottish Presbyterianism, found unwonted satisfaction in the Anglican system, in which the king became not only "defender of the faith" but also "supreme governor," including broad control of patronage. He found that the bishops stood as a firm pillar supporting royal authority. No wonder he came to think, "No bishop, no king!" When the Puritans met with him early in the reign at a conference at Hampton Court, he rejected their requests, except that for a new version of the Bible. This one project was authorized, and the result, by 1611, was the "King James Version," prepared laboriously and beautifully by over fifty scholars.

Before long it was apparent that the king and the high-church bishops were going one way, the Puritans another. When the latter began to purify Sunday and multiply Bible study and worship meetings, the king reacted with his famous Book of Sports, permitting dancing, games, and Maypoles as excellent forms of Sunday activity.

Gradually the type of the Puritan congealed. He was anything but "puritanical." He was given to self-discipline in his personal life, to avoidance of unprofitable pleasures and industrious application to his life's work, individual Bible study and devotion, family worship and group prayer meetings, simplicity and scriptural austerity in public worship, and above all to emphasis on a common adult Christian experience. Under the surface ran a thread of sectarianism. Before the march of Puritan rigor all prelacy as well as popery, all ecclesiastical frippery as well as sacramentalism, and all moral laxity must fall. The church was to be purified, root and branch.

Puritanism produced literature of historic interest and Christian faith. The Puritan experience of the Christian life found expression in that amazing spiritual autobiography by John Bunyan, *Grace Abounding to the Chief of Sinners,* while the ongoing struggle within the soul came allegorically to life in his *Pilgrim's Progress.* Beyond that one can only mention Richard Baxter's *Saints' Everlasting Rest* and the beautiful *Paradise Lost* of John Milton. The strong and abiding influence of the Reformation is seen in a comment by Bunyan on the

[101]

effect of his reading of Luther's *Commentary on Galatians:* "I found my condition in his experience so largely and so profoundly handled, as if his book had been written out of my heart. This made me marvel. . . . I do prefer this book of Martin Luther upon the Galatians, excepting the Holy Bible, before all books that ever I have seen, as most fit for a wounded conscience." [1] The other side is seen in the unremitting return to the Scriptures as a fountain of renewal and faith. And so Christian in *Pilgrim's Progress* goes through the perils of life, skirting the Slough of Despond to arrive at last in Beulah Land, the site of the Celestial City. Few books have had a more lasting and pervading influence on the thought and language of English-speaking Christians.

2. *Presbyterians.* It was of course only a matter of time until the tensions between high-church Anglicans and reforming Puritans became intolerable. This situation was exaggerated in an environment in which divine-right king and constitutional Parliament were increasingly at odds. Both conflicts came into the open in the reign of Charles I (1625-43). In fact, a curious parallel is noticeable insofar as king and high church allied against Parliament, which came more and more under the influence of Puritans. The political consequences were the Civil War and the Commonwealth; the religious results were the separatist churches. The throne and episcopacy on the one hand and the Commons and Puritans on the other were brought together not so much by common faith as by mutual antipathies against their opponents. It is difficult to say whether, for a time, the word "Presbyterian" indicated an ecclesiastical group or a political faction. Actually it meant both.

After King Charles had attempted to rule England and obtain funds without benefit of Parliament for eleven years, he was finally forced to call Parliament into session in 1640. After a brief false start (the "Short Parliament"), the Long Parliament settled down to the task of binding the king and reforming the church. A protracted period of military conflict followed, in which the royal forces were defeated through the military skill of Oliver Cromwell, member of Parliament.

---

[1] *Grace Abounding to the Chief of Sinners* (London: Religious Tract Society, 1905), pp. 76-77.

This victory gave Cromwell and the army great influence in affairs both political and religious. Since the army was religiously radical—"independent"—the ecclesiastical settlements attempted during Cromwell's protectorate were correspondingly radical. Episcopacy was abolished, vestments and liturgies simplified, and morals marshaled. When the Presbyterian majority in Parliament refused to follow the Cromwellian line, Colonel Pride and his soldiers "purged" the Commons by refusing admittance to Presbyterians. The radical independent remnant came to be known as the Rump Parliament. We need not pursue the complicated politico-religious maneuvers further. After almost twenty years of turmoil the English people yearned for peace and a normal life, even if it meant the return of the Stuarts. Charles I, who had been arrested, tried, and executed under Cromwell, had become something of a martyr. Assuredly little opposition was manifest to the return of Charles II in 1660. Thus began the period known as the Restoration.

By this time a number of divisions had appeared among the ranks of the Puritans, who were now identified as "dissenters" from the Established Church. The restrictive legislation of Charles II—the Conventicle Act, the Five-Mile Act, the Test Act—forced most of these dissenters completely out of the Church of England. They became members of the various non-Anglican churches of the English-speaking world—Presbyterian, Congregational, Baptist, Quaker. A chart may help to illustrate the steps by which these groups came into being:

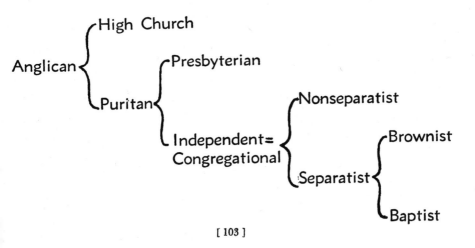

The *Presbyterian Church* looks back to Calvin, of course; but in England mainly to men like Thomas Cartwright (see above) and the Westminster Assembly and Confession (1645-49). The influence of John Knox and the Kirk of Scotland was very strong. To this day the Westminster Confession is authoritative for Presbyterian belief and church order. For a time the Presbyterians hoped to establish a national church like that of Scotland. But these hopes were dashed by Cromwell, who forced the independent-congregational system upon the nation, by the obstacles encountered under the Act of Supremacy in relations between church and state, and by the Anglican revival at the Restoration. The Presbyterians became one of several dissenting groups severely restricted under Charles II and James II, winning toleration only with the Glorious Revolution of 1688 and the Act of Toleration the next year. That not-so-glorious revolution ended the period of the Restoration with the overthrow of James II, because he was an avowed Roman Catholic.

3. Congregationalists and Baptists. Roman Catholic Bishop Bossuet in his *History of the Variations of the Protestant Churches* (1688) concluded that Protestantism contained within itself the seeds of its own dissolution, through the tendency toward the multiplication of sects. His prophecy seemed to gain support from the experience of English Protestants in the seventeenth century. For not only did the official "Protestant" body, the Church of England, continue to enjoy an established relation, but several groups dissenting from the church arose. Among these the Presbyterians have already been treated. There were others—Congregationalists, Baptists, Quakers, and several minor sects. The roots of dissent all went back into the period of the Tudors. One vocal and impatient herald of reform was Robert Browne, who in 1582 published a work carrying the informative title *A Treatise of Reformation without Tarrying for Anie, and of the Wickednesse of those preachers which will not reforme . . . till the Magistrate commaunde and compel them.* In this book he moved away from the old principle of one universal and uniform church working in collaboration with the state. He moved toward the "sect" church acting through relatively independent local congregations. Only pure Christians should be members of these congregations. One came into membership through an adult religious experience of conversion, and the act of membership was voluntary. The pure congregation should be led by a pastor who himself was converted and called to the pulpit by the congregation. The guide for ecclesiastical order and the Christian life was the Bible strictly interpreted. The inward power of the Spirit was more to be followed than mere ecclesiastical authority. Although Browne did not support complete separation of church and state, he did move toward the free-church ideal. Although the "Brownists" do not represent the central line of Congregational development, their influence was undoubtedly great.

Early in the reign of James I two congregations, one at Gainsborough under the leadership of John Smyth and the other at Scrooby under John Robinson and William Brewster, came under the unfriendly surveillance of the government. Smyth was quite radical in his outlook, suspicious of anything that smacked of rigid liturgical forms. He would have no written prayers, no written translation of the Bible, not even any written hymns. By 1607 he led his group into exile to Amsterdam, where the influence of the Mennonites came to bear. After much internal dissension this group, upon their return to England in 1611-12, formed the first *Baptist Church,* forerunner of the General Baptists of England. The Scrooby group also was forced into exile, in 1609, in this case to Leiden. These refugees were a prime source of the Congregational groups in England. Likewise, a vigorous minority made its way, via Plymouth, England, to America—the Pilgrims of 1620. It should be pointed out that these early Congregationalists were not primarily Brownists, or complete separatists. Many of them still hoped to make over the national church into the image of the true Church based on pure congregations. Gradually, however, through persecution in England and from the fact of geographical separation in America, they became a separate church, a new denomination, the *Congregationalists.*

After the Act of Toleration, 1689, all these dissenting groups were granted freedom of worship, although that freedom did not mean equality. The later changes in Stuart and Hanoverian times need not detain us, and can best be summarized in the ballad derisively revealing the confusing winds of religious fashion, the "Vicar of Bray":[2]

> In good King Charles's [II] golden days,
>   When loyalty no harm meant,
> A zealous high-churchman was I,
>   And so I got preferment.
> To teach my flock I never missed:
>   Kings were by God appointed,
> And lost are those that dare resist
>   Or touch the Lord's anointed.
>   *And this is law that I'll maintain*
>   *Until my dying day, sir,*
>   *That whatsoever king may reign,*
>   *Still I'll be the Vicar of Bray, sir.*
>
> When royal James possessed the crown,
>   And popery grew in fashion,
> The penal laws I hooted down,
>   And read the Declaration;
> The Church of Rome I found would fit
>   Full well my constitution,
> And I had been a Jesuit
>   But for the Revolution.
>   *And this is law . . . etc.*
>
> When William was our king declared,
>   To ease the nation's grievance,
> With this new wind about I steered,
>   And swore to him allegiance;
> Old principles I did revoke,
>   Set conscience at a distance;
> Passive obedience was a joke,
>   A jest was non-resistance.
>
> When royal Anne became our queen,
>   The Church of England's glory,
> Another face of things was seen,
>   And I became a Tory.

---

[2] Author unknown. Quoted in Burton E. Stevenson, ed., *The Home Book of Verse* (New York: Henry Holt & Co., 1945, 2 vols.), I, 1835-36.

Occasional conformists base,
  I blamed their moderation,
And thought the Church in danger was
  By such prevarication.

When George in pudding-time came o'er,
  And moderate men looked big, sir,
My principles I changed once more,
  And so became a Whig, sir.
And thus preferment I procured
  From our new Faith's defender,
And almost every day abjured
  The Pope and the Pretender.

The illustrious house of Hanover
  And Protestant succession,
To these I do allegiance swear—
  While they can keep possession:
For in my faith and loyalty
  I nevermore will falter,
And George my lawful king shall be—
  Until the times do alter.
    And this is law . . . etc.

4. *Quakers.* Among troubled souls in the Church of England were some who yearned for a fuller personal experience of faith that would bring God closer. They were seekers after a brighter vision of God. One of these seekers was the son of a weaver, a tall, powerfully built man of striking appearance, named George Fox. After a youth distinguished neither by prurience nor by prudery, in the year 1646 he found what he had been seeking—the "inner light" speaking to him in the very voice of God. "And when I heard it," he wrote, "my heart did leap for joy." By the inner light he meant a religious intuition that could be discerned in no church or liturgy or sacrament, nor even completely in the Holy Scriptures. Rather, God speaks to each man individually, prompting him by an inner guidance. Not that Fox repudiated the Bible, or even the Church in its pure form. But these must be understood and interpreted in terms of the inner light shining through the grace of God within oneself. With a small but growing

body of followers Fox went about England testifying to this new light in his life. The stereotype of the irenic Quaker, quietly abiding in his place and never thinking of interfering with the religious life and practice of his fellows, in no way applies to Fox. A sample of his ministry is found in his fascinating *Journal,* where he tells of interrupting a worship service in a "steeple-house"—his term for church—in Nottingham:

> Now as I passed to Nottingham on a First-day in the morning with Friends to a meeting, when I came on top of a hill, as I looked upon the town the great steeplehouse struck at my life when I spied it, a great and idolatrous temple. And the Lord said unto me, "Thou must go cry against yonder great idol, and against the worshippers therein." . . . And when I came there, all the people looked like fallow ground, and the priest, like a great lump of earth, stood in his pulpit above. He took for his text these words of Peter, "We have also a more sure word of prophecy, where unto ye do well that ye take heed, as unto a light that shineth in a dark place, until the day dawn, and the day-star arise in your hearts." And he told the people that the Scriptures were the touchstone and judge by which they were to try all doctrines, religions, and opinions and to end controversy. Now the Lord's power was so mighty upon me, and so strong in me, that I could not hold, but was made to cry out and say, "Oh, no, it is not the Scriptures." But I told them what it was, namely, the Holy Spirit, by which the holy men of God gave forth the Scriptures, whereby opinions, religions, and judgements were to be tried; for it led into all Truth. . . . Now as I spake thus amongst them, the officers came and took me away and put me into prison, a pitiful stinking place, where the wind brought all the stench of the house of office in the place, where the stench of the place was in my throat and head many days thereafter.[3]

More often than not he was clapped into jail, where he proceeded to preach to inmates and jailers alike—with good biblical precedent. Far from being a shrinking violet, he refused to doff his hat to nobility or even the king. No servility for him!

Around Fox gathered a *Society of Friends,* called *Quakers.* Rejecting most of the outward forms of organized Christianity, such as a professional ministry, sacraments, ritual, creed, preaching, etc., these seekers after the inner light developed a form of worship distinguished at first by testifyings and prophesyings, later by patient silence while awaiting

---

[3] John L. Nickalls, ed., *The Journal of George Fox* (London: Cambridge University Press, 1952) , pp. 39-40.

the inner voice that could put words of wisdom and truth in the mouth of any man. Lay preaching, then, with an emphasis on spiritual rebirth and the inner light, characterized the movement. At a later time the Quakers interested themselves in admirable programs of social service, including noncombatant war aid, antislavery teaching, work in prisons and asylums, and industrial welfare. Even so cynical a man of the world as Voltaire was forced to grudging admiration of these devoted seekers. And Cromwell had to admit they possessed an integrity all too uncommon in the disturbed England of his time: "Now I see there is a people risen that I can not win with gifts, honors, offices or places; but all other sects and people I can."

5. *The Idea of Religious Toleration.* The greater part of the history of Christianity has been the story of persecution, and that of Christians by Christians. The roots of the idea of toleration are found in antiquity; but the practice of the principle is quite modern. Even the famous Act of Toleration, 1689, gave such uncertain freedom that Methodists, when they came along later, for a time were in danger of being persecuted because they would not fit into the category of "dissenter." In America until the nineteenth century only Rhode Island and Pennsylvania did not maintain established churches. In some parts of the world the battle is being fought all over again in our own day. If the biblical justification for persecution may be found in Luke 14:23 ("Compel them to come in"), the ground for toleration lies in the parable of the wheat and weeds in Matthew 13:24-30 ("Let both grow together until the harvest"). The early Christians during the age of persecution demanded toleration, of course. But, after it had been achieved under Constantine, the inevitable sequel was the law of Theodosius I, in which all forms of religion except orthodox Christianity were proscribed. The development of the Inquisition of the Middle Ages was a logical result of the principle that, if there is one true Church, all dissidence is error. None of the major reformers of the sixteenth century questioned this long-standing principle. Respect for the idea of toleration is relatively recent, and for religious freedom even more so.

Now the dedicated persecutor must believe three things: that he is right, that the question is important, and that his efforts will be effective. The story of religious toleration is the story of the undermining of these axioms. Among outward factors favoring a spirit of toleration are: danger of reaction against persecution; secularization of politics; growing influence of minority groups; elimination of danger to the dominant group arising from toleration; economic considerations and commercial contacts; the printing press and dissemination of learning; skepticism and indifference. Behind all these factors lies another, more important: the decline of the theory of uniformity and unconditional truth as held in the Middle Ages and the consequent rise of a theory of unity within diversity. Toleration, as distinct from religious freedom, arose chiefly from the disappearance of the apparent advantages of religious uniformity and the persecution that was supposed to maintain it.

Christians in the period of the Reformation, who were still sure they were right, but were not so sure that the question was as important as others or that persecution would be effective, concluded that the best possible solutions lay in either territorialism or comprehension. The first of these was favored on the Continent and grew out of the religious wars. The second was the solution taken in England. When the Peace of Augsburg, 1555, recognized in law not one, but two, forms of the Christian faith, the all-important first step was taken. *Cuius regio, eius religio* was a poor substitute for religious freedom; but it was a step on the new road. Christians of different persuasions did not yet live in the same block; but they could live peaceably in adjoining territories. In England the Thirty-nine Articles sought to provide a room commodious enough for most reasonable folk. The motivation for toleration came mainly from the conviction that persecution was ineffective and that uniformity was impossible. The degree of toleration was quite limited, and mere toleration is a long way from true religious freedom. As Justice Holmes put it, the idea of mere toleration is an insult to mankind, because it implies that differences are not important. But the spirit of the sixteenth century was intolerant.

The grounds of complete religious freedom, another solution to the problem of religious diversity, go beyond those of toleration. The latter is negative, simply permissive. The former is positive, based on faith itself. Men like Cromwell and Milton to a degree, and Roger Williams entirely, found reason for freedom not in expediency or pragmatism, but rather in the Christian faith itself. In the first place, it is not for man to judge. Let him that is without sin cast the first stone. In the second place, in loving God we must learn to love our neighbor. And this means that we should not force him against his will to conform to one church order and creed. It means that only God can convict him of his error, and our part must be that of example and exhortation, not of force. As Roland H. Bainton has put it, "Error is not the goal, but honest error is nearer to the truth of religion than dishonest correctness." [4] The battle of religious toleration had to be won before the battle for religious freedom could become relevant to the historical situation. Toleration grew out of the dissolution of the medieval ideal of unity, the spirit of the Renaissance, the secularization of national politics, and the skepticism and indifference that characterized the Enlightenment. Religious freedom came as a vigorous expression of the Christian faith: God is loving Father as well as righteous Judge; Christ is Savior of the individual; all believers are priests; men are justified by faith; God is sovereign, even to the point of predestination. All these emphases tended to place the individual in his direct relation to God above the church as mediator of grace through the sacraments.

From the depths of conviction, and from no considerations of expediency, arose the uncompromising spirit of religious freedom in Roger Williams:

It is the will and command of God that, since the coming of his Son, the Lord Jesus, a permission of the most Paganish, Jewish, Turkish, or antichristian consciences and worships be granted to all men in all nations and countries: and they are only to be fought against with that sword which is only, in soul matters, able to conquer: to wit, the sword of God's Spirit, the word of God. . . . God requireth not an uniformity of religion to be enacted and enforced in any civil state; which enforced uniformity, sooner or later, is the greatest occasion of civil war, ravishing of conscience, persecution of Christ Jesus in his servants, and of the hypocrisy and destruction of millions of souls. . . . Lastly, true civility and Christianity may both flourish

[4] *The Travail of Religious Liberty* (Philadelphia: Westminster Press, 1951), p. 21.

in a state or kingdom, notwithstanding the permission of divers and contrary consciences, either of Jew or Gentile.[5]

The guarantees of the Virginia Statute of Religious Liberty, the Northwest Ordinance of 1787, and the principle of separation of church and state in the federal Constitution are monuments to a long and sometimes bitter struggle over the conscience of man. Some of the roots of this struggle are to be found in the rationalism of the Enlightenment. But the real source of strength for religious freedom is the Word of God itself, manifested to men in sundry human garbs.

6. *Catholicism on the Continent.* As we have seen, the Roman Catholic Church emerged from the period of the Reformation battered but unbowed. Much of Europe had been lost to the Protestant "heresies," but much had been held and some regained in the Catholic Reformation. In addition the church had been forced into thoroughgoing reform, both theological and ecclesiastical. The chief expressions of these changes were the canons and decrees of the Council of Trent. The main agents for their execution were a reformed papacy and a new monastic order, the Society of Jesus. Thus armed, the church went through the religious wars of the sixteenth and seventeenth centuries hopeful of the spiritual reunion of Europe. Kings as well as bishops were strongly motivated by religion through this whole period. Their politics appears foolish unless it is understood in terms of primary religious motivation. This consideration makes all the more startling the revolutionary innovation of that incomparable churchman and diplomat, Cardinal Richelieu, who brought Catholic France into the Thirty Years' War on the side of the Protestants—in order that the Hapsburg rivals might be discomfited. The story of this last great religious war has already been told.

In the seventeenth and eighteenth centuries the Jesuits continued to increase in influence. Whereas at their beginning they had been bound to special obedience to the papacy, within one hundred years they had come to a position of power that rivaled and sometimes thwarted that of the popes. Especially in the Hapsburg centers of

[5] *The Bloudy Tenent of Persecution* (London: Hansard Knollys Society, 1848) , p. 2.

Madrid and Vienna did they enjoy great influence. The result was that, when papal and Hapsburg policies collided, as they did more than once, the Jesuits found themselves in opposition to the papacy itself. It must be remembered that in these centuries the States of the Church held a key place in the complicated diplomatic maneuvering of European power politics. The Jesuits were also in the middle of two other important controversies, one stemming from a peculiar interpretation of the Christian ethic, the other from policy in foreign missions. The doctrine of probabilism, which stated that if any reputable moral teacher defended the morality of an act, no sin was to be imputed to it, even though others might not agree, was associated with the Jesuit moralists. Likewise, the policies followed by Matteo Ricci and other Jesuit missionaries in China led to the charge that they were diluting the Christian faith to the point of denying its central affirmations. Bishop Bossuet in France was one of many who vigorously opposed these teachings. The "rites controversy" occupied the attention of Catholics for over a century, to the middle of the eighteenth, to the detriment both of Chinese missions and of the Jesuit Order.

More important for the fate of the Jesuits, however, was the opposition that developed along political lines, beginning with Cardinal Richelieu. This statesman found intolerable any power that might be an obstacle to the growth of the French monarchy toward absolutism. No force, secular or religious, whether it be aristocratic nobles, entrenched civil servants, Protestants literally entrenched in La Rochelle, or Jesuits tainted with Hapsburgism, should be permitted to check the authority of the Bourbon dynasty. Within the French church support for this policy came from the Capuchin Order and from the Jansenist movement, insofar as both opposed the activities of the Jesuits. The barefoot friar, Père Joseph, is indeed one of the mysterious personalities of the time, holding a close yet unofficial relation to the great cardinal himself. The Jansenists, taking their name from Cornelius Jansen, a Dutch scholar at the University of Louvain, taught an Augustinian theology in some respects similar to Calvinism. They emphasized the importance of religious experience and mysticism, although within the framework of the Roman Catholic Church. They became the bitter rivals of the Jesuits and found an influential literary supporter in Blaise Pascal, who became a thorn in the side of the followers of Ignatius Loyola. The struggle came to its culmination in the eighteenth century, when, in one Catholic country after another, revulsion against the order led to its expulsion—from Portugal in 1759, from France in 1764, from Spain in 1767. Finally the papacy abolished the order in the bull *Dominus ac Redemptor*, 1773. Not until the nineteenth century was the order reborn under different conditions.

In contrast to the rising tide of religious liberty characteristic of the English Protestant scene, this period saw the growth of the typical church-state relation of Roman Catholicism—an established church in a monarchical state. France is the best example. Although the Huguenots remained strong long after the religious wars of the sixteenth century, the trend was toward political absolutism and therefore toward religious uniformity. One of the most active defenders of the new power state was Bishop Jacques Bossuet (d. 1704). "It is far less convenient," wrote he, "to suffer princes, however bad, than it is to give the least power to the people."

In such a state, where the king was the fountainhead of all power, the church should act as a bulwark of unchallengeable royal authority. That the church should itself be divided was unthinkable. Working from the biblical precedents of David and Solomon through the principle that absolute power is necessary to control anarchy, Bossuet and others rejoiced in the close relationship between an absolute state and a unified church. This had curious effects. On the one hand it set up tensions between loyalty to France and loyalty to Rome. As the French state became more absolute, the French church became more "Gallican." Although the pope should have general spiritual oversight, internal affairs of the church in France should be the concern of the French church alone. No "foreign" interference from Italy (across the Alps, hence "ultramontanism") was wanted. On the other hand it led to persecution and finally, in 1685, legal abolition of Protestantism. In the time of Louis XIV years of harrying heretics were capped by the vicious dragonnades, in which rapacious soldiers were quartered in helpless Protestant households. By this time, the king convinced himself, there were no Protestants left. Therefore the Edict of Nantes was revoked and all France was supposed to be uniformly Roman Catholic.

Unfortunately for his estimates, the Protestants were stubborn. Thousands upon thousands refused to conform, fled their native land, and took refuge in England, in the New World, and in Brandenburg, where the Great Elector, Frederick William, received them with great satisfaction. The small residue who remained in France entered upon the dread era known as the Desert, secretly cherished the Protestant faith until released in the more tolerant France of the nineteenth century.

B. Ascendancy of Reason

1. The Enlightenment. While Anglicans during the Restoration were vengefully passing laws against dissenters and Roman Catholics, one man was moving steadily toward formulation of a great principle. This principle was the law of gravitation. The man was Isaac Newton. In 1687 he published the *Principles of Mathematics,* one of the landmarks in the history of both science and philosophy. There he wrote, in the Preface:

Since the ancients (as we are told by Pappus) made great account of the science of Mechanics in the investigation of natural things; and the moderns, laying aside substantial forms and occult qualities, have endeavoured to subject the phaenomena of nature to the laws of mathematics; I have in this treatise cultivated Mathematics, so far as it regards Philosophy.[6]

And a few years later he wrote:

Now by the help of these Principles, all material Things seem to have been composed of the hard and solid Particles above mention'd, variously associated in the first Creation by the Counsel of an intelligent Agent. For it became him who created them to set them in order. And if he did so, it's unphilosophical to seek for any other Origin of the World, or to pretend that it might arise out of a Chaos by the mere Laws of Nature; though being once form'd, it may continue by those Laws for many Ages.[7]

In these works we find the scientific expression of the movement called the Enlightenment. Its roots can be traced back to the antique world

[6] (London: B. Motte, 1729), I, pp. A-A2. A revised translation is in *Sir Isaac Newton's Mathematical Principles* (Berkeley: University of California Press, 1946), p. xvii.
[7] *Idem, Opticks* (London: W. & J. Innys, 1721). Reprint, New York: Dover Publications, Inc., 1952, p. 402.

of Greece and Rome, and an early partial expression can be found in the Renaissance. But it is most clearly an intellectual outlook developed during the seventeenth and eighteenth centuries. If Newton was the scientific harbinger, so René Descartes and John Locke laid the philosophical foundation. But among the many names associated with it, that of Newton stands pre-eminent. As Alexander Pope wrote:

> Nature and Nature's laws lay hid in night:
> God said, Let Newton be, and all was light.

And later Voltaire in his *Letters on the English* praised Newton as a great figure in a great nation:

Not long since the trite and frivolous question following was debated in a very polite and learned company, viz., Who was the greatest man, Caesar, Alexander, Tamerlane, Cromwell, &c.?

Somebody answered that Sir Isaac Newton excelled them all. The gentleman's assertion was very just; for if true greatness consists in having received from heaven a mighty genius, and in having employed it to enlighten our own mind and that of others, a man like Sir Isaac Newton, whose equal is hardly found in a thousand years, is the truly great man. And those politicians and conquerors (and all ages produce some) were generally so many illustrious wicked men. That man claims our respect who commands over the minds of the rest of the world by the force of truth, not those who enslave their fellow-creatures: he who is acquainted with the universe, not they who deface it.[8]

The England of Newton and Locke was one of two chief centers —the other being France. To a lesser extent Germany and other parts of Europe were affected. Strong overtones are to be noted in both French and American revolutions. Chronologically the Enlightenment must be limited to the seventeenth and eighteenth centuries, or, more exactly, from 1687 (publication of Newton's *Principles*) to 1793 (publication of Condorcet's *Progress of the Human Mind*). These limits would include Bayle and Fontenelle, Voltaire, Montesquieu, La Mettrie, the great French Encyclopedia, Rousseau, Holbach, Gibbon, Adam Smith, and Kant, and a host of others.

Among the chief ideas of the Enlightenment are the following: First

---

[8] (New York: P. F. Collier & Son, 1889 and 1910). *Harvard Classics*, XXXIV, 99.

and foremost came reason as the force of enlightenment. All problems, if subjected to truly rational analysis, could be solved. In France this emphasis on reason was expressed in terms of mathematical forms. For example, Fontenelle put it this way:

The geometric spirit is not so attached to geometry that it cannot be disentangled and carried over into other areas of knowledge. A work on morals, on politics, on criticism, perhaps even on eloquence, will be better, all other things being equal, if it is written by the hand of a geometer. The order, the clearness and precision, the exactitude that have characterized good books . . . may well have originated in this geometric spirit.[9]

This geometric spirit would be effective beyond mathematics, in all fields of human interest.

Another leading idea, one so firmly ingrained in thought that it still governs the outlook of millions, was that of progress. It should be understood that the idea of progress has not always enjoyed the popularity so evident in the twentieth century. Other views of history, such as the cyclical and fortuitous, have long rejected progress as either impossible or undesirable. Voltaire associated progess with the Enlightenment itself. Real progress, that is, began with his own times. Then men became "enlightened," enabled through the clear light of reason to forge ahead. Given our new understanding, said Voltaire, progress will advance until even prejudices will disappear and philosophy will give consolation in times of calamity. In contrast, Turgot, famous also as a French statesman before the Revolution of 1789, believed all ages have shown gradual progress. But the ultimate *reductio ad absurdum* came with the *Progress of the Human Mind,* written during the French Revolution by Condorcet, who said that "the perfectibility of man is absolutely indefinite."

Another main idea of the Enlightenment was cosmopolitanism. If there is a universal natural order, there follows a universal human order which overcomes all differences of nation and language, comprehends all humanity. Erasmus, in the time of the Renaissance, reflected this spirit when he remarked that he would prefer to be known as a

[9] Quoted in John Wolf, *The Emergence of the Great Powers* (New York: Harper & Bros., 1951) , p. 212. From *Oeuvres de Fontenelle* (Paris, 1790) , XVI, 67-68.

citizen of the world. Along with this went another idea, toleration. Here is another root of religious toleration in the modern world. The pragmatic foundation of this principle in the Enlightenment is shown by Voltaire's word on England: Her multitude of religions prevents domination by one and civil war between two.

2. *Deism.* Deism came about as the religious aspect of the Enlightenment. It represents the principles of the Enlightenment applied to religion. Or, more concisely, Deists would consider theology a branch of physics. The best term descriptive of Deism is "natural religion." Deists were concerned to prove that true religion is in complete accord with reason and nature.

In England the Deists were by and large conservative and rather complacent. Lord Herbert of Cherbury, "the father of natural religion," in his *De Veritate,* 1624, listed five religious principles that were consonant with reason: belief in a Supreme Being; a Being to be worshiped; the center of such worship in morality; reward for obedience and repentance; and continued reward in eternal life. This much a "reasonable man" might believe. John Toland carried the movement further in his *Christianity Not Mysterious* (1696), the title of which indicates the direction of its contents. This book broke like a storm in the English-speaking world, so much so that the pulpits rang with denunciations and defenses. For clergymen were to be found on both sides. The story is told that an Irish Protestant nobleman, when asked why he had ceased going to church, replied that, whereas once in church he had heard the good news of the Lord Jesus Christ, now all he heard about was one John Toland. Matthew Tindal followed with *Christianity as Old as the Creation,* another illuminating title. Natural religion, said he, is sufficient for adequate spiritual understanding. No revelation beyond what may be observed in nature is necessary. Moreover, only the universal in religion is true. The moderation and agreeableness of English Deism is well illustrated by these lines of Alexander Pope:

> All Nature is but Art unknown to thee;
> All chance direction, which thou canst not see;
> All discord, harmony not understood;

All partial evil, universal good:
And spite of Pride, in erring Reason's spite,
One truth is clear, *Whatever is, is right*.[10]

In contrast, French Deism was radical, intolerant of all historic forms of religious expression. It should not be assumed, however, that these French radicals all became atheists. Voltaire, for example, thought of God as the "Eternal Geometrician," and made a place for general providence. But in the environment of France, caught in the midst of the Old Regime, unable to adapt to the new currents of political liberalism, economic freedom, and modern science, philosophers of the Enlightenment and Deists found themselves forced into a position of opposition, leading to revolution. The Bible was subjected to severe criticism, especially by Pierre Bayle in his *Historical and Critical Dictionary*. The ultimate expression of this French movement was materialism and atheism, positions to which men like Holbach and La Mettrie inevitably arrived.

Deism was not productive of sects. In fact, it was rather impatient with denominational differences. In France for a brief period arose a revolutionary deistic movement centered around the worship of the Supreme Being. The only important and lasting denominational influence of the Enlightenment was in the direction of unitarianism. There had been antitrinitarian heresies in the early church. The Reformation saw a revival of unitarian teachings through such leaders as Michael Servetus and the Socinians. But the organization of a *Unitarian Church* came in England in the eighteenth century, with the formation of a congregation in London, in 1778. This was the work of Theophilus Lindsay and Joseph Priestley.

It is not surprising that defenses against Deism came from many sources. Several literary figures of note, such as John Dryden and Jonathan Swift, wrote effectively. The latter composed a tract in 1708 that stands as an undeniable masterpiece of British understatement: "An Argument to Prove that the Abolishing of Christianity in England May, as things now stand, be attended with some inconveniences and perhaps not produce those many good effects proposed thereby." Prob-

[10] "An Essay on Man."

ably the heaviest artillery brought to bear against Deism was the theological work of Bishop Joseph Butler, whose *Analogy of Religion* sought to show how revealed religion—Christianity—is as reasonable as natural religion—or at least that revealed Christianity presents no more problems to the intellect than does natural religion. The conclusion is not one of exuberant faith. But the book enjoyed immense prestige down through the nineteenth century. A more destructive criticism came from the philosopher David Hume, whose analysis undercut the foundations of Deism. Unfortunately his analysis undercut also the foundations of philosophical and religious knowledge generally and arrived at something of an impasse.

The most vigorous reaction came from another movement gathering strength in the eighteenth century, the Evangelical Revival. It was manifested on the Continent in Pietism, directed against an intellectualized Protestant scholasticism. It was manifested in England in the Wesleyan reaction against Deism.

C. Ascendancy of the Heart

1. Continental Pietism. Both on the Continent and in England religion had fallen into the dry bed of Deism, or, what was just as bad, Lutheran scholasticism. Ordinary people who went to church found all too often no message directed to their condition. Among educated Germans who felt deeply the lack of contact between the religious establishment and the spiritual needs of the people were two pastors and educators, Philip Spener (d. 1705) and August Francke (d. 1727). Both of these men believed that religion was more than creedal form on the one hand and natural religion on the other. Doctrine, in fact, should be simplified. Right life was more important than right belief. Experience was more important than intellectual assent. This led them to emphasize repentance, conversion, and sanctification. In order that this new level of faith might be achieved, they advocated reform of church order to the point where the people would have a larger voice in ecclesiastical affairs, the ministers would speak from their *own* religious experience, and the disciplined life would replace the disciplined mind. Hymns, extempore prayer, lay testimony, came into prominence as means of worship. Francke especially emphasized the *Buszkampf* or penitential struggle through which Christians must pass on the way to conversion. The University of Halle became a center for this "pietistic" movement.

A little later Pietism found further support in the religious movement springing from Moravia. The *Moravian Church* finds its source in the life and work of John Huss in the fifteenth century. After his execution his followers continued in rather disorganized fashion to preserve the tradition of Bohemian Protestantism, accepting the main elements of the Lutheran Reformation. Persecution finally drove the remainder out of Bohemia to Saxony, where they were given refuge on the estates of Count Nicholas von Zinzendorf. There they founded, in 1722, the Moravian community of Herrnhut. Zinzendorf himself became the leader of the group in 1727. Characterized by a semimonastic life including the separation of children from their parents for training and education, the little group grew, spread through missionary activity, and exerted an influence far beyond the pressure of numbers. Persecution in Germany forced Zinzendorf and many of the Moravians to emigrate to western Germany, the Baltic lands, the West Indies, England, and especially to Pennsylvania, where they founded Bethlehem. Zinzendorf himself named the colony because he arrived on Christmas Eve.

A characteristic of this group, common with almost all pietistic movements, was a reluctance to separate from the whole community of Christians as an independent denomination. Only slowly did the Moravian Church as such develop from the *ecclesiolae* Zinzendorf hoped would spread like leaven in the larger and older groups. Through the Moravians pietistic influences were brought to England and played a part in the spiritual development of John Wesley.

2. *The Wesleyan Movement in England.* "At four in the afternoon," wrote John Wesley in his *Journal*, "I submitted to be more vile, and proclaimed in the highways the glad tidings of salvation, speaking from a little eminence in a ground adjoining to the city, to about three thousand people. The scripture on which I spoke was this (is it possible anyone should be ignorant that it is fulfilled in every true minister of Christ?) , 'The Spirit of the Lord is upon Me, because He hath anointed

Me to preach the gospel to the poor. He hath sent Me to heal the broken-hearted; to preach deliverance to the captives, and recovery of sight to the blind; to set at liberty them that are bruised, to proclaim the acceptable year of the Lord.' " [11] In this manner he recorded an event of primary importance in his own life and of equal importance to the history of the Evangelical Revival in England. The practice of outdoor preaching was still scandalous, although the ground had already been broken by George Whitefield. To John Wesley, strict minister of the Church of England, deeply respectful of the ancient parish system, the experience was a shock.

What force so strongly prevailed as to make him accept such a revolutionary method of preaching the gospel? That force had come into his life as a result of earlier experiences culminating in the little chapel in Aldersgate Street in London on May 24, 1738, when his heart —not his mind—was stimulated by the presence of the Holy Spirit bringing the saving grace of Christ. Born the fifteenth of seventeen children of Samuel and Suzanna Wesley, John had been brought up in the strict tradition of a pious clerical household. His systematic and disciplined character was already manifest at Oxford University, where he had his academic training. The "Holy Club," composed of a few students devoted to the principles of the orderly exhibition of the Christian life every hour of the day, has become famous through the careers of the brothers Wesley—John and Charles—who contributed so greatly to its vigor. Between 1735 and 1738 John was away from England, ministering to the spiritual needs of the people of the colony of Georgia, at that time being developed by the humanitarian James Oglethorpe. This period contributed to his spiritual growth both positively and negatively, through the helpful influence of the sturdy Moravians on shipboard and in the colony, and through the sobering and painful experiences growing out of his ill-conceived attempts to fulfill his pastoral obligations to the community, especially to the women.

John Wesley returned to England aware of two things: (1) his ineptness in pastoral care and missionary service; (2) his inner lack of a firm spiritual foundation for Christian service. How could he preach faith

[11] (London: Epworth Press, 1938), II, 172-73.

when he had none himself? Partial guidance was given by Peter Böhler, a Moravian in England, who advised him, "Preach faith till you have it; and then, because you have it, you will preach faith." One could not postpone action forever waiting for a final decision. Not until the experience in Aldersgate Street did he feel secure in the possession of that he preached. The new birth of faith he described as follows:

> The change wrought in the whole soul by the almighty Spirit of God when . . . the love of the world is changed into the love of God; pride into humility; passion into meekness; hatred, envy, malice into sincere, tender, disinterested love for all mankind. In a word, it is that change whereby the earthly sensual, devilish mind is turned into the "mind which was in Christ Jesus." This is the nature of the new birth: "So is everyone that is born of the spirit." [12]

This change had been wrought in Wesley not in an instant, although he was convinced that the event could be dated as of that evening. Significantly, he found faith while the leader was reading from Luther's preface to the book of Romans. The change had been long abuilding, through the years of cultivation at home, the experience of the disciplined life at Oxford, the purging in Georgia, the association with the Moravians, the Anglican service he attended the same morning at St. Paul's, and above all the continual influence of long years of familiarity with the Bible. John Wesley was ready to go, and now knew where he was going. Benefiting from the intellectual forces of the Enlightenment, he went far beyond it in bringing, as "a man of one Book," the revelation of God to man.

The religious societies with which he had so much to do had been in existence for some time before Wesley began his work. But now he became a leader in these unofficial groups operating within the structure of the Church of England. He had no thought of taking them out of that church. First in London, then in Bristol, then throughout the land of England he carried his message of a new birth, requiring of those who would enter only one precondition—"a desire to flee from the wrath to come, and be saved from their sins." This was regarded, however, as the beginning, not the end, of the Christian's journey to

[12] *The Standard Sermons of John Wesley* (London: Epworth Press, 1921), II, 234.

faith. The Methodist movement is seriously misunderstood if this requirement for *entrance* is regarded as the whole content of the faith. True, Wesley was impatient with theological disputation and creedal rigidity. But he held firm to the central affirmations of historic Christianity as embodied in the tradition of the Protestant Reformation. Much of Luther and much of Calvin are to be found in the sermons of Wesley, although he was neither Lutheran nor Calvinist. Working with the Societies, preaching from the pulpits when they were opened to him—at other times from the platform of the countryside—he labored indefatigably, generally from around five in the morning to late at night. For many years his life was tumultuous as opposition from on high—the clergy—and from down low—the unlettered mobs—sought to silence or at least localize him. But as he had learned not to fear the storm, so he learned not to fear men. Some 225,000 miles, much of it on horseback, around and down, between London and Bristol and Newcastle-on-Tyne and back again, then across to Ireland or up to Scotland—this comprised his work through the years till, in his eighties, worn out, when the French Revolution was sounding notes of a new world coming, he died, 1791. In association with his brother Charles, and with Whitefield, who became too Calvinistic to work well with him, and with a small army of lay preachers, class leaders, and plain men and women, John Wesley sounded a great note of another kind of revolution, creating a new world of faith. Whitefield, who had had his difficulties with Wesley, said, when asked if he would see him when they got to heaven, "No sir, I fear not, for he will be so near to the eternal throne and we shall be at such a distance, we shall hardly get a sight of him."

Among the most important of the features growing out of the Wesleyan movement were the "class" and the "lay preacher." Organized first in Bristol, the class soon became distinctive in Methodist circles. It was composed of twelve people, over whom presided a leader, who should never be a traveling minister but rather one of the number of faithful in the local religious community. The leader was to meet each week with the members of his group, inquire after their spiritual and moral welfare, accept any offering they were moved to make, reprove sinners and backsliders, and exhort to greater perfection in the

Christian life. The responsibilities and the problems of discipline and tact that fell on the shoulders of these untrained leaders are appalling! Take the case of the unfortunate Joseph Bowers, class leader in Bandon, two of whose members fell out and went to law against each other— both women. Wesley wrote in great perturbation:

For God's sake, for the gospel's sake, and for my sake, put a full stop to this vile affair, the prosecution of poor Sally Brown. If it is not stopped, I shall be under a necessity of excluding from our Society not only Eliz. Sharp but Joseph Bowers also. She would not dare to proceed thus without his connivance, if not encouragement. He can stop her if he will. . . . But I insist upon this. All of them are or were members of our Society. Therefore they were not at liberty to go to law with each other, but are under an obligation to stand to the decision of me or the Assistant. I pray, spare no pains. Put a full end to the business, that the scandal may be removed.[13]

Then there was the case of discipline at Newcastle. Wesley had been concerned about the regularity of class meetings in London, and now dealt with reports of laxity in Newcastle. Wrote he:

We must threaten no longer, but perform. In November last I told the London Society, "Our rule is to meet a class once a week, not once in two or three. I now give you warning: I will give tickets to none in February but those that have done this." I have stood to my word. Go you and do like-wise wherever you visit the classes. Begin, if need be, at Newcastle, and go on at Sunderland. Promises to meet are now out of date. Those that have not met seven times in the quarter exclude. Read their names in the Society, and inform them all you will the next quarter exclude all that have not met twelve times—that is, unless they were hindered by distance, sick-ness, or by some unavoidable business.

And I pray without fear or favour remove the leaders, whether of classes or bands, who do not watch over the souls committed to their care "as those that must give account." [14]

Lay preaching was another special characteristic of early Methodism. Wesley himself long had doubts until the evidence of results and the influence of his mother convinced him. Much of the success of Meth-

---

[13] *The Letters of the Reverend John Wesley* (London: Epworth Press, 1931), VIII, 135.
[14] *Ibid.*, VI, 208.

odism, on both sides of the Atlantic, rested in the efforts of the dedicated lay preachers who filled in the long periods when no regularly
ordained "traveling" preacher was available. There was that Yorkshire
wit, Sammy Hicks, who liked to compare the Christian life to coins
(of which he saw few in his life) :

I sometimes compare religion to the best coin of the realm. First, there is
repentance, this may be compared to a seven-shilling piece; though there is
but little of it, still it is good. Then there comes pardon; this is like half-a-
guinea. Next comes sanctification; this is like a guinea. Now, who would
be content with seven shillings, or even with half-a-guinea, when he might
just as well have a whole guinea by applying for it? [15]

It took a good many like Sammy Hicks to counteract the grim serious-
ness with which Wesley went about the business of converting souls.
A host carried on the work—James Field the soldier-class-leader,
Cornish farmers and miners of Newcastle, women like Hester Ann Roe.
Laymen and laywomen have always played a large part in the Methodist
Church.

At the center of the movement was not a changed organization or
a changed service of worship, but rather a changed person. Reference
has already been made to the historic Protestant context of Wesley's
message. Specifically, he emphasized and adapted all the major Reformed doctrines—primary authority of the Scriptures, the priesthood
of all believers, the sovereignty of God; especially justification by faith,
through the experience of conversion, the birth into a new life. It was
no coincidence that Wesley came to his own spiritual discovery during
the reading of Luther's preface to Romans! The Bible was never far
from the hand and the mind of the early Methodist, who searched it
diligently for guidance in all aspects of life. And as far as the priesthood
of all believers is concerned, the lay preachers and class leaders exemplified this doctrine rather effectively. Furthermore, the Calvinist tradition
was strong in the Wesleyan movement. The issue is sometimes confused
by the contrast drawn between Calvinists and Arminians. Actually both
were Calvinist. The difference was specific—absolute or conditional

[15] Quoted in Leslie F. Church, *The Early Methodist People* (New York: Philosophical
Library, 1949) , p. 20.

predestination, with the corollaries of irresistible grace and perseverance of the saints. Whereas Whitefield took a radical Calvinist position,
Wesley was moderate—as always in matters of theology. As he put it,
"John Calvin was a pious, learned, sensible man; and so was James
Harmens [Jacobus Arminius]. Many Calvinists are pious, learned,
sensible men; and so are many Arminians. Only the former hold absolute predestination; the latter, conditional." [16] The sovereignty of God
meant much to Wesley. He wrote a tract on it, in which he said:

It may be allowed that God acts as Sovereign in convincing some souls
of sin; arresting them in their mid career, by his resistless power. It seems
also, that, at the moment of our conversion, he acts irresistibly. There may
likewise be many irresistible touches during the course of our Christian
warfare; with regard to which every believer may say:

> "In the time of my distress
> Thou hast my succour been,
> In my utter helplessness
> Restraining me from sin."

But still, as St. Paul might have been either obedient or "disobedient to the
heavenly vision," so every individual may, after all that God has done, either
improve his grace, or make it of none effect.[17]

Wesley added something to the tradition of the Reformation as he
worked it out in the context of the Enlightenment. In justification he
emphasized much more the *experience* of being reborn into a new life
in Christ, an event or episode that could be measured and treasured.
And beyond this lay the road to sanctification, the fulfillment of the
promise of justification. Wesley was never quite sure what to do about
this difficult doctrine. To some the mere claim of Christian perfection
smacked of hypocrisy, a barrier to essential Christian humility. Wesley
never claimed the experience for himself, and sometimes severely questioned the claims of others. But he was more willing than his brother
Charles to accept testimonies at face value. If the assurance of salvation

---

[16] "What Is an Arminian?" in *Works*, ed. John Emory (New York: Carlton and Porter,
1856), VI, 134.
[17] "God's Sovereignty." *Ibid.*, VI, 136.

could lead to such perfect love that one's life continued sanctified, he was the first to rejoice.

Sanctified or not, Methodists were expected to live strictly in accordance with the "Rules," which specified a great many things the Christian should not do, and went on to advocate the doing of good works and faithful attendance upon the ordinances of God in church and family prayer. After fulfilling the one previous requirement of a desire to flee from the wrath to come, Methodist members of the Societies were expected to refrain from swearing, drinking, fighting or quarreling, smuggling, taking usury, "uncharitable or unprofitable conversation," costly or showy clothes, and all entertainment unfit for Christians, "softness and needless self-indulgence, laying up treasures on earth, borrowing without a probability of paying, or taking up goods without a probability of paying for them." The time saved was then free for positive Christian service. That many early Methodists took these rules seriously is poignantly illustrated by the story of the dairyman's daughter, Elizabeth Wallbridge:

For a while regardless of the worship of God, I looked around me, and was anxious to attract notice myself. My dress, like that of too many gay, vain and silly servant girls, was much above my station, and very different from that which becomes a humble sinner who has a modest sense of propriety and decency. The state of my mind was visible enough from the foolish finery of my apparel. At length the clergyman gave out his text: "Be ye clothed with humility." He drew a comparison between the clothing of the body and that of the soul. At a very early part of his discourse I began to feel ashamed of my passion for fine dressing and apparel; but when he came to describe the garment of salvation with which a Christian is clothed, I felt a powerful discovery of the nakedness of my soul. I saw that I had neither the humility mentioned in the text, nor any part of the true Christian character. I looked at my gay dress and blushed for shame on account of my pride.[18]

Leslie Church remarks that a later generation "might have allowed her a ribbon or two without jeopardizing her soul."

Gradually the Societies evolved into the *Methodist Church*. As long

[18] Quoted in Church, *op. cit.*, p. 203, from Elizabeth Wallbridge, *The Dairyman's Daughter*.

as John Wesley lived, he would not hear of a separation from the Church of England. Neither then nor later did Methodists want to be classed as dissenters. But separation was inevitable, once Wesley was taken from the scene. In fact, American Methodism already, through the unprecedented ordination in 1784 of men for pastoral service in the Colonies and the setting apart of Thomas Coke and Francis Asbury as "superintendents," had achieved practical independence. This action was confirmed at the famous Christmas Conference in Baltimore, when Asbury was ordained deacon and elder and elected superintendent. At this conference the *Methodist Episcopal Church* was formally organized in America. In the same year Wesley provided for the succession of authority in English Methodism by the Deed of Declaration, which set up a "conference" of ministers. When the old leader died in 1791, the *Wesleyan Methodist Church* was organized (this denomination is not to be confused with the group in America known by the same name). The separate path, strongly tinged with Calvinism, taken by George Whitefield, led to the *Countess of Huntingdon Connection,* or Calvinistic Methodists, and the *Welsh Calvinistic Methodist Church.* Both have now merged with Congregational and Presbyterian branches.

As Methodists came to play a larger part in the affairs, both ecclesiastical and political, of the British Isles, a distinctive economic and social influence is to be observed. Politically, of course, Wesley himself was conservative, in the center of the Tory tradition. His negative attitude toward the American Revolution is well known through his tract *A Calm Address to Our American Colonies,* in which he denounced the move to throw off the authority of George III and advocated rather submission to the proper constituted power. He had an ingrained, if unconscious, suspicion of representative government. He felt it to be morally bad, because it is self-centered; practically bad, because the people are incapable; and theologically bad, because it means a denial of God's providence. In this situation, however, as in the case of the political thought of Calvin, the outward teachings and attitudes of the leader did not coincide with the inner effect of the movement. The religious vigor of Methodism, its theological impact and social influence, gave rise to a radical political philosophy quite at variance with the opinions of its founder. The authority of government is strictly limited by obedience to the will of God. Beyond that, as each individual speaks for himself through his own religious experience and stands on his own before the Judgment Seat, so also he speaks for himself before the councils of men. Methodism gave to the common people a new dignity, a new self-respect, and with that a new voice.

In the field of economic activity the influence of Wesley was remarkably close to that of Calvin. Although Wesley too was a child of his own time, that of the nascent Industrial Revolution, he by no means simply reflected the current prejudices. Commercial activity was not evil in itself, he thought; but through the exercise of diligence and discipline exemplified positive Christian ethical requirements. "Without industry we are neither fit for this world nor for the world to come." At the root of his economic attitude was the recognition that God is the titleholder —all that we have is his, a trust from him. One will scarcely find anywhere a more radical doctrine of stewardship. As a result of the self-respect and new standard of ethics that accompanied the experience of conversion, Methodists gained a reputation for self-reliance, sobriety, industry. The outcome of this is neither unprecedented nor surprising: "Methodism has powerfully tended to improve those who embraced it." Wesley himself faced the problem of wealthy Methodists. The disciplined life almost inevitably issued in prosperity. Was the final service of Methodism then to play midwife to a new generation of spendthrifts? By no means. The well-known aphorism by which Wesley sought to escape from the problem was, "Earn all you can, save all you can, give all you can." If later generations of Methodists too easily forgot the last part of the advice, the result was an amazing outpouring of philanthropic energy. Although this spirit was not limited to Methodists, the Evangelical Revival in its wider context saw the development, through the work of Oglethorpe, Wilberforce, Sadler, Shaftesbury, and a host of unnamed others, of a humanitarianism that went beyond the secular concern of the Renaissance and the Enlightenment. Space prevents further consideration of the impact on many aspects of English life— personal morality, slavery, liquor, gambling, education, law, social work, prison reform, factory legislation. The testimony of historians like G. M. Trevelyan and Élie Halévy gives support.

D. The Expansion of Christianity

1. Roman Catholic Missions. While the Protestant forces under Frederick, Count Palatine, were taking a beating at the hands of Catholic Duke Maximilian of Bavaria in the Thirty Years' War, the papacy was busy with a new and exciting enterprise, the *Sacra Congregatio de Propaganda Fide,* called the "Propaganda." This institution, founded in 1622, had as its broad purpose the unremitting effort to spread the faith on all frontiers against all obstacles. It was the culmination of one hundred years of Catholic missionary expansion along the routes opened to the West and to the East from the Horn to Good Hope. Whereas the prime interest of Protestantism during the Reformation was in Europe, and most conditions worked against missionary expansion, the situation of Roman Catholicism led in the opposite direction. Catholic Spain and Portugal had led in the discoveries of the fifteenth- and sixteenth-century navigators, from Prince Henry to Ferdinand Magellan. These strong areas of Roman Catholic power were relatively unaffected by the stress of the Reformation. Many of the influential leaders, both clerical and lay, favored missions. In the Dominicans and Franciscans, and even more in the Jesuits, Catholicism had an army trained for the fray, ready to carry the gospel into the strongholds of the infidels and pagans. Politically and militarily, the sixteenth was a Catholic century.

In carrying out the urge to expand, the Roman Catholics had all the old methods and experience of the previous thousand years in Europe. In addition they had new tools, especially the Propaganda, the French Société des Missions Étrangères (founded 1663) , the Jesuits, and widespread support by monarchs who looked for the magnification of their colonial power along with the expansion of the faith. Whether consciously or not, the cross advanced in close association with the sword as Jesuit vied with conquistador to be the first to plant the standard of faith or royal authority in all the new lands said to be yearning for emancipation from superstition and barbarism. By the eighteenth century the vigor of Catholic missions languished at the very time Protestant missionary enthusiasm was just beginning to suggest the immense potentialities of the nineteenth.

The first great surge of European Christianity carried to the New World. Spanish America, Portuguese America, and later French America, all felt the impact of Christianity as it came under the guidance of friar, priest, and bishop. Columbus took friars on his second voyage. Cortes was deeply concerned about planting the faith in Mexico. Here if anywhere cross and crown went together. Spanish missions sprang up in the West Indies, Mexico, and throughout what is today the American Southwest. Of course, conflict of interest soon appeared. The story of the first priest ordained in the Americas, Bartolomé de las Casas (d. 1566), well illustrates this conflict. At first a wealthy encomendero, he slowly awoke to the evils of the encomienda system of which he was a part. Early Spanish economic development in the New World took the form of exploitation of land and of the Indians who lived on the land. An encomienda was understood to include not only title to the land but also control of the labor power of the Indians. An extremely vicious system of exploitation developed. In reaction Las Casas gave up his economic interests and devoted the rest of his life to indefatigable efforts to protect the natives, convert them to Christianity, and improve their condition. By various means, but most significantly through the legal reforms embodied in the New Laws of the Indies of the 1540's, he succeeded in effecting a gradual, and incomplete, change of attitude toward the Indians. The evil was mitigated but by no means eliminated. Indeed, the bishop of Darien was said to have subscribed to the doctrine that, since Indians were not human and hence had no souls, there was no point in converting them. Nonetheless, usually by fair means, sometimes by foul, huge masses of Indians were baptized. It must be said that in the majority of cases the baptism sat lightly. To this day one encounters in Spanish America queer mixtures of Christian faith with pagan practice. One of the most interesting episodes centers around the Jesuit mission in Paraguay. Here, far inland, remote from the coastal areas settled by whites, through the seventeenth and well into the eighteenth centuries the Jesuit fathers developed a patriarchal community in which the Indians lived, worked, and learned the Christian faith. Protected for generations against encroachment by white commercial interests, the colonies grew and lived in peace, until, as a result of colonial pressure from the east and the final abolition of the Jesuit Order in 1767, the communities came to utter disaster.

The story of expansion in Portuguese America, meaning mainly Brazil, is quite similar to that of Spain. The chief differences are to be found in the facts that throughout the broad Amazon valleys and pied-monts there were to be found no civilized Indian tribes like those of Mexico and Peru, and that the effective force of the Portuguese emigration was much less. Here also the influence of the Jesuits was large.

On the other side of the equator, in the valley of the St. Lawrence, the French in the seventeenth century began to develop missions among the Indians. In this area the relation between church and state was less evident than in the Spanish and Portuguese colonies. After several efforts that were only partially successful, a new bishop of Quebec in 1674, François Xavier de Laval-Montmorency, did much to foster missions and prepare clergy for the special tasks on a frontier. Among the most heroic missionary exploits were those of the Jesuits Jean de Brébeuf among the Hurons and Isaac Jogues, who lost his life working with the Iroquois and Mohawks. Before the end of the century the intrepid Father Marquette had helped open the upper Great Lakes and the Mississippi valley to French and Christian influences.

Elsewhere around the world Catholic missions were vigorous. Although Africa saw only limited development under Portuguese auspices, the greatest movements were in the Far East. India calls to mind the figure of Francis Xavier (d. 1552). Born of Basque parents in Spain, he early came under the influence of Ignatius Loyola and became one of the first members of the Society of Jesus. In 1541 he sailed from Portugal to India, worked among the Indians and Europeans alike in Goa and southern India. From that time on, his life was an amazing round of missionary journeys, almost every one a pioneering expedition. To Malacca and the Moluccas, back to India, then to Japan (1549), back to India, then to China, where he died—that barely touches the high points. His influence helps to explain why the Jesuits were so important so long in this broad area. The Catholic world, Loyola included, watched with avid interest the far-flung exploits of this missionary hero. In India the Jesuits for a time exercized a great influence over the court of the Great Mogul, Akbar. Robert de Nobili in the seventeenth century attempted, with some limited success, to carry the gospel to the upper classes, following the policy of associating only with Brahmins. A dispute at Rome over his policy was finally decided in his favor.

As long as the Portuguese were dominant in the East Indies, Roman Catholic missions developed in the islands. But here success was limited owing to the prior establishment of Islam and the ephemeral character of Portuguese settlement. In the Philippines the situation was reversed, as Catholic Christianity was brought there barely in time to forestall another Moslem advance. Spain, with more vigor than Portugal, fostered missions widely, and in this area with less disturbance from commercial motives. By 1591 Manila was organized into an archdiocese.

The story of Catholic missions in Japan is one of ebb and flow, according to the predilections of the rulers. In the middle of the sixteenth century the decline of the Ashikaga shogunate and the dominant influence of Oda Nobunaga favored Christianity. The latter turned to Christianity for help against his rivals, the Buddhist monks. Centering in Nagasaki, the missions grew slowly till the time of Hideyoshi, who promulgated an edict against Christianity in 1587. During the first years of the Tokugawa shogunate in the seventeenth century, Christianity again flourished; but after 1612 persecution became increasingly severe. The net result was the virtual extirpation of missions, although Christianity itself survived as a remnant until the arrival of missionaries once again in the nineteenth century.

In the Chinese Empire little was accomplished until the pioneering work of Matteo Ricci (d. 1610), a Jesuit. He followed the policy of associating with officials and scholars and of adopting many Chinese customs, including native costume, Chinese religious terminology, veneration of ancestors and of Confucius. These practices gave rise to the "rites controversy," of which the rivals of the Jesuits made the most. The debate over the question of compromise with native customs and religious forms went on for decades, and was finally settled against the Jesuits in 1742. This together with renascent persecution, greatly hindered missionary work in China, which had to wait for the great missionary century, the nineteenth.

2. Protestantism in the English Colonies. John Calvin was of the opinion that the kingdom of Christ is not the work of man, but of God alone. Luther, Melanchthon, Zwingli, were all convinced that the New Testament command to go into all the world to preach the gospel had *already* been fulfilled through the work of the Apostles, to whom alone the order had been given. The day of Doom could come any time now, for the work of preparation was complete. In this way the Reformers rationalized their reluctance to embark on any ambitious project of carrying the gospel to heathen lands. Actually, they were altogether too much involved in the serious business of self-preservation on the one hand and of formulation and definition of the faith on the other. A Luther pursued by papal excommunication and imperial ban, a Calvin busy rebuilding the synthesis of faith and reason with Augustinian rather than Thomistic blocks, had neither time for nor interest in a missionary program in the ordinary sense. Protestantism spent most of the period 1500-1800 marking time, as far as outward expansion was concerned. Little indication was given of the gathering potential that was released in so tremendous a surge of missionary vitality in the nineteenth century.

Most of the story of Protestant expansion, therefore, is associated with the actual migration of European peoples rather than with the conscious attempt to go into all the world with the gospel. For this reason the most significant expansion was in the New World, to which came English Puritans and Anglicans, Scottish Presbyterians, Swedish Lutherans, German Reformed, and a host of Quakers, Dunkers, Schwenckfelders, Moravians, Baptists, and so on—the first ingredients of the great American melting pot.

The first on the scene were Anglicans in Virginia. The early start, however, was followed by progress at the rate of the proverbial tortoise. The membership of the Anglican church in Virginia at the end of the seventeenth century was only one in twenty. Later, after the founding of the College of William and Mary in 1693, there was considerable but no spectacular improvement. Much of the trouble lay in the reluctance of the Church of England adequately to support the church in the Colonies and to provide episcopal organization.

More heartening is the familiar story of the foundation of the

Plymouth and Massachusetts Bay colonies by Englishmen of Puritan sympathies. If the Pilgrims tended to wash their hands of England as they sailed to find a new home and a new freedom of worship, not so the colonists of 1630 around Boston. "We will not say, as the separatists were wont to say at their leaving England, 'Farewell, Babylon, farewell Rome,' but we will say, 'Farewell dear England, Farewell the church of God in England and all the Christian friends there.'" [19] Even the Plymouth colonists were not entirely separatist in their religious outlook. But life in the New World soon brought them all to that practical position, for in the seventeenth century old England was far, very far away. By action of the Massachusetts General Court in 1631 the franchise was limited to members of the church. Since membership in the church was strictly limited to those who could demonstrate an adult experience of conversion, the control of both church and state came into the hands of the select few, the saints in the ark, distinct from the sinners in the world.

In this semitheocratic society several divisive religious movements soon were manifest. Thomas Hooker took one group of dissidents to the Connecticut River valley. Roger Williams founded a colony in Rhode Island, the prototype of American Baptists. From England directly came John Davenport to New Haven. In 1646 representatives of the four churches of Boston, Plymouth, Connecticut, and New Haven, assembled in the Cambridge Synod, which undertook the clarification of the Congregational system in New England. It adopted the Westminster Confession as a standard of faith and the Cambridge Platform as a standard of polity. Here is to be found the ground work of American *Congregationalism*. After some years of unhappy experience with theocracy, the rule of the saints, the bars were let down in the church with the adoption of the Half-Way Covenant, and in the state with the provision that those who were not full church members were entitled to participate in public affairs. It marked also the waning of the influence of the pastors in public affairs. But the church was very influential in New England clear down to the American Revolution.

When Roger Williams, referred to above, was exiled from Massachu-

[19] Quoted in William Warren Sweet, *The Story of Religion in America* (New York: Harper & Bros., 1950), p. 48.

setts in 1635, he had been in the Colonies just four years, was thirty-four years old. Already his experiences had led him to the conviction that the Massachusetts theocracy was not truly manifesting the revelation of God. In the new colony he helped found, Providence, he made a new beginning and received a second baptism as an adult. He came to the conclusion, not at all common in his day, that no one form of faith can lay claim to the whole of God's truth, that therefore no man should be persecuted because of his religion. His doctrine of religious freedom has already been dealt with in the section in this chapter on the idea of religious toleration. From these sources sprang the early American *Baptists*. They spread throughout the Colonies, but were persecuted in New England until the Charter of 1691 gave relative toleration to all but Roman Catholics. For their own part the colonial Baptists stood firmly on the ground of religious freedom and separation of church and state. They thus played a large part in the development of the American understanding of liberty.

Below New England, which was, religiously, relatively homogeneous, lay the Middle Colonies, which harbored all forms of Christianity, ranging from the Catholics of Maryland to the Schwenckfelders of Pennsylvania. A mere listing of the bewildering variety of denominations represented here is almost appalling. Of these some of the more significant were the Catholics of Maryland, the Dutch Reformed of New Amsterdam, the Swedish Lutherans of Delaware, and the Quakers, German Lutheran, and Reformed of Pennsylvania. The colony of Maryland under George Calvert was developed on the principle of religious toleration, similar in effect to Rhode Island, but in motivation quite different. Whereas the spirit of religious liberty as set forth by Roger Williams lay rooted in his own positive Christian faith, the practice of toleration in Maryland was the product of political necessity faced by a liberal Catholic layman. Since relatively few suitable Catholics were available for colonizing, settlers of many other faiths had to be encouraged to come. As a measure to attract population, then, religious toleration was promised in Maryland. It is an unhappy commentary on the fate of this system that the most vigorous attacks against it came from the growing Protestant population, and that by 1702 the Church of England was legally established.

Penn's proprietary colony is especially interesting, since there, and only there, the *Quakers* for a time formed a majority and enjoyed—or were burdened with—control of the government. Elsewhere and at all other times they formed a small minority. They were persecuted in New England, and even Roger Williams attacked Fox with his tract *George Fox Digged out of his Burrows*. Nonetheless Fox visited Maryland and Rhode Island in 1672. After the foundation of Pennsylvania in 1681, Quakers flocked to this attractive haven, both from England and from New Jersey. The increase in numbers, wealth, and authority had its inevitable effect in diluting their early strong enthusiasm. Along with this decline in spirit came an increase in problems. Power was something to which Quakers were unused, and they soon discovered that it brought them some very practical and unpleasant responsibilities. Chief among these was the duty of protection against the Indians. While Penn's relations with the natives had been exemplary and almost unique, the later Quakers found the situation not quite so simple. The Indians were involved in the colonial wars between England and France, which became virulent in the eighteenth century. Beset with scruples against the use of military force and with economic problems, the Quakers relinquished control of the colony, and the "world" took over.

In addition to the Quakers, Penn received Mennonites, who came to Germantown in 1683; Dunkers (German Baptists), who came in the early eighteenth century and founded the Church of the Brethren; Schwenckfelders, who fled from persecution in Silesia in 1720; Moravians at Bethlehem; and large numbers of German Reformed and Lutherans. Michael Schlatter was an important leader of the German Reformed, and the Muhlenbergs of the Lutherans.

One of the most important migrations of the eighteenth century was that of the Scotch-Irish. These inhabitants of Northern Ireland of Scottish-Presbyterian extraction were driven by economic distress in the first part of the eighteenth century to leave Ulster in large numbers; most of them came to the New World. First in Boston, then to the Middle Colonies, especially Pennsylvania, then down through the Great Valley to settle all along the Piedmont, they formed a sturdy pioneer group ready to subdue the wilderness. From them came many of the adventurous explorers who penetrated beyond the Appalachian barrier. And from them came many of the vigorous religious leaders of prerevolutionary America. Francis Makemie, William and Gilbert Tennent, the whole Log College group—these played a great part in the spread of the Great Awakening. William Tennent's school was called the Log College in derision; but it provided educational leaders for later and greater institutions like Princeton University.

How such a religious movement as the Great Awakening started is impossible to explain completely. It partook of the larger spirit of the Evangelical Revival in England, which itself grew out of the prevailing Deism and Pietism. The Great Awakening happened when the Evangelical Revival spread and took root on American shores. The wars, the general colonial unrest, the work of individuals like Jonathan Edwards and George Whitefield—all these contributed to it, but cannot explain why it happened. In New England it centered around the preaching of Jonathan Edwards, pastor at Northampton. It was in the year 1735 that he preached a tremendous sermon on justification by faith, setting the tone for a revival that increased in momentum slowly until the coming of Whitefield a few years later started an explosion. From 1740 on, a general revival spread in New England, fed by the deadly cold burn of Edwards' evangelical Calvinism and Whitefield's white-hot evangelism. The Congregationalists were split right down the middle into the New Lights, following Edwards, and the Old Lights. Edwards was actually in the middle between two fires, from the liberals on the one side and the conservative old Calvinists on the other.

While the Awakening was proceeding in New England, it was growing apace in the middle and southern colonies. It was fostered by the pietistic Germans, like Frelinghuysen, by the evangelical "Log College" group under Gilbert Tennent, and by Whitefield. Accompanied by widespread experiences of conversion, the movement resulted here also in a split, among the Presbyterians into Old Side and New Side. The former ousted the latter in a synod of 1741.

Princeton and the University of Pennsylvania sprang from the spirit of the Great Awakening. Down the Great Valley, up the Shenandoah, down the Holston and Clinch, the revival washed against the barrier of the Appalachian Mountains, affecting all denominations to some de-

THE DEVELOPMENT OF MODERN CHRISTIANITY

gree. The Methodists, having fostered the movement in England, were perhaps least affected in the Colonies, because they were late on the scene. Philip Embury was working in New York in 1766; but not till the Revolution were Methodists to be counted in any significant numbers.

This is the way in which most of the Christian churches founded in Europe since the time of the Reformation were transplanted into the rich soil of the New World. There they quickly took deep root, drank the nectar of freedom, grew in the lush climate of a vigorous frontier, and brought forth numerous progeny.

3. Protestantism Around the World. Protestants were slow in responding to the "call from Macedonia." Or rather, Macedonia was identified with needs closer to home. But, when they began to move, they went all the way from Macedonia to Mandalay. The account of Protestant missions between 1500 and 1800 is only the prelude to the main acts of the drama. They began to show signs of growth late in the eighteenth century, at a time when Catholic missions were languishing. The firm legal position of Protestants deriving from the Peace of Westphalia, the rise of Dutch and English commerce—as that of Spain and Portugal declined—the Pietism of Germany and the Evangelical Revival of England, all contributed to the surge of enthusiasm that spilled out of Europe to carry Protestant missions in all directions. The spirit of the times is well illustrated by the famous dictum of John Wesley, "I look upon all the world as my parish." This new interest took form in various organizations. The older Anglican Society for Promoting Christian Knowledge was supplemented, in 1701, by the Society for the Propagation of the Gospel in Foreign Parts. Scotland had a missionary society by 1709. These early organizations may be compared with important groups formed in the 1790's, especially the Baptist Missionary Society, the London Missionary Society, and the Church Missionary Society. One of the principal efforts of the Moravian Church lay in missions.

In surveying the development of Protestant missions, we may remark that, with the coming of the Dutch to South Africa in the seventeenth century and the English in the eighteenth, Protestantism slowly gained a foothold. Here as elsewhere, however, the nineteenth was the Protestant century. In India, where the English had decisively defeated the French and gained control of most of that subcontinent by the Treaty of Paris, 1763, the East India Company at first favored missions. This organization was one of several powerful, privileged trading companies operating under liberal charters granted by friendly governments. They exemplify the prevailing mercantilist economic outlook. For many decades the East India Company governed British-controlled parts of India and enjoyed a virtual monopoly. Even before this, German Pietists had sponsored a mission of limited appeal and success. The most notable Pietist was Christian Friedrich Schwartz (d. 1789), who was active in and around Tanjore as both administrator and minister. A few chaplains of the East India Company, predecessors of the phenomenal Henry Martyn, made some progress. But the first event suggestive of greater things to come was the debarkation at Calcutta in 1793 of William Carey, a figure decisive not only for India but for Christianity in the whole world.

What happened in India after the arrival of the English had a parallel in the East Indies when the Dutch drove out the Portuguese. Although they were not very successful in Ceylon, Dutch missions, strongly aided by the state, were established firmly in the islands of the East. This political aid came at a critical time and undoubtedly helped the cause of the faith. But the seeds of future difficulty were sown as Christianity tended to become identified with the dominant European culture.

As to those areas later famous as Protestant missionary fields, China and Japan, little indication may be found as yet of the great and sad future.

For Further Reading

GENERAL

Trevelyan, George M. *England Under the Stuarts.* New York: G. P. Putnam's Sons, 1905.

Drummond, Andrew. *German Protestantism Since Luther.* Chicago: A. R. Allenson, Inc., 1951, 282 p.

McNeill, John Thomas. *Modern Christian Movements.* Philadelphia: Westminster Press, 1954, 197 p.

————. *Unitive Protestantism. A Study in Our Religious Resources.* New York: The Abingdon Press, 1930, 354 p.

STUART ENGLAND AND ROMAN CATHOLIC EUROPE

Gwatkin, H. M. *Church and State in England to the Death of Queen Anne.* New York: Longmans, Green & Co., 1917, 416 p.

Higham, Florence. *Lancelot Andrewes.* New York: Morehouse-Gorham Co., 1952, 128 p.

Trevor-Roper, H. R. *Archbishop Laud, 1573-1645.* New York: The Macmillan Co., 1940, 464 p.

Clark, H. W. *History of English Nonconformity from Wyclif to the Close of the Nineteenth Century.* London: Chapman & Hall, 1911-13, 2 vols.

Haller, William. *The Rise of Puritanism.* New York: Columbia University Press, 1938, 464 p.

Hutchinson, Francis E. *Milton and the English Mind.* New York: The Macmillan Co., 1948, 197 p. "Teach Yourself History" series.

Buchan, J. *Oliver Cromwell.* Boston: Houghton Mifflin Co., 1934, 458 p.

Gardiner, S. R. *Oliver Cromwell.* New York: Longmans, Green & Co., 1902, 319 p.

Carlson, Leland H. "A History of the Presbyterian Party from Pride's Purge to the Dissolution of the Long Parliament," *Church History,* XI (1942), 83-122.

Stearns, Raymond P. *The Strenuous Puritan, Hugh Peter.* Urbana: University of Illinois Press, 1954, 463 p.

Whiting, C. E. *Studies in English Puritanism from the Restoration to the Revolution, 1660-1688.* New York: Macmillan Co., 584 p.

Torbet, Robert G. *A History of the Baptists.* Philadelphia: The Judson Press, 1950, 538 p.

Braithwaite, W. C. *The Beginnings of Quakerism.* New York: The Macmillan Co., 1912, 562 p.

Russell, Elbert. *A History of Quakerism.* New York: The Macmillan Co., 1942, 586 p.

Brinton, Howard. *Friends for Three Hundred Years.* New York: Harper & Bros., 1952, 239 p.

Bebb, E. D. *Nonconformity and Social Economic Life, 1660-1800.* London: Epworth Press, 1935, 198 p.

Jordan, W. K. *The Development of Religious Toleration in England from the Accession of James I to the Convention of the Long Parliament (1603-1640).* Cambridge: Harvard University Press, 1936, 542 p. Vol. II of the series.

Jordan, W. K. *The Development of Religious Toleration in England (1640-1660).* Cambridge: Harvard University Press, 1940, 499 p.

Tawney, R. H. *Religion and the Rise of Capitalism.* New York: Harcourt, Brace & Co., 1926, 337 p.

Eckhart, C. C. *The Papacy and World-Affairs as Reflected in the Secularization of Politics.* Chicago: University of Chicago Press, 1937, 310 p. Comprehensive, from Middle Ages to the present.

Preclin, E., and E. Jarry. *Les luttes politiques et doctrinales aux XVIIe et XVIIIe siècles.* Paris: Bloud & Gay, 1955, 383 p. *Histoire de l'Eglise,* XIX.

Leflon, Jean. *La crise révolutionnaire, 1789-1846.* Paris: Bloud & Gay, 1949, 524 p. *Histoire de l'Eglise,* XX.

Sanders, Ella K. *Jacques Benigne Bossuet; A Study.* New York and London: The Macmillan Co., 1921, 408 p.

Aulard, A. *Christianity and the French Revolution.* New York: Little, Brown & Co., 1927, 164 p.

Palmer, R. R. *Catholics and Unbelievers in Eighteenth Century France.* Princeton: Princeton University Press, 1939, 236 p.

Phillips, C. S. *The Church in France, 1789-1848.* New York: Morehouse-Gorham Co., 1929, 316 p.

ASCENDANCY OF REASON

Lecky, W. *History of the Rise and Influence of the Spirit of Rationalism in Europe.* New York: D. Appleton & Co., 1914, 2 vols. None better yet.

Cragg, G. R. *From Puritanism to the Age of Reason: A Study of Changes in Religious Thought within the Church of England, 1660-1700.* London: Cambridge University Press, 1950, 247 p.

Stromberg, Roland N. *Religious Liberalism in Eighteenth-century England.* New York: Oxford University Press, 1954, 192 p.

Mossner, E. C. *Bishop Butler and the Age of Reason.* New York: The Macmillan Co., 1936, 271 p.

Barker, Joseph Edmund. *Diderot's Treatment of the Christian Religion in the Encyclopédie.* New York: Columbia University Press, 1941, 143 p.

Morley, J. *Voltaire.* London: Macmillan & Co., 1923, 365 p.

Torrey, Norman L. *The Spirit of Voltaire.* New York: Columbia University Press, 1938, 314 p.

ASCENDANCY OF THE HEART

Sykes, Norman. *Church and State in England in the Eighteenth Century.* New York: The Macmillan Co., 1934, 456 p.

Elliott-Binns, L. E. *The Early Evangelicals: A Religious and Social Study.* London: Lutterworth Press, 1953, 464 p.

Nagler, Arthur. *Pietism and Methodism.* Nashville: Publishing House of the Methodist Episcopal Church, South, 1918, 200 p.

Cameron, Richard M. *The Rise of Methodism: A Source Book.* New York: Philosophical Library, 1954, 397 p.

Luccock, Halford, and Paul Hutchinson. *The Story of Methodism.* New York and Nashville: Abingdon Press, 1949, 528 p.

Piette, Maximin. *John Wesley in the Evolution of Protestantism.* New York: Sheed & Ward, 1937, 569 p.

Cannon, William. *The Theology of John Wesley.* New York and Nashville: Abingdon Press, 1946, 284 p.

Lee, Umphrey. *John Wesley and Modern Religion.* Nashville: Cokesbury Press, 1936, 354 p.

McConnell, Francis J. *John Wesley.* New York: The Abingdon Press, 1939, 355 p.

Belden, Albert D. *George Whitefield—the Awakener.* New York: The Macmillan Co., 1953, 302 p.

Candler, W. A. *Life of Thomas Coke.* Nashville: Cokesbury Press, 1923, 408 p.

Church, Leslie F. *The Early Methodist People.* London: Epworth Press, 1948, 288 p.

Bready, John. *England Before and After Wesley.* New York: Harper & Bros., 1938, 463 p. Social influence.

Edwards, Maldwyn. *John Wesley and the Eighteenth Century.* New York: The Abingdon Press, 1933, 220 p. Social influence.

———. *After Wesley.* London: Epworth Press, 1935, 190 p. Social influence, 1791-1849.

Warner, Wellman J. *Wesleyan Movement in the Industrial Revolution*. New York: Longmans, Green & Co., 1930, 299 p.

EXPANSION OF CHRISTIANITY

Weigle, L. A. *American Idealism*. New Haven: Yale University Press, 1928, 356 p.

Sweet, William. *Religion in Colonial America*. New York: Charles Scribners' Sons, 1942, 367 p. First volume of a standard American church history.

Miller, Perry. *The New England Mind: the Seventeenth Century*. New York: The Macmillan Co., 1939, 528 p.

———. *The New England Mind: from Colony to Province*. Cambridge: Harvard University Press, 1953, 513 p.

Trinterud, L. J. *The Forming of an American Tradition. A Re-examination of Colonial Presbyterianism*. Philadelphia; Westminster Press, 1949, 352 p.

Miller, Perry. *Roger Williams: His Contribution to the American Tradition*. Indianapolis: The Bobbs-Merrill Co., 1953, 273 p.

Comfort, William W. *William Penn, 1644-1716*. Philadelphia: University of Pennsylvania Press, 1944, 185 p.

Miller, Perry. *Jonathan Edwards*. New York: William Sloane, Associates, Inc., 1949, 348 p.

Boxer, C. R. *The Christian Century in Japan, 1549-1650*. Berkeley: University of California Press, 1951, 535 p.

Latourette, K. S. *A History of Christian Missions in China*. New York: The Macmillan Co., 1929, 930 p.

———. *Three Centuries of Advance, 1500-1800*. New York: Harper & Bros., 1939, 503 p. *A History of the Expansion of Christianity*, III.

Maclagan, E. *The Jesuits and the Great Mogul*. London: Burns, Oates & Washbourne, Ltd., 1932, 434 p.

Parkman, Francis. *The Jesuits in North America in the Seventeenth Century*. Boston: Little, Brown & Co., 1903, 586 p.

Rippy, J. F., and J. T. Nelson. *Crusaders of the Jungle*. Chapel Hill: University of North Carolina Press, 1936, 401 p.

FAMOUS BOOKS

Lancelot Andrewes (d. 1626). *Sermons on the Nativity; Manual of Private Devotions*.

Robert Brown (d. 1633). *A Treatise of Reformation Without Tarrying for Any*.

Blaise Pascal (d. 1662). *Thoughts*.

Jeremy Taylor (d. 1667). *Rule and Exercises of Holy Living; Rule and Exercises of Holy Dying*.

Roger Williams (d. 1684). *The Bloody Tenet of Persecution*.

John Bunyan (d. 1688). *Grace Abounding to the Chief of Sinners; Pilgrim's Progress*.

John Milton (d. 1674). *Paradise Lost*.

Richard Baxter (d. 1691). *Christian Directory; The Saint's Everlasting Rest*.

George Fox (d. 1691). *Journal*.

Jacques Bossuet (d. 1704). *History of the Variations of the Protestant Churches*.

John Locke (d. 1704). *Reasonableness of Christianity*.

Joseph Butler (d. 1752). *Analogy of Religion*.

William Law (d. 1761). *A Serious Call to a Devout and Holy Life*.

John Wesley (d. 1791). *Plain Account of the People Called Methodists; Journal; Sermons*.

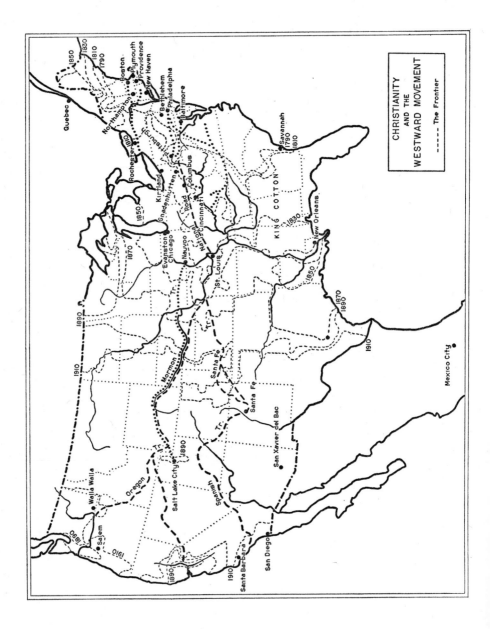

CHRISTIANITY
AND THE
WESTWARD MOVEMENT
----- The Frontier

CHAPTER IV

The Age of Progress
[1815-1914]

A. Europe

1. POLITICS AND RELIGION—THE ROMAN CATHOLIC CHURCH. THE Napoleonic cloud cast its shadow over much of Europe in the year 1799. In that year old Pope Pius VI died, carried a prisoner to France as French troops established a Roman republic. Novalis wrote in that same year, "Catholicism is almost worn out. The old papacy is buried, and Rome for the second time has become a ruin." Undoubtedly the growing power of the little man in France pressed as heavily on the prestige of the papacy as it did on the centers of political power throughout Europe.

Indicative of the impact of the new forces on the old church were the Concordat and Organic Articles of 1801 and 1802. These provided a new basis for relations between church and state in France. The pope was to appoint bishops in France, but on nomination by the state. The bishops were to appoint clergy, but the state retained the right of veto. All clerical salaries were to be paid by the state. The Organic Articles, with which Napoleon supplemented the Concordat, provided that no papal documents might be published or ecclesiastical synods held without permission of the state.

Indicative also was the experience of Pius VII, who came to Paris in 1804 for the imperial coronation. The atmosphere was redolent with memories of that other coronation a thousand years earlier, when the pope, in Rome, had crowned Charlemagne emperor. This time the pope was present and participated, but Napoleon with dramatic symbolism put the crown on his own head.

What was happening cannot be understood solely in terms of the personality of the French hero. A strong wind was blowing, of which he was but one expression, a new wind that had been hovering for some time—the vibrant wind of nationalism. Little did the world of Pius foresee the chapters of glory and of tragedy, of creation and of destruction, that would be written in the annals of nineteenth-century nationalism. The church was to discover once again that it is too much a part of that very society over which in the name of God it holds judgment. Nationalism roared over Europe like a hurricane in the years of the French Revolution, and a large part of the old political and social environment was whisked away, never to return. Oddly, the Roman Catholic Church survived, nurtured on some of the same influences that contributed to the development of nationalism. For Protestants the nineteenth was the "great century."

The outlook for papal prestige was not good at the Congress of Vienna, which gathered in 1815 to put Europe back together after the devastation wrought by Napoleon. In various ways the papacy was slighted. Symbolic of the end of many things, the Holy Roman Empire, abolished by Napoleon, was not resuscitated, although its ghost, the German Confederation or *Bund,* took its place in continuation of the age-old disunity of Teutonic Europe. The Europe that emerged from the Napoleonic fire, as repaired by the Congress of Vienna, was conservative in the extreme, even reactionary.

The symbol of reaction was Prince Clemens von Metternich, chancellor and foreign minister of the Austrian Empire in the first half of the nineteenth century. Suave and tactful, conservative in politics, aristocratic in demeanor, Metternich gave his name to an era that seemingly marked the triumph of the old way of aristocratic monarchical conservatism. Actually it adumbrated the final collapse of the old way before the rising tides of nationalism, liberalism, and social democracy. He would not tolerate any movements suggestive of revolution, reform, or any change at all. To that end the press was censored, freedom of speech denied, criticism of the government prohibited, and the slightest breath of opposition vigorously suppressed. The Concert of Europe—that is, the legitimately recognized powers acting in co-operation—should control public affairs of international concern even to the point of intervention in national politics to prevent the rise and spread of the hated virus of revolution.

In this rigid Metternich system the church had a place as the bulwark of order against anarchy. The result was a revival of ecclesiastical influence, especially of the Roman variety. The Jesuits were reconstituted in 1814. The Inquisition enjoyed a brief revival in Rome. The Index of prohibited books was found quite useful within the context of Metternichism. A series of favorable concordats, engineered by the able ecclesiastical statesman Cardinal Consalvi, increased the prestige of the papacy. A curious exception was Austria itself under Metternich, who held papal influence at a respectable distance. The church was active in politics, especially in influencing the votes of the faithful— where they had the right to vote at all. Roman Catholic secret societies, such as the Congregation of the Virgin in France and the San Fedists in Italy, were organized in opposition to liberal movements like the Carbonari.

This Roman revival received powerful support from another quite unpolitical quarter, cultural romanticism. The reaction against the prevailing classicism of the preceding century led to diverse, individualistic, emotional romanticism. Implications carried over from the cultural areas of literature, art, and music, into political theory, economic interpretation, and religious belief. Of chief importance here is the favor granted to the heritage of the Middle Ages, the "Age of Faith," as over against the admiration of ancient Greece and Rome, which was typical of classicism. This meant that the most important institution of the Middle Ages, the church, shared in the mutual admiration. And conveniently the church was still in existence, as the Middle Ages were not. The outlook has been described as "aesthetic neo-medieval Catholicism that passed for Christianity."

Roman Catholicism in England went through changes in many ways similar to those on the Continent. From a low point around the beginning of the century the papal church revived from the 1830's, and came "of age" with the elevation of Nicholas Wiseman to the office of archbishop and cardinal in 1850. This act brought another strong reaction from English Protestants, who multiplied speculation and fears about popery, Jesuits, and the ghosts of Bloody Mary, Guy Fawkes, and Titus Oates. *Punch* ran a cartoon that portrayed the prime minister chalking "no popery" on Wiseman's door and running away.

The Revolution of 1848 brought an end to the Metternich era. It provided Europe with a series of case studies in nationalism and liberalism, to say nothing of anticlericalism, and supplied the historical context for the appearance of one of the most important popes in the history of the church, Pius IX—or, as Italians impressed by the abrupt change of attitude in 1848 in this pope, already on the throne two years, would have it, *Pio Nono Secondo,* "Pius the Ninth the Second." His long pontificate (1846-78) can be described in terms of two intersecting lines, one running down from a high point at 1846 through the political and military events of the years 1848, 1861, 1866, 1870, to a low point at the end of his career as a "prisoner of the Vatican." The other line would begin at a low point marking the anticlericalism, modernism, and strong Gallicanism[1] early in the pontificate, through the ecclesiastical and dogmatic events of the years 1854, 1864, 1870, to the triumph of ultramontanism[2] in the dogma of papal infallibility. To put it another way, while the church, through the papacy, was losing both prestige and patrimony in a world of power politics, that same church, again through the papacy, was gaining strength through a new devotion to the central authority of the popes as infallible guardians of faith and morals.

Undoubtedly, from the political point of view, the era was catastrophic for the church. One may list the great events that mark the rise of nationalism as a prime force in Europe and find that list a good outline for the fall of the papacy. Begin with lay anticlericalism in all countries. Then add the unification of Italy. This process began with the skillful diplomacy of Count Cavour, prime minister of Piedmont, or Sardinia, a little kingdom occupying the headwaters of the Po River in northeastern Italy and including the major island of Sardinia. Through his determined efforts the Kingdom of Italy was proclaimed in 1861, and the ruler of Piedmont was chosen king of the united country. This was accomplished over the protests of the pope, who lost most of the Papal States to the new kingdom. Only the presence of French troops in Rome for some years prevented the obliteration of papal temporal authority. When those troops were withdrawn in 1870 at the outbreak of the Franco-Prussian War, Rome itself was annexed

[1] Opposition to papal encroachment and domination in France.
[2] Support of papal authority. Both "Gallicanism" and "ultramontanism" can be extended to apply to other countries.

and the Papal States were at an end. Pius IX retired to virtual seclusion in the Vatican, refused to recognize or deal officially with the Kingdom of Italy. He directed the decree *Non expedit* against political participation by Italian Catholics. The story ran parallel in other countries. France jumped from the anticlerical frying pan of 1848 and the Second Republic into the strong secular fire of 1871 and the Third Republic. By 1905 education had been widely secularized and church and state separated. In Austria the Concordat of 1855 was denounced at the time of the formation of the *Ausgleich,* by which the Empire became a "dual monarchy." In Germany the *Kulturkampf,* an ideological war between secular German nationalism championed by Prince Otto von Bismarck and Roman Catholic cosmopolitanism fostered by Pius IX, ended in a draw. Bismarck was unsuccessful in his attempt to secularize education and place the church under the control of the state. Pius was was equally unsuccessful in his efforts to preserve the influence and power enjoyed by the church in another age. "In the short span of twenty years," writes Robert Binkley in *Realism and Nationalism,* "the church had fallen from the first to last place in European leadership. The secular dogmas that triumphed against it in those decades were destined to stand for the remainder of the nineteenth century and into the twentieth as its most pitiless and persistent rivals." [3]

On the other hand, within the church, what amounted to a revolution occurred as the papacy won unchallenged leadership. One center of conflict concerned liberalism and modernism. Many eminent Roman Catholics, such as Lord Acton in England, Count Charles de Montalembert in France, and J. J. I. von Döllinger in Germany, favored reform and liberal religious ideas and opposed papal centralization. They were not radicals, but they were Catholics with deep respect for historical truth. This liberal movement came to public attention at a congress held at Malines, Belgium, in 1864. The pope had been viewing these "modernist" tendencies with increasing alarm, and now acted. The "Syllabus of Errors" was just that—a list of opinions and teachings considered erroneous in the tradition of the Roman Catholic Church.

[3] (New York: Harper & Bros., 1935), p. 71.

Among the errors were distaste for the old scholastic theology, freedom of religion, separation of church and state, belief in toleration, fallibility of the popes and councils, civil marriage, nonsectarian public schools. The last "error" sums up: "that the Roman pontiff can and ought to reconcile himself and agree with progress, liberalism, and modern civilization." Far from becoming a dead letter, this papal document not only continued in force through the years but increased in influence down to our own day. Repeatedly forces within the Roman church that would strike out in a new direction or depart from the conservative tradition established once for all have been beaten down.

Implicit in the Syllabus was the doctrine of papal infallibility. This was the culmination of a trend long present in the church, but by no means dominant—ultramontanism. This meant centralization and increase of authority in Rome. Part of this process was associated with the development of the cult of the Virgin. For ages Christians had been taught to look with veneration on the mother of Jesus. She might be called the Mother of God. In 1854 Pius undertook to identify himself with the trend by promulgation of the encyclical *Ineffabilis Deus,* by which the doctrine of the immaculate conception of the Virgin was made part of the unchangeable body of dogma, required belief for all Catholics. As the Virgin was exalted, so was the pope.

The final step came in 1870 with the dogma of papal infallibility. The battle for final authority had already been fought out in the days of the late medival councils, had been settled practically by the encyclicals of Pius II and others. The pope would not yield to a council. But the church at large had by no means agreed that popes cannot err in matters of faith. For example, Keenan's Catechism, widely used in the United States and England in the nineteenth century, stated as late as 1870: "Question: Must not Catholics believe the pope himself to be infallible? Answer: This is a Protestant invention; it is no article of the Catholic faith; no decision of his can oblige, under pain of heresy, unless it be received and enforced by the teaching body—that is, by the bishops of the church." [4] Gallicanism, understood here as the denial of ultramontanism, was strong not only in France but also in

[4] Quoted in Henry C. Sheldon, *History of the Christian Church* (New York: Thomas Y. Crowell Co., 1894), VI, 70.

England, the United States, and Germany. During the pontificate of Pius IX all this was changed. The Vatican Council of 1870, clearly under the influence of the pope, formally declared that the popes cannot err when speaking in their official capacity on matters of faith and morals. The language of the statement, although ambiguous on the scope of faith and morals, was clear in setting the pope apart as un-challengeable final authority on the questions of greatest concern to the church. The dilemma of honest Catholic historians like Döllinger, Montalembert, Hefele, who could admit no such clear judgment of the church in its past history, was poignant. Hefele, after deep torment, submitted. Montalembert was saved by death. He had written almost at the very end a judgment on supporters of infallibility, "who have immolated justice and truth, reason and history, in one great holocaust to the idol they have raised up for themselves at the Vatican." Döllinger lived to deny the dogma, suffer excommunication, and move to the side of the *Old Catholic Church,* although he did not join it. This church had its origin mainly in the dissidents from the Vatican Council of 1870, but it had roots in earlier movements of Gallican persuasion. Although its adherents remained small, it has continued to the present day.

The last years of Pius were saddened by the loss of the Papal States and the long-drawn-out *Kulturkampf* with Germany. He died leaving both issues unsettled. The latter was ended amicably by his successor, Leo XIII. The former continued a moot issue until the concordat signed by Mussolini in the twentieth century. Leo XIII (1878-1903), although a vigorous defender of the prestige of the church, was more practical in his approach to the unpleasant realities of the modern age. He found a *modus vivendi* in Italy, settled the quarrel in Germany, found a means of adjustment to the modern democracies, and acknowledged the proper place of science and social reform. A revival of Thomistic theology and a renewed interest in biblical and historical scholarship stem from his pontificate. He is probably most remembered, however, for the social encyclicals by which the papacy not so much accepted modern social reform as found a means of using it in the interest of the church.

Pius X (1903-14) reverted to the position of the ninth Pius in roundly condemning "modernism" in his encyclical of 1907, *Pascendi*. Severe restrictions were placed on freedom of biblical study and historical investigation. His pontificate was also much troubled with anti-clericalism in the new democracies, especially France. A man of personal blamelessness, he was horrified at the outbreak of war in 1914, an event that undoubtedly hastened his death.

2. *The Protestant Churches*. Protestants as well as Catholics were involved in the new political and economic forces of Europe in the nineteenth century. In general they adapted more successfully—too successfully, some would say. For Protestants the nineteenth was a heady century. Nations with a Protestant heritage were on the rise—England, the German Empire, the United States—while nations with strong Roman Catholic background either remained static or declined. Italy, apparently on the rise, proved soon enough to be a man of straw. The missionary impulse carried the Protestant gospel literally around the world. Many other new movements originated, from Bible societies through the World Student Christian Federation. The Wesleyan revival and evangelicalism in general provided a seemingly inexhaustible fund of spiritual energy.

This Protestant energy was most generously expended in Germany. Here in central Europe the accumulated forces building up ever since the Treaty of Westphalia, 1648, broke in wave after wave, tearing the German people from the somnolence of the Holy Roman imperial heritage, sending them on a stormy path toward national unity and intellectual and religious leadership. Romanticism, nationalism, the Industrial Revolution, intellectual vigor in the universities, theological and biblical revival—all conspired in the creation of a new Germany and a new Protestantism. Particularly in the fields of theology and biblical interpretation Germans took the initiative. In the early part of the century the name of Friedrich Schleiermacher (d. 1834) is outstanding. In him many of the divergent forces came together. He was raised in the tradition of German pietism, with its emphasis on *Gefühl*, experience. He called himself a "Herrnhuter, only of a higher order," thus testifying to his pietistic background. At the same time he received rigorous training in the critical disciplines of modern scientific and historical study. One of the high points of his career was the famous "Discourse on Religion to the Cultured Who Despise It." His theological materpiece, *The Christian Faith,* appeared in the twenties and thirties. Within the traditional framework of Christian theology Schleiermacher made room for a new approach through religious experience. One comes to religious knowledge not so much through studying and analyzing as through the living experience of it. By feeling he meant consciousness of God, a sense of absolute dependence on God, an intuitive assurance which must underlie all religious knowledge. Influenced deeply by the philosopher Kant, who had sought to reconcile divergent trends of philosophy and provide a new basis for religious knowledge, Schleiermacher sought to reconcile traditional theology with modern thought, religion with science. His influence was felt throughout the Protestant world for the rest of the century, especially in the newly developed study of the psychology of religion.

Again in the field of biblical study and interpretation Germans led. The Tübingen school, named after a series of brilliant scholars of that university, brought forth proponents and opponents from all Protestantism. F. C. Baur (d. 1860), the first of the series, applied Hegelian dialectic to the interpretation of New Testament development through the process from Peter (thesis), through Paul (antithesis), to the ancient catholic church (synthesis). This was intended to show a cause-and-effect sequence in the history of the church. David F. Strauss shook the religious world with his critical *Life of Jesus.* At Göttingen Julius Wellhausen laid the foundations for historical study of the Old Testament. The Book that had long been regarded as the central, unchanging, and unchangeable authority for the Christian faith now seemed subject to scientific judgment, reinterpretation, readjustment, and correction. Was the Bible fallible? Would it lose its age-old authority as a visible record of the Word of God? Theologians like Albrecht Ritschl (d. 1889) and church historians like Adolf von Harnack (d. 1930) were convinced that a valid foundation for Christian faith lay in the modern studies. Conservatives were fearful lest the authority of the faith be lost and took their stand in "orthodoxy" or, in the American scene, in "fundamentalism." Theological liberalism was in the process of being born.

The political involvements of the Lutheran and Reformed churches in such countries as Prussia and the later German Empire were complicated and led to a close relation between church and state. But they need not detain us here. Prussian experiments at Protestant union were forerunners of the present *Evangelische Kirche Deutschlands.*

In other Protestant countries of the Continent the story tended to run parallel to that in Germany. Of the Lutheran states of Scandinavia the smallest, Denmark, had the most lively history. There were two reasons for this: Søren Kierkegaard (d. 1855) and Nicolai Grundtvig (d. 1872). The former became better known outside Denmark; the latter had greater influence within that country. Kierkegaard, casting a shadow over the liberal optimism of his century, spoke to the condition of men in the twentieth. The world, as well as his own Denmark, was slow in discerning this genius, distorted as it was, unheralded by his contemporaries. More directly influential was Bishop Grundtvig, liberal in outlook, vigorous in administration, joyful in testimony. Through him Protestantism in Denmark came to a more active concern for the whole of life. In Norway laymen played a greater role in church affairs. In Sweden the Lutheran state church helped promote notable theological study in the universities of Uppsala and Lund, and at the same time it spawned various free-church movements, chief of which was the *Swedish Mission Covenant.*

In the Netherlands a major change in the religious complexion of the population came in 1830, when Catholic Belgium was separated from the Kingdom of the Netherlands created by the Congress of Vienna. Even so, Roman Catholics in Holland remained a large minority. The largest Protestant body was the *Netherlands Reformed Church,* which, although not completely established, enjoyed the favor and support of the government. It became more and more liberal. Partly for this reason two secessions further complicated the religious structure. One was the *Christian Reformed Church,* which held strictly to the Calvinist position of the Synod of Dort, which had expelled the moderates in the early seventeenth century. The other was the *Reformed Church of the Netherlands,* led by the eminent scholar Abraham Kuyper. This body also denounced the liberalism of the main group.

Protestantism continued a major force in Swiss life and faith. It existed in larger or smaller minorities in Poland, the Austrian Empire (especially Bohemia and Hungary, and the ancient province of Transylvania), Italy, and France. In France the prevailing Protestantism was Calvinistic, but Lutheranism was strong in Alsace. The *French Reformed Church* recovered slowly from the unhappy period of the "Desert," that era of persecution following upon the revocation of the Edict of Nantes. In spite of temporary schisms occasioned by the liberal-conservative tension and conflicts of personality, French Protestants exerted an influence on society at large far beyond the proportion of their numbers.

The Church of England trudged into the nineteenth century tired and in ill health. It was supposed to stand officially for religion in England, as did the Church of Scotland in the north. It had congealed around the comprehensive formula of the Thirty-nine Articles, and meant many things to many men. Scottish Presbyterianism, on the other hand, maintained strict forms of theological and ecclesiastical discipline. The Anglican church exhausted most of its strength in efforts to defend its inherited privileges, including public support; monopolies over marriage, burial, and the universities; and the parish system. The bishops in the House of Lords normally did not take any initiative, and tended to vote with the conservative side. As before, the church included high, low, broad, and evangelical elements. When England began to recover from the general depression consequent upon the Napoleonic wars, the church revived also. The most significant single episode was the Oxford Movement.

At the University of Oxford in the first part of the century assembled a group of able religious leaders, notably John Keble, Richard Hurrell Froude, and John Henry Newman. Beginning as a rally to defend the church against improper control by the state, it really got under way with the famous sermon "National Apostasy," preached by Keble in 1833. Specifically a protest against the act of Parliament reducing the number of dioceses of the Anglican church in Ireland, it raised the fundamental issue of the divine origin of the church. The movement was carried forward by a series of *Tracts for the Times,* to the number of ninety, at which point they abruptly ceased. The reason is seen in

Tract No. 90, in which Newman sought to interpret the Thirty-nine Articles in a catholic sense. As Newman contemplated the situation the catholic sense became the Catholic sense, and presently he and some others went over to the Roman church, much to the scandal of staid Anglicans. Before they left, however, they had driven others out of the church in the other direction, many evangelicals going into the dissenting churches. Most of the "Anglo-Catholics" remained within the Church of England, content to work toward its catholic reinterpretation. The later movement emphasized liturgical forms rather than theology, and had many spiritual benefits to offset the loss of members. After the middle of the century certain groups in the church showed a lively interest in theology and social Christianity. In both of these J. Frederick D. Maurice was an important figure. He understood both the strength and the weakness of biblical criticism and liberal theology, and always had deep sympathy for the oppressed. Christian socialism, akin to the social gospel in America, was one of the most valuable aspects of religious life during the Victorian era.

As the decades passed, the nonconformist churches became more and more important, in both numbers and influence. They increased from about one twentieth of the population to about one half. One reason for this notable growth was the removal of previous restrictions, such as the old Test and Corporation acts, Anglican monopoly of marriage ceremonies, religious tests for entrance into the universities. Presbyterians, after a deep decline resulting from the unitarian movement, recovered. Congregationalists and Baptists were strengthened through the effective preaching of such men as Robert William Dale in Birmingham and Charles Spurgeon at the Metropolitan Tabernacle. The most vigorous denomination was the Methodist, which grew apace under the dominating Jabez Bunting (d. 1858). But this vigor resulted in more than one secession, which, through a series of further splits and reunions, continued down to the First World War. One unusual development was the organization by William Booth (d. 1912) of the *Salvation Army*, directed toward Christian witness in the slums of the industrial cities.

Another strong revival came from the visit of Dwight L. Moody to England in 1873 and following years. The great Agricultural Hall at

Islington was filled with some fourteen thousand persons, and unwonted enthusiasm spread over the face of English religion. Moody's invasion of Cambridge University led to the dedication of the Cambridge Seven (students) to foreign missions. Another important organization that affected all denominations was the Young Men's Christian Association, founded by George Williams along with twelve fellow clerks in London in 1844. This little group expanded until a world organization of Y.M.C.A.'s had been formed. A Young Women's Christian Association followed soon.

3. The Eastern Orthodox Churches. Little mention has been made so far of the Eastern branch of Christianity—and for good reason. Although all branches return to the same main trunk, the Eastern group of churches after the eleventh century had relatively little to do with the development of Christianity in the West. Few contacts of any kind were made. The Tartar state of the late Middle Ages, rising with the invasion of eastern Europe by Mongol hordes out of far Asia, created a barrier between East and West that is apparent to this day. This period from the middle of the thirteenth century down to 1480 isolated Russia from the Byzantine Empire and Byzantine Christianity on the one hand, and from Western civilization and Roman Catholicism on the other.

Two major effects of the Mongol period may be seen. In the first place, Muscovy (old Russia centered around Moscow) was born of the struggle to throw off the Tartar yoke. Since the hoary Byzantine Empire had fallen to the Turks in 1453, the ambitious Muscovite princes were in a favorable position to take over in part the prestige and influence of Constantinople. The bastion of Christendom, which had withstood for a thousand years repeated attacks from the barbaric non-Christian masses of Asia, had now succumbed in heroic tragedy. Moscow assumed the mantle of Constantinople, and the grand prince became the tsar— that is, emperor.

In the second place, the *Russian Orthodox Church* emerged as the dominant partner in the Eastern Orthodox communion. Although the ecumenical patriarch of Constantinople continued to exercise limited and rather nebulous authority, the center of Orthodox Christianity moved north into the Slavic realm. In fact, as the political and religious changes ran parallel, Moscow came to be described as the "Third Rome." Classical Rome had in the early Middle Ages given way to Constantinople, the "New Rome." Now the former Byzantine capital gave way to the Muscovite city. Moscow was to be the center for the preservation of the pure strain of the Christian faith, the New Jerusalem of the faithful children of God. The faith had been soiled and adulterated in the West. Even Byzantine "Greek" Christianity was tainted by linguistic and cultural variations and by movements of the fifteenth century directed toward reunion with Rome. Since the prince of Muscovy now styled himself tsar, the leaders of the Russian church demanded the establishment of a full patriarchate in Moscow. This was done in a series of moves culminating in 1589.

The next significant development of modern times is associated with Nikon, patriarch from 1652 to 1666. Possessed of courage and determination, he lacked discretion. When he pushed through a revision of the ancient liturgical books, he stirred up violent opposition from the rigid conservative elements. The details of the controversy appear almost ridiculous on the surface—the spelling of Jesus' name, the direction of religious processions, the singing of the Alleluia two or three times, and the inevitable Eastern issue of icons. Behind them, however, lay a fundamental conflict over "Greek" influence, emanating from Constantinople via the metropolitanate of Kiev. Nikon favored many of these modern trends. The result was schism, the origin of the *Old Believers* or *Raskolniki*. They refused to permit the slightest alteration of the holy books. They believed the pure faith was preserved in the Russian church rather than in the tainted Greek church. They have continued as a separate religious group, with various vicissitudes, to this day. Cultural opposition to foreign "Greek" influences and political involvements against the Ottoman Turks and the Roman Catholic Poles also played a part.

Nikon might have succeeded completely had he not become implicated in a struggle for power against the Tsar. Relations between church and state had developed in the East in the environment of the Byzantine Empire. In principle the two authorities, emperor and patriarch, were both founded upon divine authority. The emperor was supreme in secular, the patriarch in spiritual, affairs. The two powers were co-ordinate aspects of God's sovereignty. From Patriarch Photius in the ninth century to Nikon this principle was maintained. In actuality, however, the situation was often different. If the popes in the West in the Middle Ages succeeded in part in asserting the superiority of the papacy over the imperial office, as the sun over the moon, the emperors in the East presumed to assert authority in the ecclesiastical sphere. Although courageous churchmen from time to time resisted, the emperors developed the theme of caesaropapism—that is, the authority of the secular ruler over ecclesiastical affairs. Only a few of them, however, attempted to interfere with dogma.

Nikon tried to re-establish the principle of co-ordinate spheres in Russia. In doing so he incurred the hostility of the tsar and the aristocrats, the boyars, who were jealous guardians of their ancient prerogatives. Since Nikon was endowed with an uncompromising and imperious personality, his opponents feared lest he gain actual predominance. He was overthrown in 1666 and forced into retirement.

The Old Believers continued in existence, divided into two groups, the *Popovtsy*, those with priests, and the *Bezpopovtsy*, those without. Limitations of space forbid further discussion of these groups, or of the various dissenting sects rising from biblical, ascetic, and social motives.

The deep conflicts engendered by the policies of Nikon led ultimately to the subjection of the Russian church in the time of Peter the Great (1682-1725). When the patriarchate fell vacant, Peter prevented election of a successor. Rather, he organized a new body known as the Holy Governing Synod, with a layman appointed by the tsar as its chairman. The "supreme judge" of the Holy Synod was acknowledged to be the Tsar of All the Russias. Gradually the chairman, called the Ober Prokuror, or procurator, came to dominate the Synod. Ever since then the state has controlled the church so closely that the church might be described as a department of state for religious affairs.

The story of the Russian Orthodox Church in the nineteenth century should be understood in the context of general Russian history. The solidification of the tsarist regime around the three factors of autocracy, orthodoxy, and nationalism—as expressed in the reign of Nicholas I—placed the church in the center of imperial expansion. When the Russians advanced in their "eastward movement" across northern and central Asia, they overcame and sought to assimilate many different states and cultures. Programs of Russification included emphasis on the Orthodox church as the true Russian faith. In reality the Russian Empire embraced many different faiths.

The perennial issue of Westernism versus Slavophilism involved the church. Westernizers from Peter and Catherine through the nineteenth century sought to transform Russia into a modern European power and a society influenced by "enlightened" philosophy and literature. On the one hand attempts were made to develop contact with Roman Catholic and Protestant institutions and thought. On the other hand, skepticism and social radicalism—anarchism, nihilism, later Marxism —sought to break down entirely the religious structure of faith. At its best this trend led to a truly ecumenical concept. Vladimir Soloviëv (d. 1900) dreamed of the unity of all Christians, Western as well as Eastern. He deplored blind, narrow nationalism, but he loved Russia.

Against these influences the Slavophiles fought for the preservation of all that was truly Russian. Responding to the battle cry of orthodoxy, autocracy, nationalism, they tried to eliminate and keep out foreign influences, whether political, philosophical, artistic, or religious. Men like Alexei Khomyakov (d. 1860) portrayed the Russian Orthodox Church as the achievement of true community. If the Roman Catholic tradition lost freedom in its emphasis on unity, and if the Protestant tradition found freedom at the cost of unity, only the Orthodox church exhibited the true spiritual unity referred to as *soborny,* a characteristic term difficult to translate.

‾ Not many variations may be discerned in the position of the church under different tsars. Alexander I (1801-25), by virtue of a profound spiritual experience, regarded the church highly and established a Ministry of Religious Affairs and Public Education. The Russian Bible Society was organized. Characteristically he sponsored the Holy Alliance among the victors over Napoleon in 1815, based "on the sublime truths which the Holy Religion of our Savior teaches." Prince Metternich of Austria referred to it as "a sonorous nothing." Nicholas I, Alexander's successor, in reaction suppressed the Bible Society and made the Holy Synod independent of the Ministry of Religious Affairs.

Although Alexander II (1855-81) gained a well-deserved reputation as being more liberal during the first part of his reign and actually carried through some fundamental political, social, and legal reforms, hopes for religious reform and greater freedom for the church were not realized. Partly because he was blown up by a revolutionist's bomb, the reign of his successor, Alexander III, was one of reaction. The procurator, Constantine Pobedonostsev (d. 1907), provided an able defense of autocracy and orthodoxy, and helped impose a political and religious strait-jacket. He defended with conviction and enthusiasm the divine origins of the authority of the Autocrat of All the Russias and rejected utterly any breath of liberalism or democracy. A somber background was provided for the revolutions of 1905 and 1917.

The tumultuous years of the reign of Nicholas II (1894-1917) saw repeated outbreak of revolution, the result of long-pent-up pressures. The Revolution of 1905 raised hopes for a more liberal political regime and for reforms in the church, especially local church government, a national *sobor* or assembly, and the restoration of the patriarchate. But, although some political changes were begun, nothing happened in ecclesiastical affairs. The stage was set for the great upheavals during World War I, when autocracy, orthodoxy, and nationalism alike were swallowed up in the Bolshevik Revolution.

Russia was not the only area in which Orthodox Christianity experienced troubles. Only a few words can be devoted to the complex history of Christianity in the Balkans under the domination and after the dissolution of the Ottoman Empire. After reaching a high point in the sixteenth century the Turkish Empire entered upon a long decline in which the appearance of power survived the reality. By 1815, however, the inner weakness was clear, although the Congress of Vienna refused to recognize it. For decades the Danubian world was rent by revolutions. The Greeks, after a long struggle, achieved independence in 1829 (Treaty of Adrianople) with the help of Western allies. Serbia then became autonomous within the Ottoman Empire, and in 1877 gained complete independence. The old provinces of Wallachia and Moldavia were forged into the modern nation of Rumania. Out of the Balkan Wars of 1912-13 came Bulgaria.

In the midst of this political chaos the Orthodox church threw off not only Ottoman control but also the nebulous authority of the ecumenical patriarch in Constantinople. Generally the church became autocephalous as the area gained autonomy. Full-fledged national churches appeared as the countries gained full independence. A *Greek Orthodox Church* followed upon the Treaty of Adrianople. The *Serbian Orthodox Church* dates formally from 1879. The *Rumanian Orthodox Church* achieved full autonomy in 1885. The *Bulgarian Orthodox Church,* authorized by the Ottoman Empire in 1870, encountered protracted difficulties in the Orthodox family until 1945.

Of the tremendous power of nationalism in the modern world the history of the Christian church in the Balkans provides a prime illustration.

B. The United States

1. Emancipation and Organization. When news of the repeal of the Stamp Act in March, 1766, arrived in Boston, Charles Chauncy preached on the text "As cold waters to a thirsty soul, so good news from a far country." The timeliness of this topic followed in the long tradition of political concern on the part of ministers in New England, who from 1674 were wont to preach election sermons. The stage was set for active participation by the churches in the American Revolution. On its eve the Congregationalists, strongest in New England, were the largest religious group in the Colonies. Next came the Presbyterians, then the Baptists, Anglicans, Quakers, German-Dutch Reformed, Lutherans, and Roman Catholics. The Methodists were farther down the list as a growing but still small body theoretically within the fold of the Anglican church. Hence, as far as the religious population went, the British eastern seaboard was predominantly Protestant.

The implications of this for the Revolution were clearly recognized by Edmund Burke, who in his address on "Conciliation with America," 1775, stated:

Religion, always a principle of energy in this new people, is no way worn out or impaired; and their mode of professing it is also one main cause of this free spirit. The people are Protestants; and of that kind which is the most adverse to all implicit submission of mind and opinion. This is a persuasion not only favorable to liberty, but built upon it.[5]

[5] (New York: Longmans, Green & Co., 1896), p. 23.

All the churches were involved, but in varying degrees and relationships. Congregationalists and Presbyterians were both quite active in the cause of independence. Both were strongly Calvinist and therefore vigorously concerned about political morality. The Congregationalists were in the free-church tradition. The Presbyterians were further devoted to the cause of independence from *England* because of their Scotch-Irish background. John Witherspoon, president of the College of New Jersey (to become Princeton) , was the only minister privileged to sign the Declaration of Independence. The Baptists likewise gave full support to the revolutionary cause, especially because of their devotion to the principle of religious liberty. Churches that had enjoyed in Europe an established relationship with conservative, aristocratic governments, as the Anglicans in England and the Lutherans in Germany, were in a difficult position. Many Anglican clergymen, loyal to their ordination vows if nothing else, fled to Canada or returned home. On the other hand Anglican laymen of Virginia contributed many of the most illustrious leaders of the Revolution. Although the Lutherans were known for their reluctance to reject established authority, many laymen joined the forces of independence, and two famous pastors, John Peter Gabriel Muhlenburg and his brother Frederick Augustus Conrad, defied the traditional neutralism of their old father, Henry Melchior, and took active part in the military and diplomatic struggle. John Peter Gabriel, pastor of a Lutheran church at the time, doffed his gown at the end of the service, cried, "There is a time to preach and a time to fight, and now is the time to fight," and went off to become a general under Washington. Likewise the Roman Catholics were in a difficult position. But they were led on the side of the Revolution by the highly respected Charles Carroll. As to the Methodists, one must remember they got started in the Colonies only a few years before the beginning of the War for Independence. A source of acute embarrassment was the attitude of John Wesley, who, although he sympathized with the position of the Colonists, was too much of a Tory to contemplate any limitation of royal authority there. His *Calm Address to the American Colonies* had the effect of making all American Methodists presumed loyalists. The one outstanding exception was Francis Asbury, who with great courage, albeit great reluctance, differed with his English leader. As Asbury wrote, "I am truly sorry that the venerable man ever dipped into the politics of America. My desire is to live at peace with all men; to do them no harm, but all the good I can." His influence helped keep Methodism close to the heart of America, in a position to strike out for the West along the advancing frontier after the war was over. He himself, however, took no direct part in the Revolution.

With the conclusion of the Revolution the umbilical cord was severed. With little more than theoretical precedents a new nation had to be created and organized. Likewise, churches rooted deeply in the European religious tradition were forced to strike out on their own. All groups faced problems of readjustment and reorganization. The Congregationalists continued to hold their influential position in New England. They were established in Massachusetts, Connecticut, and New Hampshire, and continued so. Much of the thought that went into the making of state constitutions came originally from Congregationalist pulpits.

The outcome for the Baptists was even happier. Without any institutional ties with ecclesiastical forces in the old world, they were free to develop as they wished, free churches in a free state. Their devotion to religious liberty, separation of church and state, and their form of ecclesiastical organization made them right at home in a government of, by, and for the people. Hence they did not go over en masse to the Federalist party, as did most of the New England ministers. The Presbyterians, Dutch Reformed, and Lutherans were able to organize nationally without serious difficulties.

The Anglicans, however, faced a crisis. The church had suffered during the Revolution, since most of the colonial clergy were missionaries rather than settled ministers. So large numbers had departed. After American independence, support from the Society for the Propagation of the Gospel in Foreign Parts was cut off. Likewise cut off was the nebulous authority of the bishop of London. Anglicans in the New World were orphans, without friends and without even a bishop and almost without clergy. Through the efforts of such leaders as William White and Samuel Seabury the church recovered gradually and in time became the *Protestant Episcopal Church*. Properly consecrated bishops were obtained, and a start was made at the development of an American Episcopalianism.

The Methodists likewise encountered serious difficulties. Most troublesome was the fact that English Methodism was not yet separated from the Established Church. After the Revolution, the Methodists in America gave Wesley to understand that the tight English connection was not to be resumed—a fact Wesley already recognized. As a result he "set apart" Thomas Coke, an ordained clergyman, as "superintendent," along with Asbury, and ordained two English lay preachers to go with Coke and help ordain ministers for the American work. At the end of 1784 it became apparent that American Methodism was on its way to complete independence, not only from the Anglican church but also from Wesley's control. The Christmas Conference in Baltimore in that year carried through the organization of the *Methodist Episcopal Church* by majority vote.

After some curious politico-ecclesiastical maneuvering the Roman Catholic Church in America was reorganized under a prefect apostolic, Father John Carroll.

Of all the Protestant groups the German Reformed and Moravians found the process of readjustment most painful and lagged longest in carrying it through. Their ties to Europe, cultural, personal, organizational, financial, were quite close. By 1800, however, almost all the churches had broken the outward bonds and become part of the surging life of America, looking henceforth not eastward toward the Old World, but westward, toward a destiny that seemed to some, though dimly, illimitable.

2. Expansion and Barbarization. The most reliable estimate of church membership in 1790 lists five per cent of the population. Ten years later the figure was less than seven per cent. The brutal fact is that a very small portion, albeit influential, of the people were officially related to the churches. And within many of them the spirit of eighteenth-century rationalism was strong in the form of Deism. Natural religion seemed to be sufficient. Established Congregationalism basked in a favored place under the New England sun, only to become embroiled in divisive and destructive quarrels occasioned by the Plan of Union, 1801, entered into with the Presbyterians for co-operation on the frontier, and by the anti-Calvinist revolt. Episcopalianism fought for breath, concentrating on the struggle for survival. The outlook for religion on the eastern seaboard was not good. It was quite otherwise on the pulsating border of the Appalachians. Lyman Beecher felt this strong pulse as he traveled west. In his *Plea for the West,* published in 1835, he wrote:

It is equally plain that the religious and political destiny of our nation is to be decided in the West. There is the territory, and there soon will be the population, the wealth, and the political power. The Atlantic commerce and manufactures may confer always some peculiar advantages on the East. But the West is destined to be the great central power of the nation, and under heaven, must affect powerfully the cause of free institutions and the liberty of the world.

The West is a young empire of mind, and power, and wealth, and free institutions, rushing up to a giant manhood, with a rapidity and a power never before witnessed below the sun. And if she carries with her the elements of her preservation, the experiment will be glorious—the joy of the nation—the joy of the whole earth, as she rises in the majesty of her intelligence and benevolence, and enterprise, for the emancipation of the world.[6]

Not much was to be expected from the old established churches. They were altogether too completely tied in with the culture and sectional interests of the East. None was equipped for an organized effort to follow the frontier the length and breadth of the country. To be sure, Congregationalism was transported westward from Connecticut. It came along with the thousands of pioneers to the great Western Reserve. Sometimes whole communities simply moved to a new area, as, for example, the inhabitants of Granville, Massachusetts, to Granville, Ohio. But it never achieved on the frontier much more than the status of bag and baggage. Obviously the staid forms of the Protestant Episcopal Church were ill adapted to the rough pioneer life.

The Presbyterians, although staid enough in the East, stood in a different relation to the challenge. They were *already* west, being settled in the upland valleys from the beginning. They already had a traveling ministry. And they had a form of organization useful in the

---

[6] (Cincinnati: Truman and Smith, 1835) , pp. 11-12.

nurture of new congregations. From western Pennsylvania, Virginia, and North Carolina they passed over the "gaps" and down the valleys into Tennessee, Kentucky, Ohio, and west. Along with them came relatively well-educated parsons ready for the rigors of frontier life. American Presbyterianism, moreover, was deeply influenced by the great awakenings already mentioned that contributed so much to expansion.

The two denominations that proved truly equal to the stupendous task posed by the westward movement were the Baptists and the Methodists. The Baptist farmer-preacher and the Methodist circuit rider have justly entered the ranks of mythical heroes. The former did not accompany the frontiersmen; he was one of them. He labored as they did to clear a sunny spot in the overawing great forest. He split rails and sowed corn and hoped for a cow and a horse, even as they did. What he lacked in equipment and lost in illiteracy he made up for in spirit and rapport with his countrymen. What his church lacked in ecclesiastical organization and system it made up in rampant democracy.

The Methodists found their strength in aspects quite different from the Baptists. Wherever the Baptist farmer-preacher settled, he was likely to find a Methodist circuit rider already at work, gaunt from the strain of frontier life, but eager to carry the gospel into the most outlying stretches of wilderness. Asbury was the prototype. He outrode even Wesley, and almost all his travels were over forest trails. Dozens of times over the multiple back of the Appalachians, up and down the Great Valley, indefatigably he rode into the hearts of countless Methodists. What he started was carried on by Peter Cartwright, James B. Finley, William McKendree, and a host of others. Tightly knit into the fabric of quarterly and annual conferences, presiding elder and bishop, the circuit rider went about his task with single-minded devotion, unhindered by family or finance, home or hotel. Within sixty years of the Christmas Conference of 1784 the Methodists had become the largest Protestant group in America.

The advance of the frontier marked the stages of the advance of religion. From the colonial seat in the East the barrier of civilization was pushed across the Appalachians during and after the Revolution; down the Ohio, Kanawha, Cumberland, and Tennessee, and up the

Mahoning, Muskingum, Scioto, Miami, and Wabash during the 1820's and 1830's; across the Mississippi into Texas, Missouri, and way out to the Far West around the middle of the century; up and down the Pacific coast back into the mountains, and finally across the broad stretches of the Great Plains from the Red River of Minnesota to the Red River of Texas. By 1890 the United States Census Bureau in its wisdom announced that the frontier had disappeared.

The churches were there. They went along, occasionally leading the way, as did Marcus Whitman, Jason Lee, and the Mormons. Inevitably the church left its mark. Wherever a log meetinghouse rose, some of the rough edges of pioneer life were rubbed off, something of decency entered to subdue the raucous barbarism. As Conrad Richter has shown so poignantly in his historical novel *The Trees,* the pioneer church meant a breath of life and hope in the midst of the primeval wilderness. Log churches sprang up all over the West, first in the forests, then in the mountains, finally on the treeless prairie. The whiskey was just as raw and just as plentiful, but now the drunkard was recognized for what he really was. Saved Christians learned to fight demon rum along with all the other devils of the wilderness, including dark loneliness. The church did not totally redeem frontier society, but it did make it a tolerable place for redeemed individuals to live.

As religion left its mark on society, so the frontier left its mark on religion. New conditions required new methods. One of these was revivalism in the camp meeting. Presbyterian ministers found their success depended not on the orthodoxy of their Calvinism, but on the fervor of their appeal. Early artists in the technique of the camp meeting were Presbyterians. Where they led, the Baptists and Methodists were close behind. The original camp meeting at Cane Ridge, Kentucky, at the beginning of the nineteenth century, soon passed from the moderate, theologically grounded preaching of the Presbyterians to the more emotional appeals that seemed natural to primitive surroundings. Emotionally starved individuals craved the heart-warming message, and the preachers were ready and willing to answer the need. There were excesses. Occasionally the violence of emotional release ran riot. But the excesses were not typical. The revival was not always followed by a debauch—in fact, the opposite was true. Charles G.

Finney (d. 1875), one-time president of Oberlin College, represents the strong evangelistic emphasis that became part of American Christianity. Wherever revivals struck root, as they did widely, there the whole life of a community was disciplined. The effect was not altogether ephemeral. Anything was better than the barbarizing influence of the untrammeled frontier. If the churches were somewhat barbarized in the process, if the wise distinctions of theology and the proper forms of liturgy were lost in the rush, that was only proof that the churches were giving themselves in direct contact with the society they sought to serve. If one speaks of the barbarization of Christianity on the frontier, one must remember as well the Christianization of a barbarous life.

One of the positive results was the rise of some new religious movements that presently congealed into denominations. Among these the most significant were the Disciples and the Mormons. The former were derived from the central tradition of trinitarian Protestant Christianity, chiefly from Presbyterians, Baptists, and Methodists. Barton W. Stone in Kentucky and Thomas and Alexander Campbell in western Pennsylvania carried through a movement that was partly a reaction against orthodox Calvinism and partly a revival of indigenous frontier origins. It combined the correlative forces of individualism and brotherhood. By a series of steps the connection with the Presbyterian Church was broken, an association with the Baptists made and then broken, and, through the adherence of some from both groups, together with some Methodists, the *Christian Church* or *Disciples of Christ* was formed. At first the intention was not to form a new denomination, but rather to provide a nondenominational center for the reunification of Christians. From the formation of the Brush Run Church in 1811 to the union in 1832 of Stoneites and Campbellites, the groups gradually took on the characteristics of a denomination, and such it is today in fact if not in theory.

Other sects had their origin in the anti-Calvinist revival atmosphere of the frontier, notably the *Cumberland Presbyterians.* Two groups, both formed at the beginning of the century, combined the American aspects of revivalism with pietism inherited from Europe: the *United Brethren in Christ* and the *Evangelical Association,* now united in the

Evangelical United Brethren Church. The founder of the former was Philip Otterbein, of the latter Jacob Albright. Both of these men were early associated with the Methodist Church, and both might well have been kept within the fold except for linguistic and personal barriers. They both came from German background. Later in the century a peculiar religious movement began in New York state which participated directly and dramatically in the westward movement: the *Church of Jesus Christ of Latter-day Saints,* the *Mormons.* The founder, Joseph Smith, grew up in the revivalistic atmosphere of western New York, but apparently had no roots in any traditional Christian organization. In 1830 he published the *Book of Mormon,* said to be a translation of documents he had dug up through the guidance of an angel. It presented a history of the early settlement of America by ancient groups from Palestine. Smith became the prophet of the new movement, organized into a church in the same year. From the original settlement the Mormons moved to Kirtland, Ohio; to Missouri; to Nauvoo, Illinois; and finally to Utah, where they founded Salt Lake City under the dynamic leadership of Brigham Young.

Another peculiar movement of American revivalistic origins sprang from the prophetic message of William Miller, a farmer of New England connected with the Baptist Church. The unique aspect of his preaching was the setting of a specific date (March 21, 1843) for the return of Christ and the end of the world. The failure of the prophecy did not end the movement, but rather led eventually to the formation of various Adventist denominations—*Seventh-Day Adventists, Advent Christian Association, Church of God,* etc.

3. Urbanization and Secularization. The War Between the States was a spiritual as well as a physical agony. In the ecclesiastical sense it began many years before the cannonade at Fort Sumter. If the maxim, "A house divided against itself cannot stand," has any application to ecclesiastical structure, some desperate blows at the house of the Lord were struck in the years leading up to the great conflict. King Cotton rent churches asunder. One of the most influential and widely distributed Protestant groups was the Baptist General Convention, formed in 1814, growing in all sections of the country. When slaveholding became an issue in connection with a candidate for foreign missions work, the southern churches broke away in 1845 to form the *Southern Baptist Convention*. In the case of the Methodists the specific issue concerned slaveholding by a bishop, and the crisis was reached in 1844. The southern annual conferences withdrew under a "Plan of Separation" to form the *Methodist Episcopal Church, South*. The Presbyterians, who had already split into Old School and New School, were also plagued by the issue of slavery. Other denominations were either split or strained. Those that avoided schism either were sectionally centralized or did not face the issue.

When war broke, therefore, most of the churches had already chosen sides. Methodists and Baptists in the North were enthusiastic in their patriotism. The southern Methodists and Baptists returned zeal for zeal. The seamless robe of Christ was rent once again, and that bloodily. American religion has carried the scars of the Irrepressible Conflict to this day.

What was the state of Christianity at the end? Around mid-century the churches lined up in the following order of size: Roman Catholic (first because of its different mode of counting members), Methodist, Baptist, Presbyterian, Congregational, Lutheran, and Disciples, all with over 100,000 members. What a change from the situation at the Revolution! Church members in 1850 comprised about 15.5 per cent of the population, as compared with 5 per cent in 1790. By 1900 they numbered 35.7 per cent. Their order in 1890 went as follows: Roman Catholic, Methodist, Baptist, Presbyterian, Lutheran, Disciples, Protestant Episcopal, Congregational. They who had been first were now last, at least in size. The changes resulted mainly from two major developments: the westward movement, and the rise of urban America. Or, to put it another way, the farmer-miner frontier was followed by the urban frontier. The churches played their part in and were affected by both movements.

In the years after the War Between the States many new influences were brought to bear upon American life in general. Probably the most powerful was the Industrial Revolution, with all that it meant in the direction of the factory system, the industrial city, the working population, and social agitation. In 1850 less than 14 per cent of the people were living in towns of five thousand population or more. This rose to 31.5 per cent in 1890, and passed 52 per cent in 1930. These few figures tell their own story. Add to this the facts of immigration in the latter nineteenth century. By the 1880's and 1890's half a million immigrants were entering every year. First came English, Irish, German; then Italian and Slav. The impact was tremendous, and that especially in the cities. Beyond this the ferment of a philosophical and scientific revolution was permeating the thinking of the country. Rationalism and humanism were supplemented by a new scientism that led to interminable, wasteful, and destructive debates on Genesis and geology, evolution, the authority of the Bible, indeed the very life of Christianity. From these conflicts, however, came a more profound understanding of the faith.

Along with society the churches were urbanized. This was more noticeable in some than in others. The Roman Catholic Church became pre-eminently a church of the great industrial city, with its teeming thousands fresh from the strongly Roman Catholic countries of Europe. The curiously polyglot character of Roman Catholicism in America is a reflection of the great melting pot. Even the Catholic ingredients of this stew, however, were only partially cooked. German, Polish, Irish, Bohemian churches rose. Meeting the challenge, American Catholicism responded with vigorous parish work among the factory workers, with new religious orders, and with an unusual American adaptation to the principles of separation of church and state and of equal freedom under law for all faiths. In the latter part of the century the outstanding figure was that of James Cardinal Gibbons (d. 1921) , who never let slip an opportunity to testify to his faith in America as a proper environment for the Roman Catholic faith. Inevitably this surge of Catholicism brought forth a countermovement in varieties of anti-Catholic organizations. The Know-Nothing party had earlier cherished this prejudice. In the eighties the American Protective Association spread in the Midwest primarily as a protest against the contamination of Roman Catholic immigrants. Other groups carried on the campaign down to the Ku Klux Klan of the 1920's.

The Protestant churches, except for the Lutherans, were not so directly affected by the tides of immigration. But they were equally drawn into the vortex of the new industrial age. In the process some of the churches, especially the larger, were transformed socially into respectable middle-class organizations. From a negative viewpoint it could be argued that they lost the fervor of the gospel in the insidious currents of secularism running through the urban life of America. The new wealth threatened to raise up new golden calves and to break once again, although less dramatically, the Ten Commandments graved upon the stone of centuries. One example is the fate of the Sabbath. That rigid institution planted by the Puritans of the seventeenth century in firm biblical soil had become by the middle of the nineteenth century more of a fetish than an ideal. It was attacked from one side by the hordes of European Roman Catholics who knew nothing of a holy and quiet Sabbath, and from the other side by the increasing demands of business and industry that Sunday be freed from its economic shackles.

On the other hand the Protestant churches responded to the industrial age with an amazing variety of activities. The Young Men's Christian Association was brought from England to the United States about the middle of the century. It expanded into a movement that influenced young lives in all the major cities of the country at a time when the old churches were losing touch with youth. From the Chicago Y.M.C.A., Dwight L. Moody went out in the years after 1870 to evangelize the land with a vigor and color reminiscent of earlier great awakenings. Finney evangelized in Rochester, New York, and around the country. The old agrarian camp meeting was transformed into first a chautauqua and finally a middle-class summer resort. But the sawdust trail was laid from Moody to Billy Sunday in city-type revivals. When the business-man came into the center of American life as the new ideal of success, laymen came to play an ever larger part in the work of the churches. The admission of laymen to the Methodist General Conference in 1872 is a symbol of the trend, always central to Methodism, that now brought greater efficiency, better organization, and "businesslike methods" to the churches. Ministers began to find much in common with their fellows in the chamber of commerce. On the other hand the problem of labor was vexing. Some even of the noblest teachers and preachers, like Horace Bushnell and Henry Ward Beecher, were blind to the demands of social justice in industrial society. Yet the churches here also responded to the challenge through the work of men like Washington Gladden and Walter Rauschenbusch, exponents of the "social gospel" in the United States.

In the great cities, teeming with people on the move, a new type of ministry was called for. It took the form of the institutional church. This became a fulcrum for a neighborhood, serving the social needs of a variegated and changing population, yet always bringing this service in terms of the Christian message. Some of the city churches became famous pulpits for great preachers. Henry Ward Beecher carried on a magnificent preaching ministry at Plymouth church, Brooklyn, until his death in 1887. His successor was the famous evolutionist Lyman Abbott. Among the older Methodist preachers perhaps the most influ-ential was Bishop Matthew Simpson, who died in 1884. A noble orator, close friend of President Lincoln, he played a part in both church and state during and after the War Between the States.

One of the most interesting effects of urban life was the rise of new denominations. Only one of many churches concerns us at this point: Christian Science. The founder, Mrs. Mary Baker Eddy, after years of affliction physical and mental, found relief through a mental healer in Portland, Maine. Adapting and reorienting the method, Mrs. Eddy wrote and published in 1875 a textbook, *Science and Health*. This set forth the basic principles of Christian Science, centered around the denial or nonexistence of matter, evil, sin, and death. From this teach-ing came a new religion, using but not relying on the Bible, the *Church of Christ, Scientist*. Its major appeal was faith healing. In 1875 the Christian Science Association was organized and presently was trans-ferred to Boston, where it took permanent root as an urban institution. When Mrs. Eddy died in 1910, she and her church had become wealthy. To this day it is urban and upper middle class in nature.

4. Diversification and Unification. The United States in the nine-teenth and twentieth centuries has seen two major and complementary forces at work in Christianity: division into multiple denominations and unification through reunions and federations. The former is chiefly characteristic of the nineteenth, the latter of the twentieth. For that reason the chief accent of this section lies in the former, while the latter becomes prominent in the next chapter. The ingredients for diversification were all present by the end of the nineteenth century.

That denominationalism was already a fully developed phenomenon by the First World War is clearly shown by the Yearbook of the Federal Council of Churches for 1916. There were 172 denominations reported. Many more had already made an appearance but were too small for notice or made no report. By 1936 the number had risen to 256, not counting the extremely small or ephemeral groups. Altogether over 400 separate groups may be discerned. Of these only 33 have had over 200,000 members. But they include well over 90 per cent of the church members of the United States. Over one half of the denominations have less than 7,000 members. The largest single denomination is of course the Roman Catholic. After that the largest Protestant church is the Methodist. Taken by denominational groups, however, the Baptists lead, with some 18,000,000 adherents, followed by the Methodists with 12,000,000, the Lutherans with almost 7,000,000, the Presbyterians with almost 4,000,000 and the Orthodox with over 2,000,000. Within a total religious population of 95,000,000 (about 60 per cent of the population) the 30 denominations of the National Council of Churches include 35,500,000. Great geographical disparity is to be noted. Congregationalists congregate in New England. Disciples live in the Ohio River watershed. Only nine church bodies are found in all states.

How did American Christianity come to such a condition? The reasons are historical, social, and doctrinal. In the first place it should be recognized that a great many of the denominations are simply imports from Europe. Whereas in Sweden there is the Swedish Lutheran Church, in the United States there are not only Swedish Lutherans but also Norwegian, Danish, and Finnish Lutherans, each in their own churches. Richard Niebuhr in his *Social Sources of Denominationalism* lists a whole page full of churches whose names alone indicate national European origin.

American history has played its part in the multiplication of sects. We have already seen what the War Between the States did. The frontier spawned a few large and many small groups. The winds of liberal philosophy and biblical criticism, of science and progress, gave rise to other groups either in support or in reaction, chiefly the latter. The age-old process of warming and cooling evangelical fervor played its part, especially in the divisions that sheered off from the Methodist Church. Race was another factor: In 1948 there were thirty-four exclusively Negro churches, almost all of them either Baptist or Methodist. Every city has seen the appearance of store-front churches, generally of the holiness or pentecostal variety. Some urban groups verge away from traditional Christianity toward mystical or philosophical or psychological vagaries. In fact, almost anything may be encountered. The Church of Daniel's Band was founded in Michigan in 1893. The Fire Baptized Holiness Church of God in the Americas was founded in South Carolina in 1898. There are the General Baptists and the Particular (Calvinistic) Baptists, the United Baptists and the Separate Baptists, the Primitive Baptists and the Seventh-Day Baptists, the Duck River (and Kindred) Association of Baptists and the Two-Seed-in-the-Spirit Predestinarian Baptists. Some denominations, especially the smallest, insist they are not even denominations. The Plymouth Brethren, for example, are split into eight branches, each denominated by a Roman numeral, but all eight firmly insist that they represent no "sectarian church," but rather a nondenominational nucleus for the reunion of all true Christians.

From this welter the prospect for Christian unity seems hopeless. And yet the Ecumenical Movement was growing in spite of denominationalism. Two factors must be kept firmly in mind: (1) Over 90 per cent of the Christians in the United States belong to some two dozen largest denominations; (2) especially in the twentieth century the opposite trend has been gaining strength, toward reunion, merger, association, federation. The Ecumenical Movement goes a long way toward overcoming the scandal of division. This movement has its roots far back in history, but as a major modern trend began in the nineteenth century and gained full prominence in the twentieth. At this point our concern is with the nineteenth-century roots in America. These go back as far as the colonial period, when the broad-minded spirit of the Enlightenment was married to the firm individualism of the Puritan tradition. The principles of religious liberty and of separation of church and state played their role. Quite early the frontier provided the churches with a missionary challenge that transcended denominations. This latter factor loomed large in the formation of the Disciples of Christ. As early as 1809 Thomas Campbell issued a memorable *Declaration and Address,* a plea for Christian unity, for going beyond the creeds to Bible truth. In this case individual Christians were to separate from the denominations and come over to the new nondenominational fellowship. Today this fellowship constitutes another denomination; but the ideal of ecumenicity perseveres.

Not only from frontier religion but also from the older churches came forces for unity. One of the most interesting developments sprang from German Reformed circles, associated especially with the Mercersburg school. In fact, here is found the first American plan for organic unity on the basis of negotiation among Lutherans, Calvinists, and Zwinglians. Samuel Schmucker, who worked on a plan for an "Apostolic Protestant Church," and Philip Schaff, church historian, editor, and ecumenical Christian of Mercersburg and Union Theological seminaries, were two leaders. As later in England, so in the United States, the Episcopalians offered to act as mediators between catholic and evangelical wings of Protestantism. The Protestant Episcopal Church sought to comprehend many varieties within a latitudinarian compromise.

Before the end of the century these efforts bore fruit in several forms of co-operation between denominations. As early as 1810 Congregationalists and Presbyterians joined in the American Board of Commissioners for Foreign Missions, an organization comparable to the London Missionary Society. A conference of missionary societies in 1893 led to the formation of the Foreign Missions Conference of North America. Around the middle of the century the student movement took form through the organization in America of the Y.M.C.A. and, later, the Y.W.C.A. By 1895 the Student Volunteer Movement and the World's Student Christian Federation had come into being. These groups nurtured such famous leaders as John R. Mott. An early experiment in a more general co-operative front was the Evangelical Alliance, the American branch of which was formed in 1867, after the War Between the States. Its purpose was for "strengthening of union and fellowship amongst Protestant Evangelicals." Its influence was limited by its mode of organization around individual Christians rather than around denominations as such. With its decline came the rise of a new experiment, the Federal Council of Churches, 1908. It was fostered through the work of a Congregationalist in New England, Elias Sanford. Here finally was an organization of denominations, one more comprehensive than the Evangelical Alliance.

On a more limited level the process of unity was furthered by a series of mergers, a series to be continued into the twentieth century. For example, the Cumberland and Northern Presbyterians united in 1906. The United Lutheran Church of 1918 grew out of long spade-work going back to the 1870's and 1880's. Even the relatively late Methodist merger of 1939 depended upon negotiations from 1876 on. Christian and Congregational talks began in the 1880's. Likewise, the United Church of Canada (Congregationalists, Methodists, and Presbyterians in 1925) was the fruit of nineteenth-century work.

Already, then, by the end of the Age of Progress, as a new and more tumultuous age dawned lugubriously in 1914, the intense individualism inherent in the Protestant tradition was being channeled and disciplined. The ground was plowed and fitted for a new harvest, to be measured not in terms of denominations and divisive revivals and controversies, but rather in the wounds healed and the rough places made plain. The Ecumenical Movement of our own day grew out of the rich and varied Protestant heritage.

C. The Expansion of Christianity

In Serampore, India, December 28, 1800, was inaugurated what Kenneth S. Latourette calls "the great century." It had been long in coming. William Carey (d. 1834), missionary to India for the Baptist Missionary Society in London, had been on the scene for seven long years, and had not yet seen one Indian converted to Christianity. But that day it happened to Krishna and Gokul, and a new generation, a Christian generation, was founded in that vast subcontinent. Previous expansion had taken the faith, mainly Roman Catholic, to many parts of the world. But now for the first time Christianity became in fact a world religion. The babel of many tongues became one through the name of Jesus Christ. The principle that John Wesley applied to his work in England came into its own in the nineteenth century: "I look upon all the world as my parish."

The end of the eighteenth century saw an amazing proliferation of Protestant societies devoted to missions. In England were the Baptist Missionary Society, the London Missionary Society, the Church Missionary Society (Anglican), the British and Foreign Bible Society (evangelical), and the Wesleyan Missionary Society. Similar organizations developed somewhat later on the Continent. In the United States in the early nineteenth century appeared the American Board of Commissioners for Foreign Missions and the American Baptist Missionary Society. This broadened vision for Protestants had its parallel in secular dreams of manifest destiny in Protestant nations like Britain and Holland. This was taking place at a time when Roman Catholic countries like Spain and Portugal were in sad retreat. Their once great empires had already given way to the new British and Dutch empires. And the Seven Years' War had decided the fate of India as between England and France.

1. *Asia.* Christianity in India was ancient and somnolent. The Nestorians had been there since the Middle Ages. When the English drove out the French in the eighteenth century and gave over control to the East India Company, the result was not immediate introduction of Christianity. This staid organization did not consider spiritual improvement one of its chief responsibilities. Not until the days of the Serampore Trio—Carey, William Ward, and Joshua Marshman—was any organized work carried on by Englishmen. It was painfully slow and hampered by commercial interests. Rival religions, Hinduism and Islam, dominated the whole culture. But gradually a little Christian community grew, the Bible was translated into numerous Indian languages, and India became one of the most hopeful areas for Protestant missionary activity. In the first half of the century Henry Martyn (d. 1812) and Alexander Duff (d. 1878) carried on works of translation and higher education.

After the disastrous Sepoy Mutiny of 1857 ended the hegemony of the East India Company and the British Colonial Office assumed responsibility for government, missionary efforts were doubled and redoubled, from England and from the United States, with notable success. In India, Protestant missions outstripped Roman Catholic. Specific attention was given to approaches through education, medicine, and agriculture. The caste system led missionaries to devote most of their service to the outcastes. With some ten million of their number spread through the enormous population, Indian Christians have acted as a leavening of great influence throughout the life of what is now an independent nation. Hinduism and Islam were far from defeated, however, and certain movements, like the Ramakrishna Mission, sought to forge, by syncretism, a religion better than Christianity itself.

The first Americans to go as missionaries to Asia were Adoniram and Ann Judson, Baptists who sailed in 1813 to Burma. They strove to preach the gospel and translate the Bible into Burmese in the midst of fearful obstacles and terrors. In this area the chief religious rival was Buddhism. Great success attended missions among the non-Buddhist Karens of the interior.

In China, ever since the sixteenth century, Christian missionaries faced an ancient and proud culture unwilling to concede inferiority in any realm, especially that dealing with the mind and spirit. Confucianism and, to a degree, Buddhism, refused to loose their hold. Not until after the Opium Wars of 1839-42 and 1856-60 did the repelling façade break down. With these events came European imperialism, extraterritoriality, and its attendant evils. Before this, however, missionaries had come. Robert Morrison (d. 1834), of the London Missionary Society, arrived in Canton as early as 1807, and began the arduous task of translating the Bible into Chinese. The American medical missionary Peter Parker landed in Canton the year Morrison died. He was the first of a notable series of Christian leaders who employed medical skill in the service of the gospel.

At first most stations were near the coast. But in 1865 the China Inland Mission, a nondenominational enterprise for penetrating the more remote areas, was organized by the English evangelical missionary J. Hudson Taylor (d. 1905). Protestantism grew apace and began to catch up with the Roman Catholic mission population, which had a head start. By 1914 China felt the full impact of the Christian gospel. The danger, as in India, was that the missionary enterprise would, consciously or not, be too closely identified with the spread of Western civilization in general. A day of reckoning was to come; but the cloud was not yet even small on the horizon.

As to the rest of the Asiatic mainland, Korea became a fertile field for Protestant missions, and also for Asiatic imperialism. The bone of Korea was worried among China and Japan and Russia until the distracted country knew not where to turn. After 1910 it was annexed by Japan. Until 1866 persecution harried Christian expansion; and not until the 1880's did Protestant missions get under way. With American Presbyterians and Methodists taking the lead, by 1914 the Protestants of Korea had outstripped the Roman Catholics.

Missions also extended into Ceylon, the Malay Peninsula, and other areas controlled by the British. The strong Buddhism of Siam prevented any notable penetration by any form of Christianity. But Indochina under the French went over heavily to Roman Catholic Christianity. In the East Indies, when Dutch rule replaced Portuguese in the seventeenth century, Dutch Reformed missions were established. It continued to expand through the nineteenth century, in spite of opposition from deeply rooted Islam.

In the Philippines, Roman Catholic missionaries had arrived in the sixteenth century in the nick of time to prevent the Moslemization of the population. With the occupation of the islands in 1898 by the United States, many important changes took place. Economically the country was developed, and a start was made toward building a mature political environment. The Roman Catholic Church was disestablished. Since the existing Roman Catholic organization was heavily Spanish, a major secession took place with the formation of the *Independent Catholic Church,* led by Filipino priests. Protestant missionaries entered and made many converts both from the nominal Roman Catholics and among the animists of remote areas. The Vatican faced the crisis by removing the old Spanish elements, sending American Catholic missionaries, and raising up an indigenous clergy, including Filipino bishops. In these ways the only really Christian people in the Far East were confirmed in their faith.

After striking reversals of fortune between 1549 and 1640, Christianity in Japan was to all appearances moribund. Except for limited trade at Nagasaki, all Japan from 1640 on was closed tight against any outside influences. After 1853-54, when Commodore Perry forced the islands open with the threat of naval power, the situation was quite different. Japan took over more and more the ways of Western civilization, along with them the Christian faith. Although Buddhism and Shinto remained strong, missions made some headway under Orthodox, Roman Catholic, and Protestant auspices. By 1873 the anti-Christian edict boards of an earlier era were removed. An American educational missionary, J. C. Hepburn (d. 1911), arrived shortly after the doors were opened to foreigners. His work in the Japanese language and in translation of the Bible was fundamental for the future missionary enterprise. Growth was especially strong in the 1880's. The strongest Russian Orthodox enterprise was in this country. Protestantism, however, had by far the greatest growth, but not spectacular in terms of the total population. The most vigorous effort came from the United States. The churches established were mainly urban, and gained most members from the professional, middle, and samurai classes. Outstanding was Joseph Hardy Neesima (d. 1890), a devoted Japanese Christian educated in America, who founded the great Doshisha, a Christian university in ancient Kyoto.

2. *Around the Rest of the World.* In the western hemisphere mission effort was chiefly of the home variety, in the United States among Indians, Negroes, and to some extent Mexicans. In Canada, James Evans (d. 1846) and Robert Rundle spread the gospel and the Bible across the windswept wastes of Manitoba and Saskatchewan. In the far Northwest, William Bompas, and in the far Northeast, Wilfred Grenfell, ministered spiritually and physically to the Indians and Eskimos. The amazing career of Sheldon Jackson as a Presbyterian missionary covered the vast prairies west of the Mississippi River and, after 1877, the newly purchased territory of Alaska. There he spent almost thirty years founding missions and schools, promoting education as United States general agent for education, and striving desperately to protect the Eskimos against exploitation and starvation.

While Roman Catholic enterprise languished in Latin America, Protestant missions were introduced in spite of recurrent opposition from the various governments. After the period of revolutions in the 1820's and 1830's, when Spanish authority was thrown off, the many new states dealt with religion as political alignments dictated. Christian churches and schools were started by James Thomson from England and David Trumbull from the United States. Agencies of Bible societies were set up, and missions among the Indians were instituted. Protestant expansion in Latin America, however, was to come chiefly in the mid twentieth century.

Some of the most dramatic episodes in the history of missions occurred in the far-flung islands of the Pacific. The early efforts of the London Missionary Society were painful and slow. Each island has its own history, and no attempt can be made here to recount the narrative. Sometimes the missionaries were gratified with mass conversions. At other times the missionaries gratified the appetites of the cannibalistic natives. Tahiti and the Tonga or Friendly Islands came over to British Christianity. John Williams (d. 1839), then twenty years old, sailed from England with his young wife to serve in Polynesia as missionary, translator of the Bible, teacher, house and church builder, shipmaker, and captain. When he sailed to the New Hebrides in Melanesia—the islands of the black people—he was slain and eaten by cannibals who were infuriated by a recent expedition of white slavers. The American missionary Hiram Bingham (d. 1908) practically created the written language of the Gilbert Islands for the purpose, carried out over long years of sacrificial work, of translating the whole Bible for the people. Others were John Patteson and John Paton in Polynesia and James Chalmers in New Guinea. Hawaii was brought over by 1870.

The big problem of Christianity in Australia and New Zealand was that of holding fast to the migrating thousands of Britishers who settled in new homes halfway around the earth. After the discovery of Botany Bay by James Cook in the eighteenth century, the British government sent shiploads of convicts to Australia. To serve the needs of these demoralized and abandoned men, Samuel Marsden (d. 1838) came as Anglican chaplain. More than any other he was responsible for the spread of Christianity to both Australia and New Zealand. The Christian population of these parts of the Commonwealth is about the same as that of Canada.

One of the most sordid chapters in the history of imperialism is found in the oppression and near extinction of the aborigines of Tasmania and Australia. The fact that they were not totally destroyed in the latter, as they actually were in Tasmania, is a tribute to the spread of the Christian faith. The remnants of the aboriginal population were by 1914 being led as they were able into the Christian fold.

The vast continent of Africa had been scarcely touched. Between Africans and Europeans the chief point of contact was the slave trade. In the North, Islam had long held sway, building a barrier against the spread of Christianity south across the Mediterranean. The Coptic Christians of Ethiopia, isolated and lacking initiative, were in no position to expand. Until the middle of the nineteenth century the unexplored interior was accessible to none but the most adventurous. Protestant activity is found earliest in the South, where the Dutch, then the English, organized an imperial bastion up from the Cape of Good Hope. About thirty per cent of the Bushmen, Hottentots, and Bantus became Protestant Christians through the efforts initiated by the London Missionary Society. Two of those who blazed a trail for others to follow were Robert and Mary Moffat, who traveled north from Capetown to found a mission at Kuruman in Bechuanaland. He died in 1883.

The problems of exploration, the terrible slave trade, and imperialistic partition among European powers all played a part in determining the course of Christian expansion. The man who encountered all these various forces was David Livingstone (d. 1873), who was drawn to Africa by Moffat. Famous in his own right as an explorer, he fought against the insidious drive for slaves, represented something of the best in British imperialism, and to the end of his life in the swamps around Lake Bangweulu sought to testify by word and act to the Christian faith. One of the results of his efforts was a flourishing mission in Uganda. Here Alexander Mackay (d. 1890), a Scottish engineer, after a difficult two-year journey, built a vigorous mission. In spite of troubles, occasioned by British-French rivalry, the arrival of Roman Catholic missionaries, and continued Moslem pressure, a thriving center of Christian influence rose. The Church Missionary Society had great success after 1877, and two years later missionaries of the French order of White Fathers, founded by Charles Lavigerie, entered to promote a

Roman Catholic mission. These monastic missionaries were effective in dealing with the Moslem culture in North Africa.

In the Congo Free State, the one great colony of Belgium, Protestants began work in the 1870's, following the pioneer Thomas Comber. They were followed by Roman Catholics, increasingly Belgian in support. With the favor of the government these had the greatest success. In British-governed Nigeria, Anglicans and Methodists, Presbyterians from Scotland, and American Southern Baptists brought large numbers over to the Christian faith. Here Samuel Adjai Crowther (d. 1891) became the first native African Anglican bishop. The courageous Mary Slessor (d. 1915), who succeeded in West Africa where others had failed, must be mentioned in passing.

In the regions south and east of the Mediterranean, Islam was dominant. When the collapse of the Ottoman Empire opened the way for European and Christian penetration, these areas resisted both with vigor. The Moslem crescent became a symbol of national loyalty against the foreigner. One method of testifying to the Christian faith lay through education. Christian colleges like those at Cairo, Beirut, and Constantinople, founded largely by American mission boards, have brought a Christian spirit into the arts, sciences, and professions of these lands.

By the time the catastrophe of Western civilization, the World War, broke in 1914, the Christian message had been preached in practically every corner of the world. The work was by no means complete, and the twentieth century was to witness disastrous setbacks. But Christ, so long ostensibly a possession of Europeans and whites, now belonged to all the world.

D. Christianity and Society

As the sixteenth century, so also the nineteenth had a revolutionary transformation of society. This revolution may be perceived in all phases. The Industrial Revolution settled with a pall of smoke over Britain, the United States, Belgium, France, and later Germany. Lady Liberty, backed by both Reason and Romance, fought on the barricades as the old order fell. At the same time she began to change fashions and manner of speech as she became the French nation, the German

Volk, or the British Empire. Outside France she changed sex and became the Fatherland. Science and materialism did their best to abolish the other world. Culture proceeded from the classicism of the Age of Enlightenment to the all-pervading romanticism of the era of Metternich. And before the century was out, cultural realism had invaded the realms of science, politics, music, economics, art, and even religion. This section can only suggest some of the manifold lines along which the church impinged on society, and society on the church.

1. The Industrial Revolution. In Charles Dickens' *Hard Times,* Coketown

was a town of red brick, or of brick that would have been red if the smoke and ashes had allowed it; but as matters stood it was a town of unnatural red and black like the painted face of the savage. It was a town of machinery and tall chimneys, out of which interminable serpents of smoke trailed themselves forever and ever, and never got uncoiled. It had a black canal in it, and a river that ran purple with ill-smelling dye, and vast piles of building full of windows where there was a rattling and a trembling all day long, and where the piston of the steam-engine worked monotonously up and down, like the head of an elephant in a state of melancholy madness. It contained several large streets all very like one another, and many small streets still more like one another inhabited by people equally like one another, who all went in and out at the same hours, with the same sound upon the same pavements, to do the same work, and to whom every day was the same as yesterday and tomorrow, and every year the counterpart of the last and the next. . . .

You saw nothing in Coketown but what was severely workful. If the members of a religious persuasion built a chapel there—as the members of eighteen religious persuasions had done—they made it a pious warehouse of red brick, with sometimes (but this is only in highly ornamented examples) a bell in a birdcage on the top of it. The solitary exception was the New Church; a stuccoed edifice with a square steeple over the door, terminating in four short pinnacles like florid wooden legs.[7]

Hard reality lay behind Dickens' fiction. The Industrial Revolution changed not only the stage setting but the inner character of life. This is seen in the country as well as in the city. Already in the eighteenth

[7] *Works* (New York: Charles Scribner's Sons, 1898), XXV, 24-25.

century the process of enclosure (for grazing rather than traditional cultivation) had almost depopulated part of the old countryside. See Oliver Goldsmith, *The Deserted Village.* The yeomen and cotters were liquidated, and the new era of scientific and efficient farming came in. From Jethro Tull to "Farmer George" (George III) the English people were subjected to a slow but violent agricultural revolution. The political troubles of the Napoleonic era had economic repercussions in the form of depression, high prices, and Corn Laws. As in England, so later in France and Germany, agricultural life was transformed by the emancipation of the serfs and the introduction of modern methods and machinery.

In industry the revolution was even more complete. With the cotton industry leading the way, manufacturing was mechanized into the factory system. The "invention of invention" brought a deluge of new devices, each disturbing the old balance between supply and demand. Each new machine created a demand for other improvements. Flying shuttles required spinning jennies. Machines created a demand for power. Power required a concentration of machines in the factory. And the consequent concentration of raw materials and products created a demand for transportation facilities. When the workers were forced to gather around the machines in the factories, the industrial city grew and cast its smoky shadow over the hitherto quiet countryside. The factory system meant dislocation, imbalance, discord—revolution. People were dislocated. Hence their institutions were thrown out of balance. Among these was the church. There was the spectacle of soaring Salisbury cathedral left high and dry in the midst of pastoral quietude, while the life of England surged into Manchester, Sheffield, Leeds, where at first scarcely a church, to say nothing of a cathedral, could be found. While many clergymen of the Establishment, following the type of relatively impecunious country gentlemen, preached in their great churches to empty pews, Wesley and Whitefield had to preach to their thousands in empty lots and street corners in the slums.

Indubitably the church was violently affected by the Industrial Revolution. Just as indubitably Christianity made its impact on society. The church has always stood in judgment upon the schemes of men, and the nineteenth century was no exception. Calvinist Christianity played its part in the rise of economic individualism, indirectly participated in the spread of the "spirit of capitalism." Heaven and hell were quite real to the Protestant merchant. But the Industrial Revolution tended to becloud heaven and hell alike. Churchmen were not only slow but loath to recognize the profound change of society. In England, on the Continent, in the United States, they tended to fall into aristocratic patterns resulting in complacency. In 1800 the church everywhere was largely rural, with a country-squire complex. In England the towns had 41 per cent of the population, only 30 per cent of the churches. Half a century later the towns had over half of the population, only 38 per cent of the churches. For a while paternalistic care for the poor maintained some contact with the working people. But after mid-century more and more the urban workers came under the influence either of Roman Catholic paternalism or of materialistic philosophies intolerant of religion. The middle class was outside both the fraternal kinship of the church with the aristocratic class and its paternal kinship with the masses. As Henry Manning said, while still in his mother church, the ministers did not influence the middle class as they did the upper class by fraternal and the lower class by paternal relations. The middle class was therefore open to the influence of secularism, social, religious, and economic.

Nevertheless, although slowly, the church became aware of the revolutionary forces and began to do something about the problems they created. This was true on the Continent and in the United States, as in England. But, since they developed earlier and with greater force in the latter, our attention is drawn primarily to the island kingdom. All varieties of Christianity, Evangelicals, Broad churchmen and High churchmen within the Established Church, and dissenting groups without, participated. Earliest attention was given to humanitarian work. Here were found men like William Wilberforce (antislavery) and John Wesley, later Richard Oastler (factory legislation) and J. R. Stephens (a Methodist minister who worked against the Poor Law of 1834), and the incomparable Earl of Shaftesbury.

In the early nineteenth century much concern was directed to legal reform and the improvement of education. One church organization, founded in 1796, was called the Society for Bettering the Condition of the Poor. Another, 1803, was the Society for Superseding Climbing Boys (chimney sweeps). Of this the bishop of Winchester was president. The Earl of Shaftesbury played a central part in the Parliamentary debates leading to electoral and factory reform. Yet he sometimes felt abandoned by the clergy themselves. He said he had more help from medical men than from ministers. The Chartists of the 1840's, who urged a program of reform through the electoral process, felt the antagonism of the clergy. They called the Establishment "Old Mother Hypocrisy," "Superstitious Old Hag." On the other hand, some individual churchmen sympathized with them and offered aid. Thomas Arnold of Rugby was one such.

Probably the most significant expression of Christian social concern in England, however, was Christian socialism. This movement stemmed from the groundwork of J. M. Ludlow, F. D. Maurice, and Charles Kingsley, the last two being clergymen. With the fall of Chartism, which was secular in nature, these men issued a "Proclamation to the Workmen of England" in 1848, the year of the surging political and social revolutions on the Continent and the year of publication of the Communist Manifesto. A literature developed, moving from *Politics for the People* through *Tracts on Christian Socialism* to *The Christian Socialist*. One continuing feature was education, beginning with night schools and culminating in a Working Men's College. They gave support to the various movements for workingmen's associations, and, till thwarted by the antireligious stand of Robert Owen, to the co-operative movement.

After the middle of the century the church in the town became aware of its own problems and its own opportunities. The result was activities foreshadowing the institutional church, agitation for regulation of housing leading to the Torrens Acts of 1866 and 1868, and participation in efforts for organization of workingmen, both town and country. The rise and fall of the National Agricultural Laborers' Union in the 1870's found Joseph Arch, a Primitive Methodist preacher, in the center of the movement; E. D. Girdlestone, a parish clergyman, among forerunners; and the vigorous Bishop Fraser of Manchester at the crisis denouncing the lockout by employers. Arch, however, was under no illusion concerning the attitude of clergymen generally:

There was a parson here and there who went with us openly; but the majority were against us; and others blew hot now cold, and flew around like weather-cocks as squire or farmer or villager grew strongest at the moment. These shining lights of the Church as by Law Established were but poor farthing rushlights to the agricultural labourer.[8]

One must qualify this antagonism, however, by noting that here a Primitive Methodist is speaking about the Church of England.

The last quarter of the century brought organization on both secular and ecclesiastical levels. Labor unions gradually forced acceptance, the Fabian Society came into being, and early forms of the Labor party appeared. From the church came the Guild of St. Matthew, organized by Stewart Headlam in 1877 with the purpose "to promote the study of social and political questions, in the light of the Incarnation." A much larger organization was the Christian Social Union, formed in 1889, largely from the impulse provided by the Lambeth Conference of 1888, the first to face social issues directly. Henry Scott Holland and Charles Gore were guiding figures, and Bishop B. F. Westcott, biblical scholar, was the influential first president.

These English developments had their counterpart in the American "social gospel." From early manifestations of social concern among the Puritans of New England and the Quakers of Pennsylvania came, in the latter part of the nineteenth century, an optimistic program of social reform called "applied Christianity." This was the term used by Washington Gladden, Congregational minister in Columbus, Ohio. Another Congregationalist, Josiah Strong (d. 1916), who was active in the Evangelical Alliance, urged the church to accept its responsibility for making the "kingdom of God come upon earth." The most famous leader was Walter Rauschenbusch (d. 1918), professor at Rochester Theological Seminary. He received an early education in the seamy side of industrial life during an eleven-year pastorate in Hell's Kitchen, on New York's West Side. His *Christianity and the Social Crisis* (1907) is the classic expression of the movement. "God had to raise up social- ism," wrote he, "because the organized church was too blind." Man does not live by bread alone; but he does not live without bread. Give

[8] From *The Story of His Life,* quoted in Donald O. Wagner, *The Church of England and Social Reform since 1854* (New York: Columbia University Press, 1930), p. 158.

him bread, said the enthusiasts, and he will be able to live as God wills. After 1890 social concern was the order of the day, at least among an influential group in the major denominations. The adoption in 1908 by the Federal Council of Churches of the "Social Creed of the Churches," taken over from the Methodist Social Creed, is symbolic of the era. Unlimited free enterprise was denounced, and the need for co-operation, mutual aid, and social concern was stressed. If the vision of the kingdom of God on earth appeared incomplete and illusory to a later age, it constituted a vigorous response to very real challenges springing from the years of the Industrial Revolution.

Meanwhile, the Roman Catholic Church was not unaware of the tremendous challenges of the new era. After the narrow and negative policy of Pius IX the outlook of Leo XIII seems enlightened. He is probably most remembered for the series of social encyclicals by which the papacy not only accepted modern social reform but also found a means of using it in the interest of the church. *Rerum novarum*, 1891, is a religious classic in its own right. Rejecting alike the extremes of socialism and capitalism, it maintained the principle of justice in relations between employers and employees, both of whom might organize for their mutual betterment. From the social and political influence of Leo XIII came the modern European forms of Catholic action through Catholic political parties and Catholic labor unions. Just before the First World War, Roman Catholics on both sides of the Atlantic organized for social action in the Catholic Social Guild in England and a Catholic Social Service Commission in the United States.

2. Liberalism and Nationalism. Political liberalism provided a fertile soil in which nationalism, ultimately illiberal, struck deep roots in the nineteenth century. As we have seen, the liberal spirit had its sources in the Enlightenment, which itself looked back to ancient Greece and Rome, and in Puritan Protestantism, which looked back to biblical Christianity. Institutions embodying that spirit sprang into prominence in this period, especially in England and the United States. The term "liberalism," which was first used in its political meaning in 1819, means here the spirit of freedom, individualism, and national self-determination. It took the form of representative government. Liberalism of the nineteenth century, then, is the conservatism of the twentieth. The role Puritan Protestantism played in the development of this spirit has been described in Chapter II, Section F. With the partial exception of Lutherans and Anglicans, the Protestant churches maintained a positive influence in favor of the modern democratic state. Much of the narrative illustrating this relation has been given in the earlier sections of this chapter and needs no repetition here. Although the Methodist Church in England under the original direction of John Wesley tended toward the authoritarian tradition, the essence of Protestantism came out in the liberal movements associated with Alexander Kilham and the Primitive Methodists in England and the organization of the Methodist Episcopal Church in America. Utilitarian political philosophy combined with the free-church tradition in such eminent statesmen as William Gladstone and Abraham Lincoln. No doubt exists as to the importance of the Baptist witness in the development of religious liberty, especially in the United States.

After the middle of the century the picture was complicated by industrial problems and the need for an economic interpretation of Christian liberalism. As political democracy became more thoroughly settled upon the states in which Protestantism predominated, industrial democracy arose to plague those who were willing to rest on their laurels. Nonetheless, through participation in local government, and through influence on the minds of great men like Lincoln, Wilson, Shaftesbury, and Gladstone, Protestant Christianity remained the ally of democracy. The great testing of this alliance was to come in the era of twentieth-century dictators.

The picture is not so clear in the case of Roman Catholicism. The turbidity is well illustrated by two documents of the 1860's, the report of the International Congress at Malines and the Syllabus of Errors. At the former, Catholic liberals like Montalembert expressed approval of Roman Catholic adaptation to democratic institutions, as in Belgium. Here was Roman Catholicism accepting, if not enthusiastically promoting, democracy, equality of individuals, separation of church and state. Liberal Catholicism in the United States, stemming from the influence of Cardinal Gibbons, showed a parallel attitude. Yet the pope himself in the famous Syllabus denounced unequivocally democratic "liberalism" and "modernism." Here was Roman Catholicism restating the age-old doctrines of moral supremacy of the one true church, authoritarian politics, clerical establishment. In the decades that followed, the Roman Catholic Church, although it prudently adapted to necessities of life in democratic states, continued to manifest an underlying antidemocratic attitude in dealing with problems of diplomatic relations, canon law, ecclesiastical property, education, and moral legislation. A tension developed that still exists between the extremes illustrated by American lay Catholic liberalism and Spanish clerical Catholic reaction.

3. Science and Materialism. When Bishop Wilberforce asked Thomas Huxley whether he considered himself "descended from a monkey on his grandmother's or grandfather's side," he fired another futile ecclesiastical gun against the "ungodly" proponents of evolution. The quality of his comment is a sufficient commentary on the quality of much of the great debate. The controversies between science and religion had perhaps better be described as a conflict between a certain kind of science (or scientism) and a certain kind of religion (or fundamentalism). The sources of both traditions go back to ancient history, and found open expression at the time of the Renaissance, particularly in the cases of Copernicus and Galileo. The nineteenth century brought the conflict into the open, because it was the century of science. This requires a word of explanation.

Many of the fundmental principles of modern science were already formulated. What took place was a filling-in process—extension of knowledge in the established sciences, introduction of new sciences, and specialization. Chemistry was put in order through the periodic chart of the elements. Physics became thermodynamic, optical, electrical, etc. Geology became identifiable as a science in its own right, as did biology. Anthropology and psychology were introduced. Semi- or pseudo sciences appeared in the form of "social sciences." But more important than any of these changes is the fact that science for the first time entered into the knowledge of the common man. The nineteenth century invented Sunday-supplement science. Men, ordinary men, for the first time took a personal interest in the findings of scientists. This fact more than any other contributed to the rise of controversy.

The great debate followed two main avenues: geology and biology. The first centered around the question of the age of the earth and of man, the second around the question of creation and human origins. The well-known biblical investigations of Archbishop Usher, who in 1684 announced that the world was created on October 26, 4004 B.C., may be contrasted to the substitle of Charles Lyell's *Principles of Geology,* published in 1830-33: "An Earnest and Patient Endeavor to Reconcile the Former Indications of Change with the Evidence of Gradual Mutations Now in Progress; it seeks an interpretation of geological monuments by comparing the changes of which they give evidence with the vicissitudes now in progress, or which may be in progress." The evidence of physical geology on the extreme slowness of geological change and yet also on the inexorability of ultimate change, brought a new concept of creation as not only very old but also dynamic. Creation is a process, not a condition, said the geologists. Historical geology gave scientists knowledge of some parts of that process, as they studied stratigraphy (the process of sedimentation), vulcanism (the process of volcanic action), and paleontology (the development of life studied through fossil remains). The conclusion was that both the earth and life on it are almost unbelievably ancient, and the world as we know it is the result of processes covering billions of years. Obviously here was a point of conflict, real or apparent, with the book of Genesis and the Christian tradition.

Even more startling to the traditionalist were the developments in biology. Charles Darwin gave a new interpretation to a very old theory, evolution, and set forth in classic form the Darwinian explanation of the origin of species: *On the Origin of Species by Means of Natural Selection; or, the Preservation of Favored Races in the Struggle for Life.* This appeared in 1859. The question here posed was difficult enough: How does this interpretation match with the biblical account of a fixed creation and static genera? Even more disruptive was the application of the principle of organic evolution to the human species. How can man be created in the image of God if, as Darwin said in his

Descent of Man: "Man still bears on his bodily frame the indelible stamp of his lowly origin"?

Darwinism revolutionized science itself with the application of the principle of *process*, with the emphasis on classification and systemization, with the drive toward knowledge of the central characteristics of life itself, with new understanding of interdependence and interrelationship—ecology. It revolutionized the social sciences, particularly through the unjustified transference of a biological principle into the realm of human social relationships. The results may be seen in the work of Herbert Spencer and automatic social evolution, William Graham Sumner and natural social selection, Walter Bagehot and the survival of the fittest empires, Karl Pearson and the beneficence of war.

Above all Darwinism made a terrific impact on religion. The Roman Catholic Church remained relatively rigid by making a distinction between the realms of irrefragable dogma and adaptable human understanding. The Protestant churches were split into "modernist" and "fundamentalist" camps. The former accepted the validated findings of science and used the new knowledge in reinterpretation and illumination of the Christian faith. The study of comparative religion and the historical evolution of Christianity, the scientific study of the Bible, and the reinterpretation of Christian theology all reflect a "modern" outlook. The fundamentalists reacted in the opposite direction and refused on principle to receive the new evidence of science. The Bible was to be taken as the literal truth in every respect. Modern science was godless. And that was that.

Scientists themselves were in similar confusion. Some, like Thomas H. Huxley, Darwin's "bulldog," went out of their way to puncture the unwise pontifications of some of the clergy. Others, like Louis Agassiz, refused to accept the theory of evolution as expressed by Darwin. One of the few high-quality debates on the subject was that between Agassiz and Asa Gray—both devout men—at Harvard. Heresy trials on the one side and uninformed attacks by materialists on the other exacerbated bitterness. As a matter of fact, educated men, both scientific and ecclesiastical, were making their way toward a basis for mutual understanding. Dogmatic materialistic scientism and fundamentalistic biblical literalism provided most of the fireworks.

4. Cultural Movements. Elements of all the foregoing are to be found in the typical cultural expressions of the nineteenth century. The movement that was subsiding as the century came in was classicism, characteristic of the politics of the French Revolution, the painting of Jacques Louis David, and the music of Gluck and Haydn. In this were to be found the following elements: above all, admiration for and imitation of Greek and Latin civilization; symmetry of form; respect for law and order; scorn of the Middle Ages and "superstition"; humanism, universalism, cosmopolitanism, and regard for reason and absolute and eternally valid truth.

With the end of the French Revolution came new forces, already well developed, diverse, and sometimes contradictory, but united in one common aim: rejection of classicism. Goethe struck the new note with his phrase, *"Hinaus ins Freie!"* Romanticists, as they were called, rebelled against the stiff formalism of the eighteenth century, against the established canons of conduct and expression. Each should seek his own medium, his own niche. The emotional took precedence over the rational, process over static condition, becoming over being. Experience, they said, goes beyond any system. Reasonableness is not the same as truth. Heart and heritage are more important than reason and utility. Let the spirit flow free! As Wordsworth put it:

> Bliss was it in that dawn to be alive,
> But to be young was very Heaven! [9]

If one seeks for the religious orientation of these cultural trends, it is to be found in the contrast between Deism and Pietism, between Lutheran scholasticism and Wesleyan revivalism. The cult of the "reasonableness of Christianity" gave way to the cult of the "Christian heritage." No longer the glory that was Greece and the grandeur that was Rome, but the Age of Faith, the Middle Ages, was the greatest era of human history. With the exaltation of the medieval period went the idealization of the Roman Catholic Church. That church was the epitome of the Middle Ages, the medieval era in modern times. Hence romanticism meant a revival of the Roman Catholic Church. Novalis in

[9] *The Prelude.*

Heinrich von Ofterdingen and Chateaubriand in *Génie du Christian-isme* illustrate the marriage of romanticism and fervent Catholicism. In the process the Roman church was altered. There were some notable conversions as individuals passed from classicism to romanticism—for example, Friedrich Schlegel.

This cultural trend took on political significance in the writings of Chateaubriand, who in 1802 expressed the opinion that the papacy was a proper tribunal for the judgment of nations. Rome had before her "the most brilliant destiny." Especially influential was the political theory of Joseph de Maistre, who regarded the papacy as the keystone of the whole structure of authority and order in society. This theory found actual expression in parts of the Metternich system. There were contradictions, however, in so inchoate a movement as romanticism. Chateaubriand is illustrative. He changed in his later years from aristocratic authoritarian conservatism to a more liberal position, associated generally with figures like Heinrich Heine, Lord Byron, Giuseppe Mazzini. Above all, romanticism lay behind the fervent nationalism and patriotism of the nineteenth century.

The pietistic tradition in Germany is closely associated with the rise of a German nationalistic spirit. Cultural nationalism led to political nationalism. That is, the German folk tales of the Grimms led to the exploits of Bismarck through devotion to the "fatherland." In extreme form nationalism became a veritable religion in itself, a rival of Christianity. Super patriots either denied the relevance of religion or sought to use it in the interests of the super state.

By this time, of course, the spirit of romanticism was dead, and its place was taken by a new cultural force, realism. The new environment was the factory system, "Coketown," power politics both nationalist and imperialist, dominant science, philosophical materialism. The age in which heaven was defined in terms of the push button had dawned. The new outlook is illustrated by Darwinism with its emphasis on natural selection from accidental variations. No guiding purpose may be discerned here—only meaningless chance. Evolution could go up or down, or around. No difference. The new outlook is also well illustrated by the economic interpretations of Karl Marx, in which things of the spirit have no place. Economic determinism meant that all aspects of history depend on the economic facts underlying. All else is mere fluff. The inexorable processes of dialectical materialism eliminate all place for either human or divine initiative. Artistic expression wandered from gross realism into the erratic and irrational paths of symbolism, expressionism, surrealism. Clearly the religious "faith" of this outlook is atheism.

All three cultural influences have been thrown into the maelstrom of the twentieth century. Two world wars, major depressions, violent nationalism, and the Russian Revolution have given heavy predominance to the last and least Christian force. The history of Christianity in our times is the history of faith in an age of tumult.

For Further Reading

EUROPE

MacCaffrey, J. *History of the Catholic Church in the Nineteenth Century, 1789-1908.* St. Louis: B. Herder Book Co., 1909, 2 vols.

Nielsen, F. *History of the Papacy in the Nineteenth Century.* New York: E. P. Dutton & Co., 1906, 2 vols. English translation.

Bury, John. *A History of the Papacy in the Nineteenth Century.* New York: The Macmillan Co., 1930, 175 p. On Pius IX.

Aubert, R. *Le pontificat de Pie IX (1846-1878).* Paris: Bloud & Gay, 1952, 510 p. *Histoire de l'Eglise,* XXI.

Phillips, C. S. *The Church in France, 1848-1907.* New York: The Macmillan Co., 1936, 341 p.

Sabatier, Paul. *Modernism.* New York: Charles Scribner's Sons, 1908, 351 p.

Carpenter, S. C. *Church and People, 1789-1889. A History of the Church of England from William Wilberforce to "Lux Mundi."* New York: The Macmillan Co., 1933, 598 p.

Cornish, F. W. *The English Church in the Nineteenth Century.* New York: The Macmillan Co., 1910. 2 vols.

Elliott-Binns, L. *Religion in the Victorian Era.* London: Lutterworth Press, 1936, 525 p.

Church, Richard W. *The Oxford Movement, Twelve Years, 1833-1845.* New York: The Macmillan Co., 1932, 416 p.

Elliott-Binns, L. *The Evangelical Movement in the English Church.* New York: Doubleday, Doran & Co., 1928, 171 p.

Knox, E. A. *The Tractarian Movement, 1833-1845.* New York: G. P. Putnam's Sons, 1934, 410 p.

Edwards, Maldwyn. *After Wesley.* London: Epworth Press, 1935, 190 p. Influence of Methodism, 1791-1849.

―――. *Methodism and England.* London: Epworth Press, 1943, 252 p. Social Influences, 1850-1932.

Gill, Frederick C. *The Romantic Movement and Methodism.* London: Epworth Press, 1937, 189 p.

Fullerton, W. Y. *C. H. Spurgeon, A Biography.* London: Williams & Norgate, 1920, 358 p.

Wood, H. G. *Frederick Denison Maurice.* London: Cambridge University Press, 1950, 170 p.

Moody, John. *John Henry Newman.* New York: Sheed & Ward, 1945, 353 p.

Fleming, J. R. *A History of the Church in Scotland, 1843-1929.* Edinburgh: T. & T. Clark, 1927-33, 2 vols.

Drummond, A. L. *German Protestantism Since Luther.* New York: Alec R. Allenson, Inc., 1951, 282 p.

Good, J. I. *History of the Swiss Reformed Church Since the Reformation.* Philadelphia: Heidelberg Press, 1913, 504 p.

Mackintosh, H. R. *Types of Modern Theology; Schleiermacher to Barth.* New York: Charles Scribner's Sons, 1937, 333 p.

Pinson, Koppel. *Pietism as a Factor in the Rise of German Nationalism.* New York: Columbia University Press, 1934, 227 p.

Lindhardt, P. G. *Grundtvig: An Introduction.* London: Society for Promoting Christian Knowledge, 1952, 141 p.

Adeney, W. F. *The Greek and Eastern Churches.* New York: Charles Scribner's Sons, 1908, 634 p. Older, but good for background.

Fedotov, George P. *The Russian Religious Mind.* Cambridge: Harvard University Press, 1946, 438 p.

Fedotov, G. P., ed. *Treasury of Russian Spirituality.* New York: Sheed & Ward, 1948, 501 p.

Masaryk, T. *The Spirit of Russia.* New York: The Macmillan Co., 1919, 2 vols.

Riasanovsky, Nicholas V. *Russia and the West in the Teaching of the Slavophiles.* Cambridge: Harvard University Press, 1952, 244 p.

Bolshakoff, S. *Russian Nonconformity.* Philadelphia: Westminster Press, 1950, 192 p.

Casey, R. P. *Religion in Russia.* New York: Harper & Bros., 1946, 198 p.

Curtiss, John S. *Church and State in Russia; the Last Years of the Empire, 1900-1917.* New York: Columbia University Press, 1940, 442 p.

Arpee, L. *A History of Armenian Christianity from the Beginning to Our Own Time.* New York: Armenian Missionary Association of America, 1946, 386 p.

Attwater, D. *The Christian Churches of the East.* Milwaukee: Bruce Publishing Co., 1947, 1948, 2 vols.

UNITED STATES

Sweet, W. W. *The Story of Religion in America.* New York: Harper & Bros., 1950, 492 p.

Niebuhr, H. R. *The Kingdom of God in America.* Chicago: Willett, Clark & Co., 1937, 210 p.

Weigle, L. A. *American Idealism.* New Haven: Yale University Press, 1928, 356 p.

Sweet, W. W. *Revivalism in America.* New York: Charles Scribner's Sons, 1944, 192 p.

Hudson, Winthrop S. *The Great Tradition of the American Churches.* New York: Harper & Bros., 1953, 282 p.

Addison, J. T. *The Episcopal Church in the United States, 1789-1931.* New York: Charles Scribner's Sons, 1951, 400 p.

Albright, R. W. *A History of the Evangelical Church.* Harrisburg, Pa.: Evangelical Press, 1942, 501 p.

Atkins, G. G., and F. L. Fagley. *History of American Congregationalism.* Boston: Pilgrim Press, 1942, 432 p.

Barnes, William Wright. *The Southern Baptist Convention, 1845-1953.* Nashville: Broadman Press, 1954, 330 p.

Clark, E. T. *The Small Sects in America.* New York and Nashville: Abingdon Press, 1949, 256 p.

Garrison, Winfred E., and A. T. DeGroot. *The Disciples of Christ, A History.* St. Louis: Bethany Press, 1948, 592 p.

Manross, W. W. *A History of the American Episcopal Church.* New York: Morehouse-Gorham Co., 1950, 415 p.

Maynard, Theodore. *The Story of American Catholicism.* New York: The Macmillan Co., 1941, 694 p.

Sweet, W. W. *Methodism in American History.* New York and Nashville: Abingdon Press, 1954, 472 p.

Torbet, Robert G. *A History of the Baptists.* Philadelphia: Judson Press, 1950, 538 p.

Wentz, A. B. *The Lutheran Church in American History.* Philadelphia: United Lutheran Publication House, 1933, 465 p.

EXPANSION OF CHRISTIANITY

Latourette, K. S. *The Great Century.* New York: Harper & Bros., 1941-44, 3 vols. *A History of the Expansion of Christianity,* IV-VI.

Schmidlin, J. *Catholic Mission History.* Techny, Ill.: Society of the Divine World, 1933, 862 p.

Richter, J. *Indische Missionsgeschichte.* Gutersloh: C. Bertelsmann, 1924, 570 p.

Farquhar, J. N. *Modern Religious Movements in India.* New York: The Macmillan Co., 1915, 471 p.

Pickett, J. W. *Christian Mass Movements in India. A Study with Recommendations.* New York: The Abingdon Press, 1933, 382 p.

Latourette, K. S. *A History of Christian Missions in China.* New York: The Macmillan Co., 1929, 930 p.

Broomhall, M. *The Jubilee Story of the China Inland Mission.* London: China Inland Mission, 1915, 386 p.

Cary, O. *A History of Christianity in Japan.* New York: Fleming H. Revell & Co., 1909, 2 vols.

Groves, C. P. *The Planting of Christianity in Africa.* Volume One, to 1840. London: Lutterworth Press, 1948, 330 p.

Richter, J. *Geschichte der evangelischen Mission in Afrika.* Gutersloh: C. Bertelsmann, 1922, 813 p.

Báez Camargo, G., and K. G. Grubb. *Religion in the Republic of Mexico.* London: World Dominion Press, 1935, 166 p.

Carey, S. P. *William Carey, D.D., Fellow of Linnaean Society.* New York: George H. Doran Co., 1923, 428 p.

Warburton, S. R. *Eastward! The Story of Adoniram Judson.* New York: Round Table Press, 1937, 240 p.

Blaikie, W. G. *The Personal Life of David Livingstone.* New York: Fleming H. Revell & Co., 1917, 508 p.

Campbell, R. J. *Livingstone.* New York: Dodd, Mead & Co., 1930, 295 p.

Richards, T. C. *Samuel J. Mills.* Boston: Pilgrim Press, 1906, 275 p.

CHRISTIANITY AND SOCIETY

Eckhardt, C. C. *The Papacy and World Affairs as Reflected in the Secularization of Politics.* Chicago: University of Chicago Press, 1937, 310 p.

Gillispie, Charles Coulston. *Genesis and Geology: A Study in the Relations of Scientific Thought, Natural Theology, and Social Opinion in Great Britain, 1790-1850.* Cambridge: Harvard University Press, 1951, 315 p.

Hopkins, C. H. *The Rise of the Social Gospel in American Protestantism, 1865-1915.* New Haven: Yale University Press, 1940, 352 p.

Hudson, Cyril E., and Maurice B. Reckitt. *The Church and the World,* Vol. III. New York: The Macmillan Co., 1940, 266 p. Deals with England, nineteenth century.

May, H. F. *Protestant Churches and Industrial America.* New York: Harper & Bros., 1949, 297 p.

Nichols, J. H. *Democracy and the Churches.* Philadelphia: Westminster Press, 1951, 298 p.

Niebuhr, H. R. *The Social Sources of Denominationalism.* New York: Henry Holt & Co., 1929, 304 p.

Stokes, A. P. *Church and State in the United States.* New York: Harper & Bros., 1950, 3 vols.

Wagner, D. O. *The Church of England and Social Reform Since 1854.* New York: Columbia University Press, 1930, 341 p.

FAMOUS BOOKS

Friedrich Schleiermacher (d. 1834). *The Christian Faith; Discourse on Religion to the Cultured Who Despise It.*

John Keble (d. 1866). *The Christian Year.*

Søren Kierkegaard (d. 1855). *Training in Christianity; Stages on Life's Way.*

David Strauss (d. 1874). *Life of Jesus.*

Horace Bushnell (d. 1876). *Christian Nurture.*

Pius IX (d. 1878). *Encyclicals; Syllabus of Errors.*

John H. Newman (d. 1890). *Apologia pro Vita Sua.*

Ernest Renan (d. 1892). *Life of Jesus.*

Leo XIII (d. 1903). *Encyclicals.*

William Booth (d. 1912). *In Darkest England and the Way Out.*

Walter Rauschenbusch (d. 1918). *Christianity and the Social Creed.*

Charles Gore, ed. (d. 1932). *Lux Mundi.*

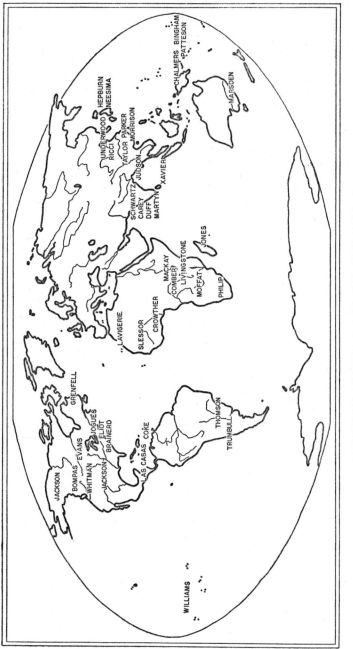

CHRISTIAN MISSIONS AROUND THE WORLD

CHAPTER V

The Age of Turmoil
[1914-55]

A. Twentieth-Century Challenges to Christianity

IN ITS ISSUE FOR AUGUST, 1914, THE COMMONWEALTH, AN ENGLISH periodical edited by Scott Holland, announced a forthcoming meeting of the International Congress of Social Christianity, to be held at the end of September in Basel. The theme was to be "Christianity and Universal Peace." Optimism was in the air, not only in Britain but also across the Atlantic. In the year 1910 a periodical called *The Journal of American History* had devoted a large part of one of its quarterly issues to plans for universal peace, and quoted part of a speech by Charles Evans Hughes, who said, "Without minimizing the conditions which still exist, threatening the peace of the world, we have reason to congratulate ourselves that the reign of war is nearly over."

The reasons for self-congratulation were short-lived. And the meeting in Basel scheduled for September, 1914, was not held. For during that fateful August most of the major nations of the world, one by one, were drawn into the vortex of a war none had specifically sought, yet none had been able to avoid. Quickly burgeoning from an unequal contest between small new Serbia and large old Austria-Hungary, the conflict inexorably involved Russia, Germany, France, Belgium, Great Britain, Japan, then Italy, the British Empire, and finally, by 1917, almost all the civilized world, including the United States. At the time few realized that this was World War I. Rather it was widely regarded as the war to end war, or at least to make the world safe for democracy. The coming of the war had been difficult to anticipate. Its significance as marking the end of an age was much more difficult to foresee. The Age of Progress tumbled unprepared, although not unwarned, into the Age of Turmoil. The twentieth century, which began in 1914, has been full of challenges. They have threatened not merely the old order of politics and economics but also the established principles of Christian civilization. Not only the British way and the American way, but also the Christian way, have been called into question. So tumultuously has the church been involved in this "time of troubles" that an introductory survey of the various challenges is in order.

In the first place stand two world wars, the second compounding with crescendo the devastation of the first. The first began in Europe in 1914 and lasted four years. The second began in China in 1937 and lasted seven years. The United States was much more deeply involved in the latter, which was in all respects more truly global. If the first gave rise to military aircraft and the League of Nations, the second contributed the atomic bomb and the United Nations. The first was entered into with patriotic fervor and sometimes bright idealism, certainly with illusions of chivalry and heroism. The second was greeted sullenly without romantic trappings, rather with a great deal of hardheaded realism and no illusions about carnage. The effects may be seen in the grayer world of mid-century. But the total effect cannot yet be measured. The returns are not all in. The full harvest has yet to be gathered.

World war was but the beginning of trouble. In its train have followed alarming forces. Among these probably the most portentous as of this writing is Marxist Communism. The story takes us back to the middle of the previous century, to that restless year 1848, the year of revolution over most of the European continent. In the midst of such excitement few noticed the publication of a little tract called a Manifesto, addressed to the workingmen of the world. The Communist Manifesto was written principally by Karl Marx (d. 1883), the founding father of Marxist, or "scientific," socialism as distinguished from the older utopian socialism. Beginning with the threat, "A spectre is haunting Europe—the spectre of Communism," the document attacked with equal vigor the principles of capitalism and of utopian socialism. In their place the author announced a Communist program. Its immediate aim was the "formation of the proletariat into a class, overthrow of the bourgeois of supremacy, conquest of political power by the proletariat." Its ultimate aim was the building of the classless society. "In place of the old bourgeois society, with its classes and class antagonisms, we shall have an association in which the free development of each is the condition for the free development of all." [1]

Thus began, with the typical double talk of propagandist technique, that strange mixture of idealism and materialism which has beguiled half the world. Before he died, Marx had formulated this program into a system in his major works, *Toward a Critique of Political Economy* (1859) and *Capital* (1867). In this system history was seen as a process of "dialectical materialism," in which each age plants the seeds of its own destruction. Every historical movement gives rise to a countermovement. This is the "dialectical" character, a swinging back and forth between extremes, each countermovement leading to a new level and another contrary force. The causal basis is materialistic. Intellectual influences, much less spiritual factors, play no part beyond that of excrescence, superstructure. Hence, "economic determinism." The real moving forces of history are economic, said Marx and his followers. And of these the determinative force is the class struggle. This struggle will continue—until the victory of the proletariat will usher in the classless society. Claiming a foundation on hard economic necessity, Communism has presented to the world a rare and alluring utopian dream. This explains much of the confusion concerning Communism in the thinking of men of good will everywhere.

The earlier efforts to organize failed ignobly. But the strategy of Communism was given a clear tactic by Nikolai Lenin (d. 1924), the leader of the Bolshevik Revolution in Russia in 1917. In his tract *What Is to Be Done?* he outlined the role of the Communist party as an advance guard of blindly devoted leaders, providing the means for seizure of power from the majority by the minority. In *The State and Revolution* he laid out a program for action. It remained for Joseph Stalin (d. 1953) to put much of this program into effect in Russia.

The Communists themselves were surprised that their first great victory came in Russia, the most economically backward major nation in Europe. By the rules, the great revolution should have developed first in the most highly industrialized capitalist countries, where presumably oppression of the masses would have proceeded to the requisite

---

[1] "Manifesto of the Communist Party," in *Introduction to Contemporary Civilization in the West* (New York: Columbia University Press, 1946), II, 415, 427, 434.

extreme. This consideration helps explain their relative inactivity in the Russian revolution of 1905 and their exceeding confusion early in 1917. By the twentieth century the Russian Communists, organized in the Social Democratic party, had split into Bolshevik (majority) and Menshevik (minority) factions, the former representing the power of Lenin.

Not until Lenin returned from exile and took over control, taking advantage of the chaos brought about by World War I and the previous overthrow of the tsar by liberals, was ultimate victory in sight. The subsequent adjustment of theory, to fit the new set of facts and the exploitation of suffering in other backward rather than advanced areas, well illustrates the fundamental opportunism of all Communist theories. Eschewing for a time the drive for world revolution, Stalin was content to build Communism in one country. That he did, at least if industrial development and figures of production are relevant. By the time of World War II the Union of Soviet Socialist Republics had grown into a major industrial and military power. The story of Russian and Communist advance by military conquest on the one hand and by political infiltration on the other is part of the story of current events and need not be recounted here. As we shall see, this movement constituted probably the greatest challenge to Christianity in the twentieth century.

World War I brought in its train many other troubles. Europe had been hard hit economically. The vast combination of the British imperial trade block was shaken, and the economies of some Continental countries were almost or entirely shattered. Britain never quite recovered from the First World War. Political and economic difficulties and rivalries kept Europe in turmoil throughout the twenties, while the United States went through its spectacular cycle of "boom and bust." The League of Nations, the fairest fruit of the war, was given a desperate blow by the refusal of the United States, its godparent, to enter. More and more it became the arena for struggle between the great powers, especially France, which sought to use it as a means of keeping Germany down. Italy first showed signs of chronic sickness. By 1922 the monarchy was so shaky that it could not prevent the seizure of power through the mere threat of force by the Black Shirts of Benito Mussolini. The world began to hear a word new in popular usage, "Fascism." The leader of the Italian Fascists, Mussolini, disgusted with liberalism, democracy, and socialism, turned to a principle he described as one of "action." "Fascism," wrote he in *The Political and Social Doctrine of Fascism* (1932), "believes neither in the possibility nor the utility of perpetual peace. . . . War alone brings up to its highest tension all human energy and puts the stamp of nobility upon the peoples who have the courage to meet it." [2] The foundation of his political program was the absolute state, "in comparison with which all individuals and groups are relative." This is totalitarianism. Mussolini also fostered the leadership principle—a tightly knit Fascist party dominated by a leader, *il Duce*. The totalitarian dictator had no more use for Russian Communism than he had for American democracy and capitalism.

After Mussolini had been beating the drums of Fascism for many years, in the midst of the great world depression of the thirties there arose in Germany a new brand of Fascism, symbolized by the marching storm trooper and the banner of the swastika, Nazism. Adolf Hitler, emerging from a nondescript past in Austria and World War I, grasped the means of public influence in Germany and shortly whipped the people into a frenzy of hatred against the fomenters of the Peace of Versailles and of devotion to the concept of the *Volk*, that mystical representation of all that was truly German. Using the settlement of Versailles, the world depression, prejudice against the Jews, and the ever-present penchant for militarism, Hitler in 1933 took over (by constitutional means but with the threat of force) the organs of authority. Within a brief time the constitutional forms of government were abolished, and there remained in undisputed power the one party, the "National Socialist" party. Of this Hitler himself was the leader, *der Führer*. Many features of Italian Fascism were taken over and reinforced by German Nazism. Once more central Europe throbbed to the tune of marching boots, and now also the shouts of *"Duce! Duce!"* and *"Heil Hitler! Sieg heil!"* The democratic countries seemingly

[2] A. Zimmern, ed., *Modern Political Doctrines* (London: Oxford University Press, 1939), pp. 33, 36. This article is a translation of an article in the *Enciclopedia Italiana*, 1932.

could do nothing but stand aghast, fearful of the shadows flitting over the dark wall of the future.

In the midst of all this the world was plunged into a great economic depression. In the United States midsummer of 1929 was a season of bright prosperity. Most people were too busy trying to get their share and more to notice that all was not well, that the stock market was feverish, that banks in Minnesota already felt the pressure of failures. In October these pressures broke loose. Overnight fortunes were lost, ambitious enterprises failed. Banks began to feel the loss of funds. In October of that year unemployed were estimated at one million; by 1933 the figure had risen to over twelve million. Franklin D. Roosevelt was elected president in the midst of depression with a mandate to *do something*. This economic disaster reverberated over the world, affected deeply all the major nations except Soviet Russia, which was busy with its Five-Year Plans.

The stage was set for the second world-wide conflict, which ended with the fearsome unleashing of the atomic bomb over Hiroshima and Nagasaki.

B. Christianity in Europe and America

The time of troubles called for a strong spiritual voice, full of faith and hope. Was the voice heard? Sometimes a clarion did rise above the roar, but too frequently that voice was muffled by the spreading clouds of secularism. The old cultural movements of the nineteenth century—classicism and romanticism—had given way after 1850 to the new "realism." The era of back-alley art, and after that of irrational symbolism and impressionism and cubism, had arrived. Science had become the new god of power and enlightenment. Its wonders beguiled the people as telegraphs and telephones silently, and locomotives and the Model T Ford noisily, wove them closer and closer together. This world was so full of a number of things that no time was left for consideration of another world—if any such existed. The new temper led many to question or reject traditional religion. Europe and America were full of professed or quiescent agnostics and atheists. Many of these continued to go to church, out of habit or design. Too infrequently were they jarred into acute awareness of the fundamental opposition between their way of life and the Christian way. Secularism lay like a blight over the Western world, a spiritual counterpart of the political and social blight of Communism, Fascism, Nazism. The Church, then, had to struggle against not only the principalities and powers of the world, enemies readily identified and resisted, but also against the more insidious rot within. In too many ways the Church stood not only in the world but of it. Was a voice heard? Yes. Although lost from time to time in the clash of arms and muted by inner spiritual conflict, the Church spoke to a troubled world, and in thus speaking came to a clearer understanding of her own evangel.

1. Europe. Of the nations not affected internally by totalitarianism Great Britain was the most vigorous. During World War I the churches, as everywhere, had difficulty adjusting to a wartime situation. In general they did not go to excesses of patriotism and hate-mongering. The relatively large number of conscientious objectors constituted a problem, but only in Scotland were they ill treated.

The war brought with it the inevitable increase in popular religion —or superstition. Much more significant, however, was the spiritual impact of the war itself, which left, altogether, some eight million people killed and three million more dead of epidemics. Problems of postwar depression and housing down through the great general strike of 1926 kept alive the social problems raised by the war. During this period the Church of England responded with various efforts to bring spiritual strength to bear. When the archbishop of Canterbury expressed sympathy for the working people during the strike, he had the rare experience of being hailed in the streets by workers and hooted by members of the middle class. The most vigorous action was COPEC (Conference on Christian Politics, Economics, and Citizenship), designed to speak to the workingman. In the years between the wars several notable leaders appeared, among them William Temple (d. 1944), who as archbishop of York and later of Canterbury exerted powerful influence in the directions of social Christianity and the Ecumenical Movement. His *Christianity and the Social Order* (1942) became a best seller. Other figures were P. T. Forsyth in theology and Charles Gore the Anglo-Catholic. The church experienced more and more difficulty as a result of its establishment. This became apparent in the efforts toward revision of the Prayer Book and measures for episcopal reform.

The nonconformist churches continued to play a large part in the religious life of the country, especially from outstanding pulpits in the large cities. One of the most influential leaders was L. P. Jacks, the Unitarian editor of the *Hibbert Journal*. Of special interest was the phenomenal growth of the Salvation Army, commanded by General William Booth for sixteen years after 1912. It spread into eighty-two countries and carried its message of comfort to the disinherited in sixty-nine languages.

The Roman Catholic population increased in both England and Scotland, but in the process tended to become more "English" and less suspect of foreign influences. Around Glasgow the Roman Catholics were especially strong. With the proclamation of the Irish Free State in 1921, Roman Catholicism surged forward as the faith of the vast majority in the new nation. In contrast the Church of Ireland (Anglican) sadly declined. Many Protestants were forced to emigrate to Northern Ireland, where they reinforced the non-Catholic population of Ulster. Protestants there, chiefly Presbyterians and Anglicans, succeeded in maintaining a clear majority over the vocal Roman Catholic minority.

During World War II the churches in Britain suffered along with the rest of the country. Many hundreds of edifices were destroyed or blasted beyond repair. Of these the cathedral of Coventry, reduced to a bare shell open to the sky, has become a symbol of the strength of faith against all the evil forces of the world. It has been estimated that some 2,600 Methodist churches were damaged or destroyed.

On the Continent some countries, at least for a while, escaped the direct impact of totalitarianism. Of these France was the largest. The Roman Catholic Church there began the twentieth century low in spirit. Separation of church and state in 1905 symbolized the dominance of secular anticlerical forces in the government. The people, especially in the cities, were broadly apathetic. Only ten per cent were active in the church. A symptom of spiritual sickness was the popularity of existentialism in its French form, an almost nihilist, certainly non-

Christian philosophy. World War II brought to France more than to some other parts of Europe great suffering and despair, in the midst of which the Christian faith, for all its temporal losses, found once again the power of the grace of God. Especially heartening was the temper of French Reformed Protestantism, which was reunited into a single church. CIMADE (Comité Inter-Mouvements auprès des Évacués) was a Protestant youth organization devoted to relief and evangelistic work among refugees. Attempts were made, in France and the Netherlands especially, to reach the secularized working people.

In Spain, Roman Catholicism remained fixed in its uncompromising conservatism under the monarchy. The period of the republic, 1931 to 1939, brought anticlerical forces to the front, revealing the depths of resentment against the church. The Civil War, a prelude to World War II, brought Francisco Franco and the *Falange* to power in reaction. With this victory the church returned to its favored position as an example of extreme clerical reaction. The few Spanish Protestants suffered throughout.

Lutheranism in Scandinavia continued into the twentieth century in much the same form it had taken during the earlier periods. With the decline of Germany, Swedish theological influence loomed ever larger. One of the outstanding leaders of the Ecumenical Movement was Archbishop Nathan Söderblom of the Church of Sweden. During World War II Denmark and Norway felt the brunt of Nazi conquest and occupation. In the latter Lutheranism exhibited an unwonted activism in resistance, especially through the courageous stand of Bishop Eivind Berggrav, who defied the Nazis and was imprisoned.

The most important and the most poignant aspects of church history in Europe lay farther east, in the countries of the dictators. The very homeland of the papacy was rent with the tensions of Fascism. The stage for trouble was set during the pontificates of Benedict XV (1914-22) and Pius XI (1922-39). The Roman Catholic Church with its world-wide ramifications was subject to powerful strains in World War I, and Benedict with difficulty preserved the universal ideal of Catholicism. Between the wars a series of eucharistic congresses symbolized the claim of the Roman faith to universality. Theological revival, especially along Thomistic lines, and liturgical reform invigorated intellectual and spiritual life. The papacy itself continued to centralize authority and prestige in the Vatican. This trend was re-emphasized when on November 1, 1950, through the sole, infallible authority of the pope, the new dogma of the bodily assumption of the Virgin was promulgated. Contradictory forces, however, continued to disprove the pretense that Roman Catholicism stood in one unbroken façade. French Catholics, even to the upper hierarchy, were loath to defer to the papacy on such matters as worker priests, etc. Significant differences remained among Spanish, Irish, British, American, East European forms of Roman Catholicism, and among rival organizations and movements.

In Italy itself the church faced at an early date an ambitious and half-pagan Fascism. Mussolini attempted to reconcile the contrary forces of Roman Christianity and Italian Fascism by making a place for the special faith of the people. This bore fruit in 1929 with the signing of a concordat by which the papacy was finally freed from the self-imposed restrictions dating from the conquest of Rome and abolition of the Papal States in 1870. The concordat was at least a *modus vivendi*. But it was evident that no treaty could obsure the fundamental conflict of ideology. Soon the pope was forced to protest the progressive totalitarian measures by which control of youth and education were wrested from the church. In 1931 Pius XI published the famous encyclical *Quadragesimo anno,* on the fortieth anniversary of *Rerum novarum,* which it restated and reinforced. The church maintained its right to speak freely on political and social issues, even in opposition to political authority. Little love was lost between the pope and *il Duce,* although an uneasy truce was maintained that led some to suspect the papacy of sympathy with Fascism, at least as a bulwark against Communism. And the encyclical was far from rejecting the Fascist state.

World War II devastated Italian churches. Among the most vivid episodes of the whole war was the battle that surged around the ancient monastery of Monte Cassino, defended by the Germans until scarce one stone was left on another. Rome itself was spared the full treatment, largely through the efforts of the pope to declare it an open city. Florence, on the other hand, suffered heavy damage. After the war a major threat to Italian Christianity appeared in the form of Communism, which received such support from the industrial workers as to threaten control of Italian political life. The church took an active part in the campaign to prevent Communist expansion and reduce its influence.

If Christianity faced a rival in Italy, it faced a monster in Germany. The fact that Nazism descended there later than Fascism in Italy does not reduce the violence of the impact. The churches, here both Catholic and Protestant, were subjected to the most violent persecution. Hitler would tolerate no limitation on the totalitarian state. In the years before 1933 Christianity had had a normal existence. Roman Catholics were active in political life through the Center party, in economic life through Roman Catholic labor unions, and in cultural life through the press and education. Among the Protestants the ecumenical spirit was manifested in the formation in 1922 of the German Evangelical Church Federation, a combination of some twenty-eight *Landeskirchen*, territorial ecclesiastical units reflecting the earlier divided history of Germany, together with the Moravians. When Hitler took over the government in 1933, a change came almost immediately. The churches, Catholic and Protestant, discovered that they faced a rival, a ruthless rival, for the total allegiance of the German people. The Nazi party stood as the uncompromising advance guard of the new faith. As Hitler said in a speech at Nuremberg in 1934, it would be inflexible in its teaching, hard in its organization, supple in its tactics, but as a whole it would resemble an Order. Or, as Alfred Rosenberg put it in *The Myth of the Twentieth Century*, the new faith is the myth of blood. The nordic blood has replaced the old sacraments. Many Nazis left the Christian fold completely, followed the German Faith Movement, formed in 1933. A Nazi Aryan distortion of Christianity appeared with the German Christians, organized in 1932 by a Nazi pastor. The German Evangelical Church Federation, after a brief period of non-co-operation, was brought in part under the domination of the new Reichsbishop, Ludwig Müller, a Nazi. The Protestants answered with defiance. A Pastors' Emergency Federation was organized to combat the influence of Müller. Pastor Martin Niemöller denounced Nazism from his pulpit in Berlin itself. And in 1934 there appeared Confessional Synods, which in a few months formed the *Evangelische Kirche Deutschlands* (*Evan-*

gelical Church of Germany), composed of Lutheran and Reformed elements. The struggle continued into 1935, when a Reich ministry for church affairs was organized for the purpose of dominating them completely. Many pastors were arrested, including Niemöller in 1937. The war brought more troubles, with renewed emphasis on German paganism and political totalitarianism. Some eighty-five per cent of the pastors were taken directly into the army.

If sufferings of the German Protestants were great, devotion was strengthened by war and persecution. After the end of fighting the church emerged with renewed faith in God as over against the uncertainties and limitations of earthly security. In 1948 the Evangelical Church was reorganized. Bishop Otto Dibelius took a vigorous lead in preserving a Christian fellowship across the Iron Curtain. That German Protestantism has been able to make a positive contribution in any respect to the Christian faith is little short of a miracle. Nevertheless, men like Niemöller have been widely heard on both sides of the Atlantic. Works in the field of *Formgeschichte* (dealing with formation of the New Testament) and eschatology were followed by the major contributions of the German-Swiss theologian Karl Barth, who began his work of theological recall with a *Commentary on the Epistle to the Romans* in 1918. Rejecting the long trend of liberal thought stemming from Schleiermacher, Barth called men back to the Word of God mediated through the Bible. Men must cease thinking of God, he said, as a helpful partner in building the Kingdom on earth. God is sovereign, not man. Barth's influence has been enormous, both in Europe and in the United States.

Roman Catholics did not find life under Nazism easy. The Center party disbanded in 1933, and a concordat with some favorable features was signed with the new regime. But conflict was inevitable. First in Bavaria, then throughout Catholic Germany, the state took over the schools, tried to control the youth organizations, suppressed the Catholic press, engaged in practices repugnant to Catholics and Protestants alike, such as antisemitism and sterilization. By 1936 the Roman Catholic bishops gathered at Fulda united in denunciation of political control of the schools. Problems were doubled in 1938 when the Nazis annexed Austria.

We saw in the preceding chapter how the Russian Orthodox Church took on the aspect of a department of state for religious affairs. This was the condition of the church at the time of World War I and the Revolution. When the tsarist regime fell in March, 1917, the liberal provisional government abolished the office of procurator, established that of minister of confessions, and permitted the assembly of the ecclesiastical Sobor, which restored the patriarchate and elected Tikhon patriarch. The October Revolution (November in the Western calendar) changed this, along with everything else. Overnight the tightly organized Bolsheviks, led by Lenin, took control. Almost immediately an attack on the church was instigated. The new patriarch, who had been elected in the middle of the Revolution, had the enormous responsibility of defending the church against a hostile state. Church lands were nationalized along with all the rest. The extensive educational institutions of the church were taken over. Civil marriage was required, and all matters of probate were placed under the state. Financial aid was cut off. Finally church and state were legally separated. Although the church had been liberated from tsarist pressure, it now encountered a new and more intense pressure. Patriarch Tikhon early in 1918 was forced to describe the situation in a pastoral letter, in which he reported ruthless persecution of helpless people, openly and without shame, without any pretense of law or justice. Churches were desecrated and ridiculed. Clergymen were arrested and schools turned into anti-God museums. The answer of the government to the protests of the church was bitter persecution. Priests were deprived of civil rights. Sunday was abolished. Churches were turned to secular or antireligious uses. A League of Militant Godless was organized.

As a result of these blows the church reeled. In the twenties a Living Church Movement came into being which was willing to co-operate with the Soviet state. It gained some limited support and was favored by the Communists as a means of dividing clerical opposition. Patriarch Tikhon was forced to "confess" disloyalty before charges of active hostility against the state were dropped. Right after the Revolution and then again during the campaign to sovietize agriculture in the Five-Year Plans, 1928 and after, vigorous efforts were made to suppress Christianity and promote atheism. After 1936 a relaxation of persecution was noticeable, a trend much fostered by World War II. Sunday was restored in 1940. But in that year it was estimated that over ninety per cent of the churches open in 1917 were closed or used for other purposes. The number of priests had declined in the same proportion.

The Second World War brought extensive changes in relations between church and state. With an eye directed toward allies friendly to religion, in the Balkans and in the West, and with another directed toward moral support by the church in wartime, the Soviet government increasingly favored the church and, conversely, became indifferent to anti-God activity. Religious journals appeared as antireligious publications disappeared. These privileges were bought with a price. The church was tied more closely to the state and served more completely its interests.

After the war the fundamental opportunism of the Soviet regime again became apparent as religious affairs began to return to the former state of conflict. Attempts were renewed to supplant Christianity with materialistic atheism in such organizations as the "All-Union Society for the Dissemination of Political and Scientific Knowledge." As the church moved closer to the Soviet government, it moved away from ecumenical Christianity. The Iron Curtain has drawn a barrier that has kept Orthodox Christians in Russia away from the Amsterdam and Evanston meetings of the World Council of Churches. The question is still unanswered, whether a church that is permitted little more than worship according to its liturgical forms can survive pressure from the Communist masters. Within its exceedingly narrow confines the Orthodox Church in Russia continues to minister to its devout millions with richly beautiful liturgical worship, sensitive mystical awareness of Christ in the midst of sorrow and suffering, and the unheralded but eloquent testimony of martyrdom.

The other forms of Christianity in the Soviet Union, especially the Baptists and the Roman Catholics, shared the fate of the Orthodox Church, except insofar as it served the purposes of the Communists to set one church against another. There were said to be over three million Protestants in 1950. All groups by that year had been assimilated into the Soviet propaganda machine. The situation is well stated by a publication of the youth movement, which said that the church is disestablished and religion is a private matter for the ordinary citizen; but it is not a private matter for members of the Bolshevik Party, who maintain "the only true, scientific, materialistic world outlook."

Since the end of World War II the Western world has looked aghast as Soviet power has swallowed up country after country in east and central Europe, and has reached its tentacles into the Latin countries of western Europe. The story of the fate of Christianity in these countries behind the Iron Curtain is tragic and poignant. Nowhere has this struggle been more dramatic than in East Germany. When Russia occupied this area at the end of World War II, many clergymen, both Protestant and Roman Catholic, were killed. The constitution that was promulgated provides for religious freedom and separation of church and state, with specific limitations against political or social influence. An Office of Religious Affairs is supposed to deal with complaints, but actually serves as an agency for enlisting compliant churchmen. In many ways Christianity is restricted and hampered in religious education, ministerial training, intellectual isolation of the clergy, etc. Curiously, the religious welfare groups—Innere Mission, Evangelisches Hilfswerk, Caritas—are still permitted to operate. Moreover, both Roman Catholics and Protestants have been able to hold great synods and mass meetings. One remembers especially the Protestant *Kirchentag* in 1951 in East Berlin, attended by over 100,000. The Communists have been diligent in their attempts to draw Lutheran youth away from the *Junge Gemeinde* into the Communist *Freie deutsche Jugend*. Bishop Dibelius has traveled freely back and forth between his East German and West German constituents, has spoken forthrightly against all forms of oppression, and has joined with his Roman Catholic compeers in repeated protests. German Christianity behind the Iron Curtain is surprisingly vocal and vigorous.

More lugubrious is the picture in Czechoslovakia. This brightest dream of modern democracy has fallen to low estate. The Communists are not the only force to blame. Weaknesses were present from the beginning—as even its name indicates. Lack of inner unity among Slavic elements, pressure from a strong and discontented German minority, and above all a twice-repeated tale of abandonment by the West, all contributed to the debacle. About three quarters of the population were Roman Catholic. During the Republic about 800,000 broke from Rome to form a *Czechoslovak National Church*. The Protestants remained in a rather small minority, about 1,000,000, the *Czech Brethren* being largest. When the Soviet Union annexed Ruthenia, the Greek Catholics there were placed under pressure to move over to the Russian Orthodox Church. The strong Roman Catholic population of Slovakia was persecuted. The outcome was already in sight when the Communists won the election of 1948. A Bureau for Ecclesiastical Affairs was established the following year, and action was started to gain control of the church in the typical fashion. Ecclesiastical property was nationalized, attempts were made to divide the higher and lower clergy, and priests were arrested. In spite of protests from Archbishop Josef Beran, the process went on, with arrests of thousands of priests, leaving about three quarters of the parishes empty. Beran himself was accused of treason and banished from Prague in 1951. At last report some of the bishops had largely succumbed to the pressure, even to the point of defying papal excommunication. Once again Christianity suffered from too much involvement with the world. Here as elsewhere the Roman Catholic Church had accumulated vast land holdings, over 400,000 acres. For this and other reasons it was a relatively easy victim of Communist propaganda.

The *Church of the Czech Brethren,* numbering about 750,000, traces its origin to John Huss in the fifteenth century, but in organization and theology it is clearly Reformed. Its most potent voice recently has been that of Professor J. L. Hromadka. He has maintained that the church dare not withdraw from society, even Communist society. It must, rather, maintain contact with and influence on all societies, and yet remain steadfast in its primary loyalty to Christ and the things not of this world. As a result these Protestants have not yet come to the point of direct opposition to the state or to complete subjection under it. They are living on a tightrope.

The Czech National Church has apparently accepted the new regime and has not offered opposition to it.

Poland has been the most unhappily situated country in Europe, caught between the Slavic power to the East and the Teutonic power to the West. The long tragedy of Polish national history was continued in the period after World War I. Even the brief respite of freedom embodied in the Republic between the two wars was marred by an aggressive nationalism and a reactionary social structure. The best Poland could do was to spawn another dictatorship. Approximately three quarters of the people were Roman Catholic, ten per cent Orthodox, and ten per cent Jewish. Protestants were a small minority, totaling about one million. World War II brought disaster to all. The Polish Lutheran Church (mostly in the western area) was obliterated, the Roman Catholic Church suffered bitterly, and the Jews were well-nigh exterminated.

When the Russians occupied all of Poland after the war, one of the first acts was the formation of a "Committee of Initiative for the Transfer of Greek Catholics to the Orthodox Church." The purpose of this was to force Uniats into the Russian Orthodox community. The chief effect of this action was felt in the eastern parts annexed to the Soviet Union. The Roman Catholics in Poland proper remained for a long time adamant, under the leadership of Cardinal August Hlond. Repeatedly the Communists tried to use minority religious groups against the Roman Catholic majority—the Polish National Catholics and even the Jehovah's Witnesses. While the latter were being persecuted in East Germany, they were being highly favored in Poland. By 1949 laws placed religion in much the same place it had under the Soviet constitution. Church lands—again a source of embarrassment—were confiscated, and religious welfare work was obstructed. Progressively the government sapped the strength of the churches.

Down the Danube, Hungary fell to the Russian advance. Here the Roman Catholics, although a substantial majority, about sixty-five per cent, lived with an influential Protestant minority, about twenty per cent, chiefly Hungarian Reformed. The old story was repeated in the matter of church land holdings, for the Roman Catholic Church had about one eighteenth of the best land. During the Nazi occupation the churches experienced relatively less persecution than in Poland or Czechoslovakia. Christians of all persuasions denounced the Nazi persecution of the Jews. Cardinal Joseph Mindszenty spoke out clearly against the outrages, and Jews were sometimes even hidden away in monasteries. After the war, by 1948, the Communists had gained control of the government, and the usual tactics were employed against religion. The tragic aspect of the land reform of 1945 was that it had to be carried through by the Communists.

Along with land the churches lost control over religious education and charity. A state office for ecclesiastical affairs was set up. In the midst of all these changes stood Cardinal Mindszenty, who had become primate in 1945, the very year Hungary faced her new masters. Typical of his courage was his proclamation of a Marian year in 1948, beginning with a Feast of the Assumption scheduled to offset a Communist patriotic observance of the centennial of the Revolution of 1848. The day after Christmas, 1948, he was arrested and held for one of the most spectacular trials in modern history. Of course he confessed to crimes against the state and was imprisoned.

The vigorous Lutheran and Calvinist churches were subjected to the same pressures. Curiously, the former, usually more obedient to political authority in the tradition of Luther, rejected more actively the aggression of the state than did the Reformed group. In 1948 Lutheran Bishop Lajos Ordass was convicted and imprisoned because of his uncompromising stand. Among the Reformed churches Albert Bereczky, strongly influenced by Karl Barth, advocated compromise. In the resulting uncertainty Bishop László Ravasz resigned in protest. But the Hungarian Reformed Church came more and more under the control of the Communist state.

Space lacks to describe the subjugation of Christian churches in the Balkans. In Yugoslavia the Roman Catholic archbishop of Zagreb, Aloysius Stepinac, stood firm against repeated waves of persecution, Fascist, Nazi, and Partisan Communist. He was imprisoned by Tito but later released under surveillance. The sizable Orthodox Church in the country was more resilient here than in other areas of the Balkans. Both Roman Catholics and Orthodox were plagued by problems arising from their landed holdings and aristocratic connections. A similar fate descended on Christianity throughout the Balkans (except in Greece) and in the little Baltic states.

The general character of the Soviet tactic has become clear. Beginning from the first principle that Marxist Communists themselves will profess atheism and reject the church completely, the policy in countries under their control will vary according to the opportunities of the moment. The ultimate aim is always the complete subjugation of the church and its eventual liquidation. Steps and methods will vary, but almost always include setting one group against another by alluring promises, striking at the entrenched economic power of the churches, especially landed property, constraining opposition as treason and the ecumenical spirit as disloyalty, and wearing down the resistance of leaders by unremitting and intolerable pressure. The main reason for this bitter rejection of Christianity is that Communism is really a rival religion, claiming the total devotion of its followers. The rivalry is all the more acute in that both Communism and Christianity share, although for entirely different reasons, certain common concerns in the field of social justice. More and more Communist mores have been taking on the aspects of religious symbolism. Philosophical atheism is in process of being transformed into a religious faith, crassly materialistic but fervent. Marx is the new Moses, Lenin the new Joshua.

2. The United States. Religion in the United States has not been subjected to the violent stresses such as have been described in Europe. In many ways twentieth-century church history is a continuation of nineteenth. For this reason much less space will be necessary.

World War I found the churches unprepared. Unlike England and, for the most part, the Continent, American churches tended to go to extremes. Some were not content to support the program for chaplains to the armed forces and minister to the spiritual needs of those left behind. War fever penetrated the sanctuaries, which witnessed patriotic rallies for recruiting and sale of war bonds. In too many cases the gospel of good news was confused with the glitter of global destiny. After the conflict an embittered reaction set in, as war boom gave way to postwar depression, optimistic idealism to pessimistic disillusionment, militarism to pacifism. Influential churchmen like Harry Emerson Fosdick confessed the sinfulness of the military spirit and went over to an extreme pacifist position. Never again should the church be caught in the evil meshes of war and violence. Not the war hero but the conscientious objector was the true Christian. War became to these men the worst of all possible evils.

Another result of the reaction was the feverish activity of the "gay twenties." The moral discipline concerning alcoholic beverages that had led to the Volstead Act and the eighteenth amendment to the Constitution was followed by the era of bootleg liquor and the speak-easy, accompanied by that strange aberration of American womanhood, the flapper, and the age of jazz. Burgeoning prosperity gave more and more prominence to the ideal of the successful businessman. Churches were caught up in the spirit of the times and began to use high-pressure methods of "selling" their "product." Revival meetings of the type conducted by Billy Sunday (d. 1935) were supplemented by highly organized campaigns and "crusades" for funds and members, employing the latest advertising techniques, radio, and the motion picture. The Oxford Group Movement appeared on the American scene, led by Frank Buchman. It sought to bring a new faith by means of personal evangelism and small group meetings. After 1938 it was transformed into what was called "Moral Rearmament." During the twenties theological liberalism reigned supreme in most of the Protestant churches, and had its influence on Roman Catholics.

Then came the great depression of 1929, destroying forever the optimistic dreams of the twenties. As in Europe, so in America, the churches suffered losses of all kinds, although they were spared the persecutions blighting Europe. The economic distress of the times did not drive people into the churches. But Christians were forced to re-examine their beliefs and to renew the central devotion to the gospel. During the thirties the influences of Continental theology, especially Karl Barth, began to penetrate American religious thinking. Reinhold Niebuhr left a pastorate in Detroit to begin a notable career at Union Theological Seminary as mediator of "crisis theology," or neo-orthodoxy, to American liberal Christianity. Strong liberal forces rejected this new trend, as did also the vocal but smaller force of fundamentalism. The social gospel was not so much rejected as reinterpreted.

Membership increased apace until by 1950 about fifty-seven per cent of the people were church members. But as membership increased, the standards for admission tended to decline. It became possible to join a church as one would join a social club or the chamber of commerce. Of special significance was the continuing growth of Roman

Catholicism, especially in the cities, both in membership and in property. A network of parochial schools covered the country.

Among the problems faced were the moral issues of prohibition and divorce, the ecclesiastical issues arising out of Roman Catholic pressures such as diplomatic relations with the Vatican and public aid to parochial schools, and the underlying issue of prevailing secularism. If Protestants became alarmed at the growing influence of Roman Catholicism, and if fundamentalists strove against liberals and both against the neo-orthodox, all the Christian forces of America were forced to acknowledge the common peril of secularism. In the center of the problem lay the public schools, forbidden to introduce any "sectarian" teaching into the curriculum.

World War II and the appalling problems of life in the atomic age brought Christianity back into the center of American life. The churches grew not only in membership but also in prestige. Scientists were not so certain of their self-sufficiency. Some revivals, notably those of Billy Graham in the United States and Europe, appeared to lead a mass return to religion. Whether this religion was in every case really Christianity was not so apparent. Nevertheless, throughout the war and the prolonged period of world-wide suffering afterward, American Christianity remained true to its ideal of service and benevolence. All the churches, but especially those with strong ties in Europe, joined in ambitious programs of relief for victims of war, and later for the hordes of refugees in Europe, Asia, and the Near East. The American Friends Service Committee and Church World Service were outstanding among agencies enjoying interdenominational support. The World Council of Churches quickly assumed responsibility for the correlation of the many programs with the many areas of need.

In the total picture of Christianity in the twentieth century in America the most significant trend has been the Ecumenical Movement. Whereas the former history of Protestantism had been largely that of division and disunity, the most recent era has seen a return toward the fundamental principle of unity in Christ. The story of how this has been taking place through church union, co-operative service agencies, federations, and the World Council of Churches, is deferred to the final section of this book.

C. World Christianity

1. Expansion and Contraction. A letter mailed by a West Virginian soldier from wartime New Guinea on December 18, 1942, described an interesting little episode almost lost in the crash of guns.

> Last night our camp had about a half dozen visitors. These visitors were natives. They came on their own. I would like to give you a minute description of them, but we aren't allowed to elaborate too much. These visitors came and started singing. Soon there was a crowd about. They sat in a little circle inside the big circle. All this was in the moonlight. The moon was filtering through the palms. They started off singing "When the Roll Is Called up Yonder." They didn't know all the words, but they did know the tune. Some of them couldn't speak English, but they knew the English words to this. Then they sang many more songs and danced a little for us. Just about the end of their visit they thought to do just the thing that every one of us had been too busy to think of. They sang two Christmas carols, "Hark, the Herald Angels Sing" and "O Little Town of Bethlehem." [3]

The young man from West Virginia had found Christianity in a most improbable environment. And that was symbolic of a twentieth-century fact. By the time World War II broke, Christianity had literally circled the globe. That the faith was world wide was indisputable.

The great unanswered question was: Was Christianity sufficiently vigorous in the Orient to withstand such deadly blows as it was suffering in Europe? Would the multitude of tender young missionary plants be trampled under the march of nationalism, racism, and Communism? At mid-century the issue was still uncertain. But three heartening developments could be listed: (1) The Christian faith had penetrated every corner and every culture to a greater or lesser degree; (2) in several areas the "younger churches," born of the missionary effort, were growing muscular and becoming self-sufficient; (3) the Ecumenical Movement was tying together the disparate parts of Christendom in a wider fellowship. These factors must be set over against the disasters of recent years and the foreboding of the future. We may begin with a brief survey of the process of expansion, pursued so notably in the nineteenth century and continued into the twentieth.

[3] From *Pastor's Journal*, XV (1943), 12.

India, with a long history, a highly developed culture, and a population of some 400,000,000, occupies a vast subcontinent virtually cut off by the massive Himalayas from the rest of Asia. In 1914 Christianity was the faith of about 1 per cent of the total, but carried its influence deep into Indian life. By mid-century the proportion had risen to about 2½ per cent. Included were members of various groups, the ancient Syrian Church and its nineteenth-century branch, the Mar Thoma Church, and Roman Catholic and Protestant churches. These increased through missionary effort in ascending order of vigor and success. The Roman Catholics faced peculiar problems. Both world wars brought difficulties when contact with Europe was cut off. The old problem of the *padroado* in India, the original Portuguese control of patronage, continued to interfere with ecclesiastical efficiency, even after the concordat of 1928 eliminated the worst features. Most of the missionary personnel came from the European continent, and most of the work was done south of the region of Goa-Madras. Relatively few converts were made, and most attention was given to the existing congregations.

Protestant missions continued along much the same lines as they had in the nineteenth century with continued success but many new problems. Emphasis on education resulted by 1930 in the establishment of some fifty-five colleges and thousands of high and elementary schools. Although Protestantism carried great influence into the life and thought of India, it faced serious problems for this very reason. Many of the Hindus were sympathetic toward the Christian message and accepted Christ after a fashion, but refused to accept Christianity as the *only* way. The most notable example was Mohandas K. Gandhi. Was he a Christian in the context of Hinduism? Or was he a Hindu with a Christian flavor? Adaptation and adulteration could go only so far. Far more serious for the immediate situation of the church was the political transformation of India from a subject colony of the British Empire to an independent self-governing state and the creation of a Moslem state, Pakistan. The impact of this change is best understood in terms of the development of the younger churches. At this point it may be said that the resurgence of India has caused a fundamental readjustment of missions, particularly with regard to relations with fostering societies and to renewed emphasis on medical and educational work. This readjustment would in all probability have come in any case. But the process has been hastened by the political factors. Obstacles have been placed in the way of missionaries, especially against active evangelism among Hindus. The situation is different and somewhat easier in Pakistan.

Equal to India in all respects of area, population, antiquity, and culture is China. Here the all-important development has been the disintegration of the ancient culture based on Confucianism. The process began long before the advent of the Communists, in fact finds its roots in the nineteenth century and the opening of China to the West. Manifestations of the change increased after 1911 with the revolution ending the Chinese Empire and introducing the new Republic under the leadership of that dominating figure, Sun Yat-sen (d. 1925), a Protestant Christian. The anti-Western movements and the organization of the Kuomintang in the twenties carried the social revolution further. The end of the old China was completed with the Japanese invasion and World War II. The beginning of the new China was seen in the Nationalist movement under Chiang Kai-shek and the Communist movement under Mao Tse-tung. The only thing they had in common was mutual distaste for the old imperial China.

In the midst of these world- (not merely China-) shaking events the Christian church had a rough time. Although it had been present for a thousand years, off and on, only in the nineteenth century had it really taken root. Christians by then numbered about 1/2 per cent of the total population. In the course of another century they had increased to about 1 per cent. Roman Catholics, building on earlier work, were able to maintain leadership, but Protestants were rapidly gaining. In 1914 the former counted some 1,500,000 members; by 1947 they numbered about 3,250,000. Roman Catholics, like Protestants, were severely attacked during the anti-Western demonstrations of the twenties. Through this period they tended to emphasize the responsibility of building up the church and its institutions. Not nearly so much as Protestants did they influence the entirety of Chinese society.

Protestants counted fewer members, about 250,000 in 1914 and something over 500,000 in 1936. The constituency, however, was very much larger. The same denominations and organizations remained active, but after 1914 the Seventh Day Adventists and the China Inland Mission became more prominent. The latter maintained more missionaries than any other, and were the largest Protestant group outside the National Christian Council, which represented the major denominations. This fact bears upon the strong conflict between liberals and fundamentalists in missionary and national circles. The issues of "modernism" and fundamentalism ran through most missionary areas of the twentieth century, but were more troublesome in China. Then came the Communist invasion of Nationalist China and the defeat of Chiang Kai-shek, who retreated to the island of Formosa. China lay fallow beneath the Communist boot. The latter immediately set about building a new China in the image of the Marxist-Leninist ideal. The fact that here again Marxism was planted in one of the least industrially developed countries in the world did not hinder its ruthless Communization. The Christian church was now regarded as representative of the most insidious Western capitalist influence. Rapidly enterprises were curtailed or shut down or taken over. Missionaries were imprisoned or exiled. Native Christian congregations were swallowed up in the waves of propaganda. By 1952 almost all missionaries were gone. Schools, hospitals, and educational institutions were gone. Churches were open for worship, although under surveillance. No one could tell, however, how much faith would live on in the fellowship and in the secret recesses of the mind. Christianity had survived repeated and brutal persecution in the past. Christianity had survived the direct anti-God pressures in Russia. Could it survive in an oriental society? Had the Chinese Christ become real enough?

The third great aggregation of power in the Orient is Japan. The fate of Christianity in these three countries might well determine its fate in the entire nonwhite world. Its effective introduction into Japan came only about one hundred years ago. In that relatively short time it has made a deep impression on Japanese religion and society. The same organizations and methods continued in the twentieth century. By 1936 Roman Catholics numbered about 100,000, Protestants 200,000. Both have emphasized education and both have established full-fledged universities. Sunday schools have also played an important part. One of the most colorful figures, both in East and West, has been Toyohiko Kagawa, who inaugurated an ambitious Kingdom of God Movement in 1928. With the thirties came increasing disfavor on the part of the government, which was coming under the domination of militant greater-Japan elements. Upon the heels of the invasion of Manchuria came condemnation by the League of Nations and the withdrawal of Japan from that organization. In the Orient, World War II began in 1937 with full conflict between China and Japan. During this difficult period all Japanese, including Christians, were forced to attend upon the ceremonies of Shinto. The only factor that made the situation tolerable for Christians was the definition by the government that these ceremonies were purely patriotic, not religious. With the collapse of Japan and the end of the war came new opportunities, beclouded, however, by wartime destruction, by the frightful memories of Hiroshima and Nagasaki, and by the increasing threat of Communist infiltration. So far the Roman Catholic Church seems to have responded more energetically than the Protestants. The Russian Orthodox mission, which had uniquely testified to Orthodox vigor in the nineteenth century, sadly declined, for manifest reasons. As in India and China, national leadership came more and more to the front in organizing the "younger" churches discussed in the next section.

An adjunct of Japan during most of the twentieth century was Korea. In spite of difficulties posed by Japanese imperial control the Christian population approximately doubled. But by 1940, as a result of increasing pressure from the Japanese, now deeply involved in "greater East Asia" expansion, most of the missionaries had left. The country suffered through the long years of war, then, with scarce a chance of recovery, was plunged into the catastrophic Korean War, which left it north and south alike, devastated beyond imagination. In 1954 the Methodist Church, always specially interested in Korea, collected over a million dollars beyond its usual support for the rebuilding of churches.

A glance around the other areas of the Far East reveals further evidence of new forces, mainly nationalistic and Communistic, at work undermining both colonial and indigenous authority. In Ceylon affairs remained relatively quiet; but in Burma, Indonesia, and Indochina revolution seethed. In spite of all the turmoil, however, Christians in Burma, chiefly Baptists, maintained their foothold. The Protestant church survived the ordeal of independence in Indonesia and achieved independence itself as the *Protestant Church of the East Indies*. And Roman Catholics held on to something like a lost cause in Indochina.

The other huge nonwhite continent is Africa. Africa is stirring. Last of the colonial areas to be exploited, it is apparently the last in the world to feel the dangerous modern forces of disruption. But they have finally come, are growing, and may well be building up to an explosion. From French Morocco on the Northwest to Cape Colony in the extreme South, the native peoples are on the move. France maintains uneasy hegemony south of the Mediterranean, and the Union of South Africa is a powder keg. Kenya keeps the British on edge. Christianity faces another potential crisis.

In some ways the changes have provided opportunities for the church. The disintegration of primitive native cultures have sometimes resulted in mass conversions of whole tribes. In the Union of South Africa, in the midst of racist troubles, the Christian population has risen from about one third to one half, mostly Protestant. Except for the Dutch Reformed Church, which is less a missionary agency than a representative of the dominant Boer culture, the churches have deplored the trend toward *apartheid* (racial segregation) and the reduction of the African to menial status. In equatorial regions the Roman Catholics have been eminently successful, especially in Belgian Congo. Most provinces had become from ten per cent to fifty per cent Christian by 1950. The problem in Nigeria was special, because of the strongly entrenched Islam previously introduced from the north. Although the situation was still somewhat amorphous, African Christians have felt the pressure toward autonomy and national leadership. Christian converts are numbered in the millions.

As to the southern quadrant of the western hemisphere, Roman Catholicism remained the predominant form of faith throughout Latin America. But it continued to reveal weaknesses. When Mexico passed through a social revolution early in the twentieth century, the church suffered much from anticlericalism, directed against ecclesiastical influence in political affairs and against church lands. This anticlericalism, associated with political and social radicalism, moderated in the 1940's. But it was a continuous issue throughout much of Latin America.

Protestant missions were strongly supported from the United States, but the most interesting aspect was the development of energetic national leadership, especially in Mexico and Brazil. In spite of opposition from governments under the influence of Roman Catholicism the Protestant churches advanced. In some countries, notably Colombia, persecution of Protestants aroused considerable unfavorable attention.

In the twentieth century, however, the real story of the expansion of Christianity was not to be found in missions per se. Far more important for the future were the twin developments, indigenous churches on the one hand, and the world-wide Ecumenical Movement on the other. Increasingly it became clear that Christianity outside Europe and North America would not survive if it remained tied to the apron strings of a colonial authority or a "foreign" church, however benevolent. And it became even more clear that Christianity anywhere might not survive the storms of the Age of Turmoil if all its parts, hitherto ever more divided and competitive, did not stand together, East with West, dark with light, in obedience to our unity in Christ. "For by one Spirit we were all baptized into one body—Jews or Greeks, slaves or free—and all were made to drink of one Spirit" (I Cor. 12:13, R.S.V.).

2. Rise of the Younger Churches. During the autumn months of 1932 the British people were treated to an unusual spectacle. Some devoted Indian Christians were carrying the gospel to *them.* The itinerary of the missioners looked like that of John Wesley, from Newcastle-on-Tyne through Bristol to Manchester and London, to most of the large cities and some of the small in England and Ireland. It all came about as a result of the Mission of Fellowship from the Churches of India and Burma to the Churches of Great Britain and Ireland, sponsored by the Indian National Christian Council. This was no mere device for increasing interest in and support of missions by displaying briefly some of the products. The purpose was rather to deepen the Christian faith of Great Britain and Ireland by means of evangelical testimony from Christians of the Orient. Christ crucified and resurrected was still preached. But now those who had been ministered unto came to minister. As the Report of the Jerusalem meeting of the International Missionary Council, where the idea had hatched, put it: "We believe that the time is come when all would gain if the younger churches were invited to send missions of help to the churches of Europe and America, that they may minister from their treasure to the spiritual life of those to whom they come."

If some Christians in the Occident began to speak in the mid-twentieth century of a "post-Christian age," this was not the temper of Christians in the Orient. However great the dangers with which they were surrounded, they diligently served in preserving and strengthening the tender but vibrant institutions which by now were manifestly "younger churches." The missionary enterprises of earlier years had finally sent out runners to be rooted and nourished in native soil. That this could be in a world increasingly characterized by instability was one of the most heartening aspects of contemporary Christian history. The full story is yet to be told; but it need not take long in the telling.

India well illustrates the parallel trends toward national independence from colonial control and ecclesiastical autonomy as against missionary control. This vast and populous land received repeated shocks in the period after World War I as it moved ponderously and painfully toward freedom. The British may be credited with providing the foundations upon which the Indians found it possible to build a new nation. The Morley-Minto Reforms of the prewar years, which began the process of opening places in the government to qualified Indians, were followed in order by the Montagu-Chelmsford Reforms of 1919 and the Government of India Act of 1935. All these limited forms of self-government failed to satisfy the supporters of the Indian National Congress, organized politically in the Congress party. Mohandas K. Gandhi was the fountainhead of power for most of the period between the two world wars. The process was hastened by World War II. In 1947 Great Britain withdrew viceregal control and vested authority in two dominions, India and Pakistan. The former soon took the short further step to complete independence.

While the land was shaking under these revolutionary changes, Christianity was trying to find a place not dependent on the continuation of missionary support. The ancient Syrian Church of course had been for a long time indigenous. But Protestant influence in the nineteenth century brought about a schism resulting in the formation of the

Mar Thoma Church. Among the congregations formed by Protestants arose a new native leadership, proud of Indian ancestry and ambitious to take greater responsibility. These leaders were torn between the insistent demands of nationalists claiming India for the Indians, which included Hindu demands of India for the Hindus, and their own fundamental dedication to the Christian faith. In fact, the Indian National Congress began to reflect Hindu pressure to limit Christian missions and win Christians back to the "national" faith. This pressure embarrassed Moslems as well as Christians, and the former suffered painfully in the conflict between India and Pakistan. All branches of Protestant Christianity were affected by the trend toward autonomy. Indian Methodists grew in self-reliance. By 1935 Baptists were almost completely under Indian leadership. Anglicans gained greater freedom at the same time. Meanwhile, denominational differences, which appeared meaningless to Indians, were de-emphasized. With encouragement from J. H. Oldham a National Christian Council was formed in 1923. It was an important step on the way to ecumenical Christianity in India. One of the most effective illustrations of a reversal of flow in the missionary movement was the Mission of Fellowship from India to the British Isles mentioned above. It was a sign of an ever-amplifying voice to be heard most clearly in the days of the World Council of Churches.

For all their differences, both India and China were moving in the same direction. In different ways both had been subject to strong European colonial influence, and now both were striving under great burdens to achieve national self-expression. In China even more than in India many of the political leaders were Protestant Christians. Chinese Christianity, like Indian, was striving toward self-support. A National Christian Council was formed in 1922 which led in 1927 to the *Church of Christ in China.* During this period Chinese law required that the heads of all educational institutions and a majority of board members be Chinese. The transfer to national leadership was sufficiently rapid to cause wide-spread insecurity among the ranks of foreign missionaries. As early as 1918 a Chinese Missionary Society had existed.

When the Communists descended like wolves on the fold in the years after World War II, some curious and many tragic changes were made. Missionaries were imprisoned or expelled as representatives of Western imperialism and hence inimical to Chinese welfare. They were almost all gone by 1952. Pressure was exerted to bring Chinese Christians under the influence of the Communists. Behind and beyond this policy lay the anti-Christian and antireligious philosophy, amounting to a religion in itself, of Marxism, still quite foreign to the Chinese mind. A catastrophe had broken in one of the crucial areas of the globe. The final outcome is yet to be discerned. Christians have continued their witness, even under difficult conditions.

Scarcely less violent was the experience of Christians in Japan. The same trends toward freedom from missionary support are to be observed. By 1929 something over one half of the Protestant congregations had become financially independent. In the year immediately preceding the merging of World War II in the East with World War II in the West at Pearl Harbor, two developments increased this trend. The government applied pressure to terminate foreign support of Japanese churches. And Japanese Protestants brought themselves together under government pressure in the *Nippon Kirisuto Kyodan,* or the *Church of Christ in Japan,* known as the *Kyodan.* Most congregations of most denominations were united in this hopeful example of ecumenicity. And even after the withdrawal of the Anglicans and Lutherans it represented two thirds of Japanese Protestants. Unfortunately the churches have been troubled with more than their share of quarrels between liberals and fundamentalists.

In all three of the great Asian nations the Roman Catholic Church moved toward such autonomy as was consistent with the hierarchical structure centering in Rome. In China in the 1920's six bishops were consecrated, and later a cardnial and a hierarchy were established.

Movements toward ecclesiastical independence were not limited to the main areas discussed. In Indonesia strong nationalism found a counterpart in the Protestant Church of the East Indies. A *United Protestant Church of Madagascar* was formed in 1934. In Africa generally more and more native clergy were trained and given responsibility by both Roman Catholics and Protestants. Christian councils were formed here also, some with representation in the International Missionary Council. Wherever native leadership was nurtured to a point of self-reliance, the younger churches demonstrated a powerful tendency to break away from tutelage and an equally powerful tendency to grow together in ecumenical fellowship. This final and most significant phase of modern Christian history now claims our attention.

3. *The Ecumenical Movement.* Ever since Paul took the Corinthians to task (I Cor. 1) for multiplying factions around him, of Apollos, and of Cephas, the Christian faith has been ecumenical in its appeal. No ultimate divisions can exist among the children of the Kingdom. Protestants especially have been scandalized by the multiplication of sects. That in the latter days this situation at least has been recognized as a great sin of human willfulness is a harbinger of hope.

The general trend away from exclusive denominationalism has been manifested in various ways. One of these has been merger, the original and most nearly complete form of ecumenicity, although not necessarily the best. The number and significance of church unions seem to be increasing. In the last one hundred years about one hundred unions and reunions have been consummated. About two thirds of these have taken place within "families" of denominations. The rest have crossed such lines to build a larger fellowship. Most of the latter type have come into being since World War I, and the largest of them have occurred among the younger churches. Mergers have been especially notable in the United States, until now a forest of sectarianism. Only a few may be mentioned by way of illustration.

Lutherans came together through the *United Lutheran Church,* formed in 1918 from three groups, and the *American Lutheran Church,* 1931, from three German synods. The American Lutheran Conference of 1934 joined the latter with Norwegian and Augustana Swedish Lutheran churches in a loose federation. In the 1950's negotiations for further mergers continued, with the prospect that most Lutherans might find themselves in one of three groups: United, Missouri Synod, and a new larger church.

Another notable union occurred in 1934 when the Reformed Church in the United States and the Evangelical Synod of North America joined in the *Evangelical and Reformed Church.* Here was a marriage between families. Discussions were continuing in 1955 between the Evangelical and Reformed and Congregational Christian Churches.

The latter was a merger of two churches in 1931. The prospect for a *United Church of Christ* by the end of the decade was good.

The most impressive reunion, although one entirely within the "family," was that consummated in 1939 between the Methodist Episcopal Church, the Methodist Episcopal Church, South, and the Methodist Protestant Church, to form the largest single Protestant denomination, the *Methodist Church*. In England, Methodists reunited through a devious process whereby three smaller groups came together in 1907 to form the *United Methodist Church,* and the latter joined with the Wesleyan Methodists and the Primitive Methodists to form the *Methodist Church* in 1932. A more comprehensive merger, one of the best examples crossing family lines, took place in Canada in 1925 with the formation of the *United Church of Canada* from Methodists, Congregationalists, and most Presbyterians.

More significant still were the unions consummated on the mission fields within the younger churches. In India the *United Church of North India,* composed of Presbyterians and Congregationalists, was organized in 1924. The *South India United Church* brought together in 1908 Presbyterians, Reformed, and Congregationalists. This was the organization expanded spectacularly in 1947 into the *Church of South India,* including Methodists and Anglicans. Here was an experiment in church union that would gather together free churches and one adhering to the historic episcopate. A *Church of Christ in China* was formed in 1927 from Presbyterian, United Brethren, United Church of Canada, some Congregationalist, and Baptists sources. This was said at the time to be the most comprehensive union in the world. The *Kyodan* in Japan, listed earlier, should also be mentioned.

During the nineteenth and twentieth centuries Christians were brought closer together in a myriad voluntary organizations for cooperation in one field of endeavor or another. To list them would be monotonous and unrewarding. Some, such as the Y.M.C.A. and the Y.W.C.A., have already been discussed in other connections. Earliest and most numerous were those related to missions. Some were devoted to work with young people, as the Student Volunteer Movement and the World's Student Christian Federation (1895). Others were primarily interested in Christian education or evangelism. The American

Bible Society (1816), the American Tract Society, The British and Foreign Bible Society (1804), and the Society for Promoting Christian Knowledge may be mentioned. When in 1910 the all-important World Missionary Conference convened in Edinburgh, the leaders of these sundry strains were coming into closer touch with one another and beginning to catch the vision of a greater future when all might be one. Some of these groups were interdenominational fellowships limited to one country, pre-eminently exemplified by the Federal Council of the Churches of Christ in America, organized in 1908. By 1950 this had merged into a more comprehensive and well-knit body, the National Council of Churches, including also the former Missions Council of North America (Foreign and Home), the International Council of Religious Education, and several other agencies. Councils were formed in other countries—the Canadian Council of Churches, the British Council of Churches, the Ecumenical Council of Churches in the Netherlands, etc. The major mission areas followed suit.

Henry P. Van Dusen has classified the multitude of associations under eight categories:[4] (1) associations of individuals of different communions, like the prototype of missionary organizations, the London Missionary Society (1795), Bible societies, and the Evangelical Alliance; (2) conferences of individuals of different denominations, like the world missionary conference in New York (1854) and others down to 1910 at Edinburgh (by which time missionary societies themselves took part); (3) nondenominational associations, like the Y.M.C.A. and later youth organizations; (4) interdenominational conferences of official representatives, again seen earliest in missions, first on the mission fields and then among sponsoring societies at home, but including some of the most crucial gatherings of the Ecumenical Movement, in life and work and faith and order; (5) interdenominational organizations with specific purposes, such as missionary councils on the field, the World's Christian Endeavor Union (1895), the World's Sunday School Association (1907); (6) denominational world associations, such as the Lutheran World Federation, the Baptist World Alliance, the International Congregational Council; (7) federations

[4] *World Christianity* (New York and Nashville: Abingdon Press, 1947), pp. 84-97. Used by permission of the publishers.

of churches, from national down to local and up to the World Council of Churches; (8) church unions, which have already been discussed.

The central facet of the history of the Ecumenical Movement, however, resides in the series of episodes leading to the formation of the World Council of Churches. The antecedents were complicated; the organizations involved were many; and various meetings and conferences were endless. The Evangelical Alliance, an association of individuals in England from 1846 and the United States from 1867, was the most comprehensive of many noble experiments that cleared the way. But the story may be simplified without too much violence to the truth by following four main lines: missions, youth, life and work, and faith and order. The accompanying chart lays out these lines in schematic and chronological form. The focal point of this sequence was the great World Missionary Conference at Edinburgh, 1910, when over thirteen hundred delegates from missionary societies heard John R. Mott urge the formation of a continuation committee that led directly to the organization of the permanent International Missionary Council in 1921. Here also Charles H. Brent and William Temple were fired with enthusiasm for the work of Christian unity.

About Eastertime in 1928 the members of the Jerusalem Conference found close fellowship in their pilgrimage through the holy places and in the impressive joint communion held on Good Friday. The Madras Conference demonstrated dramatically the shift of concern and influence through the presence of representatives of the younger churches amounting to a full one half of the delegates. Although Japan and China were already at war, both were represented by numerous delegates who did not allow their national animosities to break the bond of Christian unity. New problems of an age of turmoil were faced frankly in recognition both of the perils of the present and of the shadows of the future. The contrast between the old and the new in Christianity, between the West and the East, was never so apparent. But even clearer was the strong voice in favor of unity, a major force in the formation of the World Council of Churches.

One may doubt, however, whether the latter would have come into being before the middle of the twentieth century without the impatient insistence and bold experimentation of the interdenominational movements directed toward youth. Developing from the Y.M. and Y.W. of earlier times through their respective world organizations of 1855 and 1894 and the American Intercollegiate Christian Movement to the Student Volunteer Movement and the World's Student Christian Federation, the enthusiasm and optimism of youth were brought to bear on ecumenical discussion in a way that could not be ignored. Here was a school ready for training leaders in ecumenicity, students who grew up to be ecumenical statesmen. The massive world conferences of Christian youth at Amsterdam in 1939 and Oslo in 1947 acted as catalytic agents.

From such sources as the Federal Council of Churches in the United States and the British Conference on Politics, Economics, and Citizenship in 1924 arose the socially concerned Life and Work Movement. One of the forceful personalities was Archbishop Nathan Söderblom of the Church of Sweden, vigorous and learned, with a striking presence. The Conference in Stockholm in 1925 was a tribute to his prestige. There representatives from ninety-one churches from thirty-three countries discussed international affairs, especially war, social problems, education, and economic issues. An impressive communion service, more truly ecumenical through the intercommunion of the Church of Sweden and the Church of England, crowned the conference. A tendency to avoid controversial areas lest unity be disrupted was balanced by common concern with the problems of the Church and the world. The well-planned and managed conference at Oxford in 1937 was a continuation of this movement. J. H. Oldham and other key participants were in their prime. Discussion was centered around five general topics: church and community, church and state, church and economic order, church and education, and the Universal Church and the world of nations. German Christians were represented by Baptists and Methodist only. Each topic brought the Church into the center of the issue. Here already was an indication of the way in which the concerns of the Life and Work Movement were approaching those of the Faith and Order Movement. One of the chief results of the Oxford meeting was a call for a World Council of Churches, anticipating that of the Madras Conference held the following year.

Bishop Brent at Edinburgh in 1910 realized that ultimate unity could not be realized in the presence of unresolved conflicts and mis-

ORIGIN OF THE WORLD COUNCIL OF CHURCHES

From a Millennium of Ecumenical Efforts and Experiments

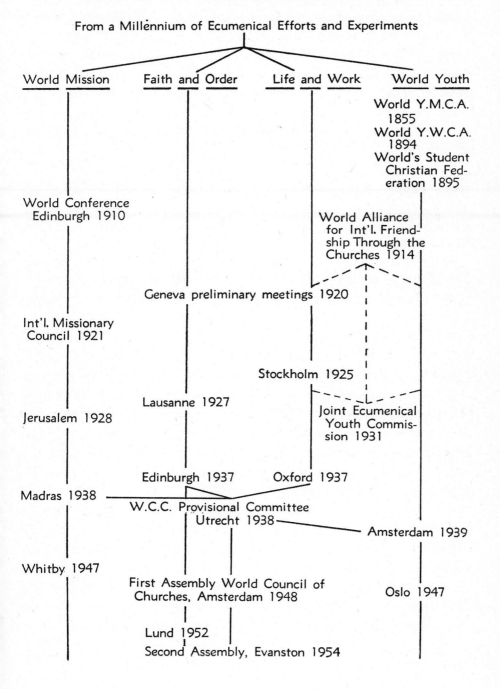

understandings over doctrinal issues, especially those involving the ministry, the sacraments, and the Church. Others of like mind joined in a series of theological discussions parallel to the Life and Work meetings. The first general conference was that at Lausanne in 1927. Under local difficulties the delegates agreed unanimously on a superb Message to the World, prepared in large part by Adolf Deissmann.

Jesus Christ, as the crucified and living One, as Saviour and Lord, is also the centre of the world-wide Gospel of the Apostles and the Church. Because He Himself is the Gospel, the Gospel is the message of the Church to the world. . . . The Gospel is . . . the gift of a new world from God to this old world of sin and death; still more, it is the victory over sin and death, the revelation of eternal life in Him who has knit together the whole family in heaven and on earth in the communion of saints, united in the fellowship of service, of prayer, and of praise.[5]

They found themselves in deep waters, however, in specific discussions of the Church, ministry, and sacraments. The many disagreements revealed in part here were carried into the discussions at Edinburgh in 1937, for which careful preparation was made. Nevertheless a remarkable consensus was reached on the doctrine of grace and on the principle that, since episcopal, presbyteral, and congregational forms of church order have all been practiced since the days of the early church, all three forms must find a place in ecumenical unity. The closest approximation to this principle in actuality today is the Church of South India. In spite of difficulties over the obstacles of the ministry and the sacraments, the delegates strongly supported the movement for federation through a World Council of Churches.

Preliminary discussions of the thirties in which William Temple as archbishop of York played a vigorous role resulted in a constituting assembly at Utrecht in 1938, which drafted a constitution for a World Council of Churches. With Faith and Order and Life and Work movements at the center, the new body was to be "a fellowship of churches which accept our Lord Jesus Christ as God and Savior." Churches directly and officially were to be members, but the new organization was

[5] The message is printed as an appendix to William A. Brown, *Toward a United Church* (New York: Charles Scribner's Sons, 1946), pp. 211-12.

not to have binding legal authority. Because World War II broke before the machinery could be set up, a continuation committee carried on effective work not only in preserving the plan of Utrecht but in actually serving the churches during the difficult years of the war. A compromise was achieved on the question of geographical or denominational representation. It was provided that one third of the assembly be laymen. The official launching of the World Council came in 1948 at the great First Assembly, held in Amsterdam. Over one hundred churches were accepted for membership, including not only the preponderance of Protestant denominations in Europe and America but also the larger younger churches and some of the Orthodox and other Catholic churches. Although the International Missionary Council was still outside, the two were said to be in "association." A similar relationship was held with the World's Student Christian Federation and other bodies. By the time of the Second Assembly in 1954 its membership included 161 churches in 48 countries.

After six fruitful years of official life the World Council held its Second General Assembly in August, 1954, at Evanston, Illinois. Concerning itself with the themes of evangelism, unity, responsible society, international affairs, racial and ethnic tensions, and Christian vocation, with special attention to the main theme, "Christ, the hope of the world," it stood as one of the few hopeful signs as the world fearfully found its way into the last half of the twentieth century. Of one thing the delegates were sure: Whatever happened to the world, the Church of God, coming closer to unity in these days than at any time since the Apostles, would, through his grace, continue to testify to the εὐαγγέλιον, the glad tidings. As the 125,000 persons assembled in huge Soldiers' Field the evening of August 15 began the impressive "Festival of Faith," Marc Boegner of France, a President of the World Council of Churches, led in a responsive reading:

President: Who are you to have come here?
Congregation: We are Christians. We have come from many different traditions.
President: What is it to be Christian?
Congregation: It is to believe in God the Father; in his only Son, our Lord; who is the hope of the world . . . and in the Holy Spirit.

President: From where have you come?
Congregation: From 161 member churches from 48 countries on five continents.
President: Why have you come?
Congregation: We have come to worship God.

A fitting conclusion to this story of Christianity in modern history may well be found in that word that has come to signify the determination of ecumenical Christians *to stay together* in a world that bids fair to fall apart—Evanston.

For Further Reading

CHRISTIANITY IN EUROPE AND AMERICA

Keller, Adolf. *Christian Europe Today.* New York: Harper & Bros., 1942, 310 p.
———. *Church and State on the European Continent.* Chicago: Willett, Clark & Co., 1936, 382 p.
Horton, W. M. *Contemporary Continental Theology. An Interpretation for Anglo-Saxons.* New York: Harper & Bros., 1938, 246 p.
Beck, G. A., ed. *The English Catholics, 1850-1950.* London: Burns Oates & Washbourne, Ltd., 1950, 640 p.
Edwards, Maldwyn. *Methodism and England.* London: Epworth Press, 1943, 252 p. Social influence, 1850-1932.
Highet, John. *The Churches in Scotland Today.* Glasgow: Jackson, Son & Co., 1950, 257 p.
Horton, W. M. *Contemporary English Theology.* New York: Harper & Bros., 1936, 186 p.
Lloyd, Roger. *The Church of England in the Twentieth Century,* Vol. I. New York: Longmans, Green & Co., 270 p.
Spinks, G. S. *Religion in Britain since 1900.* London: Andrew Dakers, Ltd., 1952, 256 p.
Binchy, D. A. *Church and State in Fascist Italy.* New York: Oxford University Press, 1941, 774 p.
Guilday, P. *The Catholic Church in Contemporary Europe, 1919-1931. Papers of the American Catholic Historical Association,* Vol. II. New York: P. J. Kenedy & Sons, 1932, 354 p.
Manhattan, A. *The Vatican in World Politics.* New York: Gaer Associates, Inc., 1949, 444 p.
Pichon, Charles. *The Vatican and Its Role in World Affairs.* New York: E. P. Dutton & Co., 1950, 382 p.
Herman, Stewart W. *The Rebirth of the German Church.* New York: Harper & Bros., 1946, 297 p.
Höye, Bjarne, and Trygve Ager. *The Fight of the Norwegian Church Against Nazism.* New York: The Macmillan Co., 1943, 180 p.
Cockburn, J. Hutchison. *Religious Freedom in Eastern Europe.* Richmond, Va.: John Knox Press, 1953, 140 p.
Shuster, George N. *Religion Behind the Iron Curtain.* New York: The Macmillan Co., 1954, 281 p.

Curtiss, John Shelton. *The Russian Church and the Soviet State, 1917-1950.* Boston: Little Brown & Co., 1953, 387 p.

Spinka, Matthew. *The Church and the Russian Revolution.* New York: The Macmillan Co., 1927, 330 p.

Anderson, Paul B. *People, Church and State in Modern Russia.* New York: The Macmillan Co., 1944, 240 p. Under Soviet system.

Spinka, Matthew. *Nicolas Berdyaev: Captive of Freedom.* Philadelphia: Westminster Press, 1950, 220 p.

Hunt, R. N. Carew. *The Theory and Practice of Communism. An Introduction.* New York: The Macmillan Co., 1950, 231 p.

MacEóin, Gary. *The Communist War on Religion.* New York: The Devin-Adair Co., 1951, 264 p. Historical survey, country by country.

Denominational histories of American churches listed in Chapter IV.

Allen, Frederick L. *Since Yesterday.* New York: Harper & Bros., 1940, 362 p.

Wector, Dixon. *Age of the Great Depression, 1929-1941.* New York: The Macmillan Co., 1948, 362 p.

Kincheloe, S. C. *Research Memorandum on Religion in the Depression.* New York: Social Science Research Council, 1937, 158 p.

Blanshard, Paul. *American Freedom and Catholic Power.* Boston: Beacon Press, 1949, 350 p. Critical of Roman Catholic Church.

Furniss, Norman F. *The Fundamentalist Controversy, 1918-1931.* New Haven: Yale University Press, 1954, 199 p.

WORLD CHRISTIANITY

Beach, H. P., and C. H. Fahs, eds. *World Missionary Atlas.* New York: Institute of Social and Religious Research, 1925, 251 p.

Grubb, K. G., and E. J. Bingle, eds. *World Christian Handbook.* New York: Friendship Press, 1949, 405 p.

Latourette, K. S. *Advance Through Storm.* New York: Harper & Bros., 1945, 542 p. *A History of the Expansion of Christianity,* VII.

Chirgwin, Arthur M. *Under Fire; the Christian Church in a Hostile World.* New York: The Macmillan Co., 1941, 188 p.

Bell, G. K. A., ed. *Documents on Christian Unity, 1920-24.* New York: Oxford University Press, 1924, 382 p.

———. *Documents on Christian Unity, First-Second Series, 1920-24; 1924-1930.* New York: Oxford University Press, 1930, 636 p.

———. *Documents on Christian Unity: Third Series, 1930-1948.* New York: Oxford University Press, 1948, 300 p.

Rouse, Ruth, and Stephen Charles Neill, eds. *A History of the Ecumenical Movement, 1517-1948.* Philadelphia: Westminster Press, 1954, 822 p.

Brown, William A. *Toward a United Church; Three Decades of Ecumenical Christianity.* New York: Charles Scribner's Sons, 1946, 264 p.

Van Dusen, Henry P. *World Christianity, Yesterday, Today, Tomorrow.* New York and Nashville: Abingdon Press, 1947, 302 p.

Hogg, W. R. *Ecumenical Foundations. A History of the International Missionary Council and Its Nineteenth-Century Background.* New York: Harper & Bros., 1952, 466 p.

Sundkler, Bengt. *Church of South India.* London: Lutterworth Press, 1954, 460 p.

Iremonger, F. A. *William Temple, Archbishop of Canterbury: His Life and Letters.* New York: Oxford University Press, 1948, 663 p.

Index